Language, Nations, and Multilingualism

Language, Nations, and Multilingualism explores the legacy of Herder's ideas about the relationship between language and nationalism in the post-colonial world. Focusing on how anti-colonial and post-colonial nations reconcile their myriad multilingualisms with the Herderian model of one nation-one language, it shows how Herder's model is both attractive and problematic for such nations.

Why then does the Herderian model have such valency? How has the Herderian ideal of one nation-one language continued to survive beneath the uncomfortable resolution struck by new multilingual nations as they create fictions of a singular national mother tongue? To what extent is Herder still relevant in our contemporary world? How have different nations negotiated the Herderian ideal in different ways? What does the way in which multilingual post-colonial nations deal with this crisis tell us about a possible alternative framework for understanding the relationship between language and nation?

By approaching this investigation from diverse archives across Asia, Africa, Europe, Latin America, and the Caribbean, *Language, Nations, and Multilingualism* proposes answers to the aforementioned questions from a global perspective that takes into account the specificities of a range of colonial experiences and political regimes. And by extending the discussion backwards in time to offer a more historical reading of the making of modern nations, it allows us to see how multilingualism has always disrupted constructions of monoglot nations.

Ying-Ying Tan is Associate Professor of Linguistics and Multilingual Studies at Nanyang Technological University, Singapore.

Pritipuspa Mishra is Associate Professor in the Department of History at the University of Southampton, the United Kingdom.

Routledge Studies in Sociolinguistics

For more information about this series, please visit www.routledge.com/
Routledge-Studies-in-Sociolinguistics/book-series/RSSL

Language, Nations, and Multilingualism

Questioning the Herderian Ideal

Edited by Ying-Ying Tan and Pritipuspa Mishra

Routledge
Taylor & Francis Group

LONDON AND NEW YORK

First published 2021
by Routledge
2 Park Square, Milton Park, Abingdon, Oxon OX14 4RN

and by Routledge
52 Vanderbilt Avenue, New York, NY 10017

Routledge is an imprint of the Taylor & Francis Group, an informa business

British Library Cataloguing-in-Publication Data
A catalogue record for this book is available from the British Library

Library of Congress Cataloging-in-Publication Data
Names: Ying-Ying, Tan, editor. | Pritipuspa, Mishra, editor.
Title: Language, nations and multilingualism : questioning the Herderian ideal / edited by Tan Ying-Ying and Mishra Pritipuspa.
Description: Abingdon, Oxon ; New York, NY : Routledge, 2021. | Series: Routledge studies in sociolinguistics | Includes bibliographical references and index.
Identifiers: LCCN 2020031124 (print) | LCCN 2020031125 (ebook) | ISBN 9781138322639 (hbk) | ISBN 9780429451911 (ebk)
Subjects: LCSH: Language and languages—Political aspects. | Language planning—History. | Language policy—History. | Language and culture. | Multilingualism. | Nationalism. | Herder, Johann Gottfried, 1744–1803.
Classification: LCC P119.3 .L353 2020 (print) | LCC P119.3 (ebook) | DDC 306.44/6—dc23
LC record available at https://lccn.loc.gov/2020031124
LC ebook record available at https://lccn.loc.gov/2020031125

ISBN: 978-1-138-32263-9 (hbk)
ISBN: 978-0-429-45191-1 (ebk)

Typeset in Times New Roman
by Apex CoVantage, LLC

Contents

Figures

Contributors

Janet Y. Chen is Associate Professor of History and East Asian Studies at Princeton University.

Tony Crowley is Professor of English Language at the University of Leeds.

Andrew M. Daily is Associate Professor of Modern French and Global History in the Department of History at the University of Memphis.

Nkonko Kamwangamalu is Professor of Linguistics in the Department of English at Howard University.

Rosina Lozano is Associate Professor of History in the Department of History at Princeton University.

Stephen May is Professor in Te Puna Wānanga (School of Māori and Indigenous Education) in the Faculty of Education and Social Work at the University of Auckland.

Pritipuspa Mishra (editor) is Associate Professor of History at the University of Southampton.

Helder De Schutter is Professor of Social and Political Philosophy at KU Leuven.

Ying-Ying Tan (editor) is Associate Professor of Linguistics and Multilingual Studies in the School of Humanities at Nanyang Technological University, Singapore.

Acknowledgements

This volume happened because an amazing group of scholars came together and met for two days in Princeton in the fall of 2017. It was, however, no chance meeting. This meeting would not have happened without the funding of the Fung Global Fellows Network Grant and co-funding from Nanyang Technological University, Singapore, and Southampton University. We are incredibly grateful to Princeton Institute for International and Regional Studies (PIIRS), Beate Witzler, and Nicole Bergman for hosting and organizing the workshop. We are also indebted to Michael Gordin and Gyan Prakash for supporting this work.

We thank our workshop participants, Linda Cardinal, Janet Y. Chen, Tony Crowley, Andrew M. Daily, Helder De Schutter, Nkonko Kamwangamalu, Rosina Lozano, and Stephen May, who have shaped the conversations that have culminated in this volume we have.

We are also grateful to Katie Peace and Jacy Hui at Taylor & Francis for their editorial help and patience. Special thanks to Sophia Tan at the Nanyang Technological University, Singapore, for her careful reading and detailed editorial work on the drafts.

This research is supported by the Ministry of Education, Singapore, under its Academic Research Fund Tier 1 (RG63/18).

1 Questioning the Herderian ideal[1]

Pritipuspa Mishra and Ying-Ying Tan

What is the Herderian ideal? The most (in)famous aspect of Herderian philosophy is perhaps his take on language and nationalism, embodied in the slogan "one people, one fatherland, one language" (cited in Bauman and Briggs, 2003, p. 193). The Herderian ideal is grounded on the belief that a common language is a primordial and necessary condition for building a nation. Bauman and Briggs (2003), in their exposition on Herder's philosophy, explain this idea as follows:

> The desired goal of unification rests upon discursive unity, provided by the authority of tradition and a unified adherence to the national spirit. And here too, linguistic homogeneity is a necessary condition: "One people, one fatherland, one language".
>
> (p. 193)

The Herderian ideal form of the nation-state has been predominantly characterized as a monoglot one. Herder has been known to promote the idea that language forms the *soul* of the nation and language enables the existence of the nation by providing national continuity. For Herder, a nation or a people (*Volk*) is a cultural entity with distinct characteristics and a shared language, and the national character of the people is embodied in its language (De Schutter, 2013, p. 393). In Herder's view, the relationship between language and the nation is very much organic, as "a people is a plant of nature, just one with more branches" (1969, p. 324). The nation, in "the most natural state" is therefore also "*one* people, with one national character" (Herder, 2004, p. 128). This means that a nation necessarily has to have a single national language. To push it to an extreme reading, what Herder has done then is to have enabled a notion of a world of monolingual people. Bauman and Briggs (2003) sum this up by painting a picture of Herder as the purveyor of an "ideology of a monoglot and monologic standard . . . demand[ing] one language, one metadiscursive order, one voice . . . denying the legitimacy of multiple voices and multiple languages in public discourse" (p. 194). One can see why there is an uncomfortable association between Herder and multilingualism or linguistic diversity. It is in fact tempting for proponents of nationalistic agenda to read the Herderian model as one that promotes a monolingual nationhood and thereby pushing for homogeneity in terms of both language and ways of living. In recent years, and across different disciplines, scholars have shown how the future of language in an increasingly multilingual Europe, and even the world, challenges the purportedly Herderian model of "monoglot nations" (e.g. Wright, 2004; Blommaert, 2005; Canagarajah, 2012). This critique also exposes the theoretical limitations of thinking that nation-states should be built upon the ideal of monolingualism. The inadequacy of the "monoglot nation" model becomes especially acute when scholars are faced with the complex linguistic ecologies of non-western, multilingual nation-states.

And it is especially within the post-colonial context that Herder's legacy persists in a fraught position. Scholars have illustrated how his insistence of cultural particularism based on common language both enables the argument for the formation of new post-colonial nation-states while also serving as a spectre of European modular idea of nation-state that often leaves post-colonial nations with a sense of inadequacy due to the multilingual nature of their citizens (e.g. Padgen, 1994; Robinette, 2011; Noyes, 2014; Young, 1995; Muthu, 2003; Chatterjee, 1984; Goswami, 2004). In his description of the nation, Herder insisted that "nothing therefore appears so directly opposite to the end of government as the unnatural enlargement of states, the wild mixture of various races and nations under one sceptre" (1969, p. 324).

This argument against "unnatural enlargement of states" was made in service of his critique of imperialism and slavery (Muthu, 2003; Young, 1995) This critique was based on the idea that when people were alienated from their native tongue or their native land, they degenerated as a collective and this constituted an unethical violence against the colonized peoples. Clearly, this was the sort of argument that would gain support from even the staunchest anti-colonialists like Fanon or Gandhi (see, e.g. Fanon, 1963; Mishra, 2012). However, in arguing that a multilingual collective was unnatural, Herderian thought effectively rendered illegitimate all nations that are formed through the happenstance of empire and therefore consist of a variety of peoples. Why then, does the Herderian model continue to have such valency? How has the Herderian ideal of one nation-one language continued to survive beneath the uncomfortable resolution struck by new multilingual nations as they create fictions of a singular national mother tongue? To what extent then is Herder still relevant in our contemporary world? How have different nations negotiated the Herderian ideal in different ways? What does the way in which multilingual post-colonial nations deal with this crisis tell us about a possible alternative framework for understanding the relationship between language and nation? These are questions that this book seeks to explore. This volume therefore also seeks to address the afterlife of Herderian linguistic nationalism by drawing attention to the ways in which non-European or post-colonial nation-states have contended with the Herderian model. What sorts of adjustments, compromises, and departures did this contention involve? Ultimately, what does this tell us about the linguistic nature of the modern nation-state?

Herder's monolingual claim and post-coloniality

Even though the Herderian claim has been a monolingual one, curiously, at the same time, Herder has also been lauded as a trailblazer for promoting linguistic diversity. Fishman (1982) hailed Herder as the first "genuine pluralist" (p. 7). Others such as Berlin (2001), Taylor (2016), and Kymlicka (2001) also argue for the value of multiculturalism and pluralism, and their works have been linked to or credited to Herder's influence. There is in fact an inherent irreconcilability in Herder's view on nationalism and what Sikka (2011) would describe as Herder's "linguistic constitutivism" (p. 160). Linguists would understand this as Whorfianism (Whorf, 1956). The Whorfian idea is a well-rehearsed one, namely, language determines thought, and therefore language is a manifestation of values and ideas. Language communities therefore conceptualize the world in ways that are different from speakers of other languages. In this view, language is absolutely critical to the development of thought and human consciousness. Fishman (1982) goes as far as to attribute Whorf's ideas to Herder, calling Whorf a student of Herder and "a neo-Herderian champion" (p. 5). What is this idea and in what ways can Herder be seen as a pluralist? It is useful, at this point, to draw out some of the key points of Herder's argument on language. We are by no means trying to reinvent a new reading or provide a comprehensive review of Herder's philosophy here. De Schutter, in this volume, has provided an excellent reconstruction of Herder's philosophy; see Forster (2010, 2018) and Sikka (2011) for detailed readings of Herder's writings. Rather, this section tries to reconcile the apparent contradiction in Herder's views on language and nationalism and to tease out the points of disjuncture that have created this inconsistency.

For Herder, language is intrinsic to man and is what makes man human. In *Treatise on the Origin on Language*, Herder draws out the distinction between animal sounds and human language. Human language, in Herder's view, is what differentiates man from other animals, and "language would become as essential to the human being as—he is a human being" (2002, p. 80). Yet for Herder, language is not something that is "invented by a higher being" (2002, p. 72). Language has to be learnt, and language can only be learnt in the community, and more specifically, from one's parents.

The links between language learning, socialization, and the formation of thought becomes clear when Herder explains how children are brought up. The infant learns not only language from his parents but also "the whole soul, the whole manner of thinking, of his begetters gets communicated to him with the language" (2002, p. 140). Consequently, the child, through the learning of the language of the parents, also experiences the feelings and thoughts of the parents.

> The infant who stammers his first words, stammers a repetition of the feelings of his parents, and swears with each early stammering, in accordance with which his tongue and soul forms itself, that he will make these feelings endure eternally, as truly as he calls them father- or mother-tongue.
>
> (Herder, 2002, p. 140)

One can now see a strong link between the formation of the language and the soul of the human. While language is being acquired, for Herder, the soul is being formed. The soul, specifically, encompasses the feelings, sensations, and ways of life.

> For our mother-tongue was simultaneously the first world that we saw, the first sensations that we felt, the first efficacy and joy that we tasted! The side ideas of place and time, of love and hate, of joy and activity, and whatever the fiery, turbulent soul of youth thought to itself in the process, all gets made eternal along with it. Now *language really becomes tribal core* [Stamm]!
>
> (Herder, 2002, p. 143)

This is where the signs of Whorfianism become obvious. And we can see now how language represents not just the child's and the parents' thoughts and feelings, but also by extension, of the community or the *tribe* the child is part of. If the tribe or community is the nation, then language is the soul of the nation.

And because language for Herder is, as Spencer (1996) would describe as "expressivist", language is "credited with constituting the very contents of our consciousness" (p. 249). For Herder, thinking and reasoning can only be done with language, for language "must be regarded as inherent in, or the natural corollary of, the very first act of human reasoning" (Herder, 1969, p. 20). Because language expresses thoughts, this process also makes language the conduit for values, habits, and practices.

> Each race will bring into its language the sound belonging to its house and family; . . . Climate, air and water, food and drink, will have an influence on the linguistic organs and naturally also on language. Society's ethics and the mighty goddess Habit will soon introduce these peculiarities and those differences in accordance with behavior and decency.
>
> (Herder, 2002, p. 148)

What we have here is language and thought in a symbiotic relationship. Man needs language in order to think and to express his thoughts. The world that one lives in is being shaped by the language one knows, "that cave in which the inventors of language and all their followers thought: the plastic shapes of those small worlds from out of which they looked into the great world" (Herder, 2002, p. 144). At the same time, language will bear characteristics of each community, race, and cultural group. These different groups will bring into their language their ways of life, their habits, behaviours, and values. It is also through their language that we will have glimpses of different worlds. Every individual's worldview is shaped by their language, and in turn, language is the tool to experience these worldviews.

Just as humans are different, Herder believes that there exists as many languages as there are different human groups. Herder makes this very explicit:

> [T]he whole human species could not possibly remain a single herd, likewise it could not retain a single language either. So there arises a formation of different national languages.
>
> (Herder, 2002, p. 147)

It is clear that Herder does not believe in a monolingual world. He is, as Fishman (1982) would believe, in favour "of a multilingual, multicultural", world in which "little peoples" and "little languages" would not only be respected but valued (p. 5). And there is real basis in Fishman's belief, for Herder believes that language is the treasure trove which holds a community's art, history, culture, and sense of being.

> And what a treasure familial language is for a developing race! In almost all small nations of all parts of the world, however little cultivated [*gebildet*] they may be, ballads of their fathers, songs of the deeds of their ancestors, are the treasure of their language and history and poetic art, [they are] their wisdom and their encouragement, their instruction and their games and dances.
>
> (Herder, 2002, p. 147)

Herder's advocacy for language, in this conception, can then be used by language activists arguing for language recognition, promotion of linguistic diversity, and protection of language rights. After all, protecting languages would be the way to uphold cultures and preserve different ways of seeing the world. And it is in fact an argument that is used by many, Fishman (1982) being one of them. In fact, linguistic pluralism does exist for Herder, but only insofar as this pluralism is presented as distinct nations, in well-defined territories. He believes that every nation has its own territory: "Does the earth not have space for us all? Does not one land lie peacefully beside the other?" (Herder, 2002, p. 379). Linguistic pluralism is, for Herder, a way "to enable each people to maintain its own national character" (p. 385). This is not an unfamiliar idea. Van Parijs (2011) in his argument for linguistic justice sees territoriality as a way for languages to survive and for linguistic groups to assert their right to their languages. However, as we will see in May (this volume), territoriality is by no means an adequate response to the kinds of linguistic complexity we see in modern nation-states, nor a solution to questions of linguistic justice (see De Schutter, also in this volume).

Problems notwithstanding, how can one man be known for encouraging both linguistic pluralism and monolingualism? How did Herder land himself into what Crowley in this volume brilliantly calls "Herder's language trap"? In some way, this trap is an inevitable consequence of his argument. For language to be the soul of a man, it necessarily follows that language will be the soul of the nation. The act of language acquisition, for Herder, is no random act. The acquisition of language starts from a mother to a child, via the mother tongue. This same mother tongue is shared by members of the same community. We can call it a community, or we can call it a nation. What this means is that if Language X is the soul of a man, and this man belongs to a community in which all speak Language X, then Language X becomes the soul of this community. If we call this community a nation, then Language X necessarily becomes the soul of the nation.

There is nothing wrong with this argument except that it is primarily a monolingual claim. The fact that Herder sees a world with many languages does not mean that he sees multilingualism within a nation or within individuals. Piller (2016), in her defence of Herder, claims that Herder is a proponent for multilingualism for he was himself a speaker of multiple languages. However, being a speaker of multiple tongues does not detract from his failure to acknowledge that people can have multiple mother tongues. To be fair, this failure is not Herder's alone. The term "mother tongue" is highly problematic as it necessarily invokes only one language. One only has one birth mother, and as an extension of that metaphor, one can therefore only have one mother tongue.

The monoglot nation is birthed when this one singular language is then tied to the nation. Even if Herder believes in a multilingual world, his argument leaves no room for a nation with multiple languages. His strong belief that language is a manifestation of a worldview or identity is inherently at odds with the realities of a multilingual nation. If a man has only one soul, so does the nation. And the nation can only articulate in one language. As Crowley (see Chapter 4 of this volume) rightly observes, "the identification of 'the national language' as the key to 'national identity' is based on an elision of the cultural differences within the nation". And one can imagine why this is problematic, especially in spaces where multilingualism is integral to the character of nations (e.g. most nations in Asia and Africa). And we can see this tension across time and territories. Despite being multilingual, new nation-states saw the need to embrace the Herderian model, often leading to a frantic search for the soul that would be in the form of a national language. Rather than dismissing the need for a common tongue, the national language came to serve as both a claim and an anxiety for nationalist movements of the twentieth century. For instance, in India, leaders argued for making Hindustani, an amalgamation of Hindu, Urdu, and elements from regional Indian languages, into the national language. And in the Philippines, leaders created a political fiction that Filipino, a construction based on Tagalog and its regional languages such as Ilocano, can serve as a common language for the whole nation. The anxieties of having a national language that can speak *to* and *for* the nation can be felt most acutely in post-colonial states as these nations strive to create a new national identity while climbing out of the shadows of colonialism.

Yet the quest for the singular national tongue, as we will learn from the various chapters in this volume—from the United States (Lozano) to India (Mishra) and China (Chen), from Africa (Kawangamalu) to the Caribbean (Daily), and to a tiny island in Southeast Asia (Tan)—is not without its challenges. We are reminded, through these chapters, of Derrida's claim, "I have only one language and it is not mine . . . Or better still I am monolingual" (1998, p. 1). By drawing attention to the alienation of his self from his language, Derrida provokes us to think about the connections between the purported monolingualism of the modern subject and the realities and legacies of imperialism. For Derrida, the status of the French language is deeply embattled, for it is both the language of the other and the language of the self. Derrida's discussion of the colonized and post-colonial condition troubles our understanding of the legacies of Herderian nationalism by forcing us to think about the relationship between the imperial language and the colonized subject.

And this provocation opens up a far more complex linguistic field where the imperial language interacts with the national and minority languages of now post-colonial nations by establishing a hierarchical relationship between the imperial and native tongue. As studies on colonial linguistics (Errington, 2008; Irvine, 1995) have revealed, the relationship between imperial languages such as English or French and native languages such as Arabic or Tamil was often mired in the politics of the European civilizational mission. Young (1995), for instance, has discussed the European understanding of culture and its relationship with the non-West at length. This imperative has often led to the idea that colonized languages are somehow less equipped for modern life than imperial languages. Apart from a distinction in ability, the rise of colonial linguistics also places the languages of the world in familial relationships with each other. The result of this was that there emerged an alliance between colonial linguistics and liberal imperialism where familial adjacency between European languages and Indian languages for instance gave rise to an imperial project of liberal development where systems of imperial rule worked towards "developing" native languages up-to the standard of the imperial language. Borrowing Dipesh Chakrabarty's (2000) formulation of colonial temporality, this liberal project effectively placed the imperial and native language in two different times—in the modern and the non-modern respectively. In order to inhabit the colonized modern world, the colonial subject has had to espouse the modern imperial language which in turn relegated the native language to a more native and private sphere. For instance, the history of press in India illustrates how two parallel public spheres emerged and the vernacular public sphere was qualitatively different from the European public sphere as it was imagined by Jurgen Habermas (Bhargava & Reifeld, 2005). Hence, in terms of language, the colonized subject was split down the middle—between a modern European language speaking self and a native language speaking non-modern self. However, as Homi Bhabha's (1984) discussion of mimicry suggests, this separation was not airtight. The articulation of one self often spilled over in that of the other. This slippage is further complicated when we consider the existing hierarchies within native languages and the operations of power and exclusion at play within fundamentally multilingual colonized societies. Modern monolingualism therefore was neither natural nor painless for newly post-colonial nations of the world.

If monolingualism was not natural to non-European states, then why did it serve as the governing template for the relationship between language and nation in the post-colonial world? The reason, we would like to suggest, has to do with the politics of anti-colonialism and decolonization in a twofold way. First, as May's chapter (Chapter 3) in this volume illustrates, the modular form of the modernist nation-state has always been monolingual. The political reception of Herder and the German Romanticism arguments on the construction of the European ideal of nationhood has meant that for a nation to qualify as a nation-state, it has to have a common language. This need for a common language is both ideological (borrowing from a German Romantic idea of language as the repository of national culture) and administrative (in order to enable modern governmentality) (Ngũgĩ, 1986). As the ideal model of a nation-state came to be seen as a monoglot entity, new nations in the making in the colonized world had to buy into and make real the myth of monolingualism within their boundaries. The struggle to claim a national language in colonized and quasi-colonized spaces in Asia, Latin America, and the Caribbean is tied to this need to assimilate to the dominant model for nationhood (Chatterjee, 1984; Goswami, 2004). The determining power of this model is evident in the interwar period, when global discussions on self-determination for the colonized people clearly linked self-determination with linguistic identity (Manela, 2007).

The linking of self-determination with linguistic identity brings us to the second way in the legacy of Herder that has had an impact on the politics of anticolonialism and decolonization. The process of decolonization had much to thank Herder for his strident critique of imperialism which was founded on an impassioned defence of the particularity of non-western cultures. Berlin and Hardy (2000) have argued that Herder was a "counter enlightenment" thinker. They drew attention to Herder's resistance to the universalizing tendencies within Enlightenment thought that often judged non-European peoples through a set of European standards. Herder, according to Berlin and Hardy, believed that the human community was made up of a variety of cultures and they should be valued equally. In his famous treatise on history, "This too a Philosophy for the Formation of Humanity", Herder argues that we need to acknowledge the multiplicity of ways in which various cultures have developed.

> Should there not be manifest *progress* and *development* but in a higher sense than people have imagined it? Do you see this *river current* [*Strom*] swimming along—how it sprang forth from a little source, grows, breaks off there, begins here, ever meanders, and bores further and deeper—but always remains *water!, river current!*, drop always only drop, until it plunges into the ocean—what if it were like that with the human species?
>
> (Herder, 2002, pp. 298–299)

By comparing human development to a river, Herder hoped to counter the dominant linear narrative of human progress where Europe provided the template for human civilization. In doing so, he illustrated that cultures could be different from European culture and yet be valid in their own terms.

Recently, as the scholarship on the Enlightenment has illustrated that there was no singular enlightenment, scholars such as Zammito, Menges, and Menze (2010) have come to emphasize the complexity of Herder's take on culture. Both Muthu (2003) and Sikka (2011) have also drawn our attention to how Herder deftly balanced his argument for the validity of multiple cultures and the insistence on the idea of a common humanity spanning the globe. The latter draws on the central impulses of Enlightenment thought which argued that all human beings share a common humanity and hence, any difference amongst them has to be understood as a variance in a spectrum of development. This take on humanity framed the relationship between the European and non-European cultures as one of model versus not-yet-there prototype while the argument of cultural particularism flew in the face of Enlightenment thought.

Padgen (1994) has illustrated how Herder's move away from Enlightenment thought was effected through a move to "detach the process of change from any direct causal link with the temporal" (p. 144). That is, rather than thinking about cultural formation as a result of temporal progress in the singular direction, Herder situated cultural formation in the spatial realm. Geography, he argued, had an immense impact on how cultures were formed. For instance, while discussing the difference between the Egyptians and the Greek, he suggested that in consideration of the difference between Greek and Egyptian art and skill we need to think about the differences in ecology.

> Egypt *had no pastures*—hence the inhabitant had to *well learn* agriculture; and how much Providence facilitated this difficult learning for him through the *fecund Nile*. Egypt had *no wood*, people had to learn to build with stone; *there were stone-quarries enough there*, the *Nile was comfortably there* to transport them thence—how high the art rose!, how much it developed other arts! . . . Here again too, stupidity to tear a *single Egyptian virtue* out of the land, the time, and the boyhood of the human spirit and to measure it with the *criterion of another time*! If, as was shown, it was already possible for the Greek to be so mistaken about the Egyptian and for the Oriental to hate the Egyptian, then, it seems to me, it really ought to be one's first thought to see him merely *in his place*, otherwise one sees, especially looking hither from Europe, the most distorted caricature.
>
> (Herder, 2002, p. 282)

By moving from the temporal to the spatial, Herder provided a substantive basis for anti-colonial arguments against Empire. The imperial civilizing mission that promised progress to the colonized peoples could be refuted on the grounds that civilizations are multiple and European civilization need not be transplanted to the non-West. Europe, as Dipesh Chakrabarty (2000) puts it, is simply a province of humanity. Furthermore, the spatial argument for cultural particularism also allowed anti-colonial thinkers to draw alternative boundaries and borders to undermine modern imperial geographies.

However, this anti-imperial argument for cultural particularism was also founded on an argument for linguistic identity of emergent nation-states. Hence, anti-colonial movements had to account for their own unitary linguistic identity in order to participate in the world republic of nations. In fact, the drive to produce a monoglot image of the new nation can be seen in the strong nationalist movements in India and China in modern history. In this volume, some of the chapters bring into discussion contemporary critiques of monolingualism and how they can be put in conversation with histories of the Empire, anti-colonial nationalism, and post-colonial language policies. This opens us up to the complexity of the status of monolingualism and multilingualism in the post-colonial world, where the desire for monolingualism in a multilingual reality vies against the need to interrogate the applicability of the Herder model to their national context.

Summaries of chapters

This book therefore is a research conversation informed by a shared concern about the limitations of existing conceptual literature on the relationship between language and nationalism. We propose that the current reassessment of the Herderian model can be fruitfully extended in two complementary directions: in space, beyond Europe, and in time, beyond the contemporary. The authors in this volume work from diverse archives across Asia, Africa, Europe, Latin America, and the Caribbean, and by doing so, we propose answers to the aforementioned questions from a global perspective that takes into account the specificities of a range of colonial experiences and political regimes. And by extending the discussion backwards in time, a more historical reading of the making of modern nations can allow us to see how multilingualism has always disrupted constructions of monoglot nations. As it is, most conversations about our research questions have been field and language specific. This volume also seeks to unite multiple strands of inquiry and disciplinary approaches, which could lead to alternative readings of the relationship between language and nation. We trust that this innovation will provoke further cross-fertilization of ideas across diverse fields and disciplines.

We begin the conversation with Helder De Schutter, whose chapter is an examination of the contemporary relevance of the philosophy of Herder, and how Herder's philosophy can be used to justify the recognition and protection of languages today. De Schutter outlines clearly Herder's philosophy on how language opens a "life-world", and how within this argument presents a dilemma—one that assumes and favours monolingualism, which in essence goes against the idea of linguistic diversity. De Schutter proposes how Herder can be used effectively to defend language recognition as it is possible to reject the monolingual understanding while still holding on to the life-world account by allowing individuals and territories characterized by linguistic hybridity to be constitutively embedded in their linguistic horizon(s). Purifying Herder's life-world argument from its monolingual bias, and thus injecting the hybridity conception of language into Herder's life-world argument, De Schutter renews the reading of Herder's theory, making it fit for contemporary language recognition projects.

Stephen May pushes the applicability of the Herderian model further by unravelling the Herderian idea of a reified national language and thereby arguing for an alternative linguistic ideology for the contemporary nation-state. In May's discussion, he takes us through the history of how the Herderian juxtaposition of language and nation has produced a hierarchy of languages with the national language at the top and minority as well as regional languages lagging at the bottom has led to the migrant languages. As a counterpoint to recent scholarly responses using the Vertovec's (2007) idea of superdiversity, May proposes that we draw on Kraus' notion of complex diversity that allows for the fluid and constructed nature of language identity while also recognizing that these identities exist in social, cultural, and political contexts. Complex diversity allows us to question the modernist state's monolingualism while continuing to enable group-based linguistic activism that recognizes the claims of both migrants and indigenous peoples.

Through a history of language politics in the nineteenth- and twentieth-century Ireland, Tony Crowley explores the legacies of Herder's monolingualism in Ireland. He argues that the politics of this period illustrates how Ireland falls into what he calls Herder's "language trap". Crowley shows how Herder's philosophy of language has enabled Irish nationalism through its insistence of the importance of cultural particularism founded on the Irish language. Through a history of the language debates in the Irish public sphere and English- and Irish-driven language policy from the eighteenth century to contemporary times, Crowley illustrates how this early dependence of Herderian monoglossia has meant that everyday heteroglossia has had to be denied in the service of the monoglot Irish nation. This is essentially the Herderian language trap as it does not allow everyday multilingual realities to inform nationalist linguistic politics. In fact, this insistence on monoglossia has served as an alibi for reactionary politics amongst some sections of the post-independence Irish political sphere.

Rosina Lozano's chapter questions the monoglot nature of the modern American State through the framework of settler colonialism. This approach allows Lozano to unravel the notion that the United States of America is and has been a monolingual English-speaking nation. By focusing on the State and Territorial Legislative Session laws from the 1830s to the 1930s, Lozano illustrates how the emergent American state was able to absorb linguistic differences amongst its settler population of European language speakers by keeping the stipulations on the language of governance fairly broad. To make her case, Lozano carefully tracks the use of translation of official documents from English to European languages like German and Spanish to illustrate how the State sought to accommodate other language speakers. By coupling the history of American language policy and settler colonialism, Lozano has illustrated the complex legacies of Herderian linguistic and nationalist thought.

Pritipuspa Mishra explores these complex legacies of Herderian thought through a focus on India's search for a common national language. At the centre of this search was a language called Hindustani. Through a history of the debates around this language, Mishra illustrates the profound impact of the Herderian dictum of one nation-one language on how the nation dealt with contentious nature of linguistic politics in India. Drawing on Peter Novack's discussion of historical objectivity as myth, Mishra shows how a common national language served as an organizing myth that would hold at bay the disintegration threatened by linguistic politics across regional India through a promise of unity. Like a myth, this common national language was simply a noble dream and not a reality. However, even as the promise of Hindustani dissipated by the 1970s, the underlying narratives of common cultural origin remained dominant in Indian nationalist thought. Therefore, for India, the impact of normative Herderian ideas of linguistic nationalism was in the realm of ideology rather than in the realm of linguistic policy making as the multilingual reality of India could never really measure up to the Herderian ideal.

Janet Y. Chen's paper tells the story of *putonghua*. This is a story of how the Chinese, at both the state level and the level of the speech communities, come to terms with the learning of this imposed "standard" or "common language" in China in the 1950s. This paper is held together by the idea of "laughing", or perhaps more negatively, of "mockery". And yet this is no joking matter, as the learning of *putonghua* was and remains a state project that belies the Herderian ideal. And this social history of *promoting* and *learning* Putonghua opens up a few questions that are not only historically interesting but also linguistically significant. The construction of a national identity, as we have been led to believe, by Herder no less, is one that is bound to the idea of the national language. Janet elucidated that the *putonghua* is really a repackaged form of the national language—and the appeal lies precisely in the moving away from the discourse of the "nation" (i.e. state) to one that is of the people (common language). And this is a rhetorical move that seemingly gives power to the people in the process of linguistic unity.

Nkonko Kamwangamalu's paper presents a view of how Herder can be applied in post-colonial Africa. Despite his championing linguistic homogeneity, Herder arguably never envisioned one continent colonizing and imposing its languages on another, as happened with Europe's colonization and imposition of its languages in the African continent. It is against the background of Herder's view of linguistic diversity and of his criticism of colonial powers that this paper seeks to propose an alternative to inherited colonial language ideologies, including the ideology of the nation-state and the ideology of development, both of which have informed Africa's language-in-education policies since colonialism ended 60 years ago to the present. Kanwangamalu, in essence, explores why, in post-colonial Africa, the inherited monolingual model favouring European languages as the sole medium of instruction in school persists. Drawing on theoretical developments in language economics and critical theory, Kanwangamalu proposes that prestige planning for African languages is the way forward to changing the status quo.

Andrew M. Daily's chapter illustrates how the history of slavery and diaspora in the Caribbean unravels the Herderian framework for linguistic nationalism. By focusing on Eduardo Glissant's engagement with the question of what should be the language of the Caribbean, Daily has shown how the need to have a uniting national language left the region with no prior models to build upon. Caribbean peoples, formed from histories of violence, displacement, slavery, and creolization, do not easily fit into Herder's organic account of the nation. There were only two choices available in the Caribbean—a construction of national language based on African languages through a celebration of negritude, or a language drawn from the creole experience of the Caribbean people. And yet neither of these options fits the Herderian model. Daily argues that Glissant can help us to understand how the Caribbean experience of modernity challenges organicist nationalism and poses new models of national identity and cultural belonging.

Ying-Ying Tan's paper is an application of the Herderian philosophy to the small, seemingly multilingual, post-colonial state of Singapore. Her paper outlines a story of how the state negotiates and presents multilingualism in language policies that are seemingly un-Herderian. Unpacking and outlining the state's different strategies to manage linguistic diversity, Tan highlights a new nation's struggles to maintain the facade of multilingualism while promoting the use of the colonial language. She also shows how the carefully crafted multilingual policies are multilingual only in form, but monolingual in practice. Using sociolinguistic data as evidence, Tan presents a picture of how Singapore today is confronted by a set of linguistic realities that seem to move away from multilingualism. Her paper argues how multilingual Singapore is a myth created to balance the development of the Herderian ideal and the realities of how languages come to represent the nation.

Note

1 This research is supported by the Ministry of Education, Singapore, under its Academic Research Fund Tier 1 (RG63/18).

References

Bauman, R., & Briggs, C. L. (2003). *Voices of modernity: Language ideologies and the politics of inequality*. Cambridge: Cambridge University Press.

Berlin, I. (2001). *The roots of romanticism*. Princeton, NJ: Princeton University Press.

Berlin, I., & Hardy, H. (2000). *Three critics of the enlightenment: Vico, Hamann, Herder*. Princeton, NJ: Princeton University Press.

Bhabha, H. (1984). Of mimicry and man: The ambivalence of colonial discourse. *October*, *28*, 125–133.

Bhargava, R., & Reifeld, H. (2005). *Civil society, public sphere and citizenship: Dialogues and perceptions*. New Delhi: Sage.

Blommaert, J. (2005). Situating language rights: English and Swahili in Tanzania revisited. *Journal of Sociolinguistics*, *9*(3), 390–417.

Canagarajah, S. (2012). *Translingual practice: Global Englishes and cosmopolitan relations*. London: Routledge.

Chakrabarty, D. (2000). *Provincializing Europe: Postcolonial thought and historical difference*. Princeton, NJ: Princeton University Press.

Chatterjee, P. (1984). *Nationalist thought and the colonial world: A derivative discourse?* Minneapolis: University of Minnesota Press.

Derrida, J. (1998). *Monolingualism of the other, or, the prosthesis of origin* (P. Mensah, Trans.). Stanford: Stanford University Press.

De Schutter, H. (2013). *Herder, Johann Gottfried, encyclopedia of modern political thought* (G. Claeys, Ed., pp. 393–394). Washington, DC: CQ Press.

Errington, J. J. (2008). *Linguistics in a colonial world: A story of language, meaning, and power*. Oxford: Blackwell.

Fanon, F. (1963). *The wretched of the earth*. New York: Penguin Books.

Fishman, J. (1982). Whorfianism of the third kind: Ethnolinguistic diversity as a worldwide societal asset. *Language in Society*, *11*(1), 1–14.

Forster, M. N. (2010). *After Herder: Philosophy of language in the German tradition*. Oxford: Oxford University Press.

Forster, M. N. (2018). *Herder's philosophy*. Oxford: Oxford University Press.

Goswami, M. (2004). *Producing India: From colonial economy to national space*. Chicago, IL: University of Chicago Press.

Herder, J. G. (1969). *J. G. Herder on social and political culture* (F. Barnard, Ed. & Trans.). Cambridge: Cambridge University Press.

Herder, J. G. (2002). *Philosophical writings* (M. N. Forster, Ed. & Trans.). Cambridge: Cambridge University Press.

Herder, J. G. (2004). *Another philosophy of history and selected political writings* (I. D. Evrigenis & D. Pellerin, Ed. & Trans.). Indianapolis/Cambridge: Hackett.

Irvine, J. T. (1995). The family Romance of colonial linguistics: Gender and family in nineteenth century representations of African languages. *Pragmatics, 5*(2), 139–153.

Kymlicka, W. (2001). *Politics in the vernacular: Nationalism, multiculturalism and citizenship.* Oxford: Oxford University Press.

Manela, E. (2007). *The Wilsonian moment: Self-determination and the international origins of anticolonial nationalism.* Oxford: Oxford University Press.

Mishra, P. (2012). The mortality of Hindustani. *Parallax, 18*(3), 71–83.

Muthu, S. (2003). *Enlightenment against empire.* Princeton, NJ: Princeton University Press.

Ngũgĩ, T. W. (1986). *Decolonizing the mind: The politics of language in African literature.* Portsmouth, NH: Heinemann.

Noyes, J. K. (2014). Herder, postcolonial theory and the antinomy of universal reason. *The Cambridge Journal of Postcolonial Literary Inquiry, 1*, 107–122.

Padgen, A. (1994). The effacement of difference: Colonialism and the origins of nationalism in Diderot and Herder. In G. Prakash (Ed.), *After colonialism: Imperial histories and postcolonial displacements* (pp. 129–152). Princeton, NJ: Princeton University Press.

Piller, I. (2016, March 4). Herder: An explainer for linguists. In *Language on the move.* Retrieved from www.languageonthemove.com/herder-an-explainer-for-linguists/

Robinette, N. (2011). The world laid waste: Herder, language labor, empire. *New Literary History, 42*(1), 193–203.

Sikka, S. (2011). *Herder on humanity and cultural difference.* Cambridge: Cambridge University Press.

Spencer, V. (1996). Towards an ontology of holistic individualism: Herder's theory of identity, culture and community. *History of European Ideas, 22*, 245–260.

Taylor, C. (2016). *The language animal: The full shape of the human linguistic capacity.* Cambridge: Belknap Press.

Van Parijs, P. (2011). *Linguistic justice for Europe and the world.* Oxford: Oxford University Press.

Vertovec, S. (2007). Super-diversity and its implications. *Ethnic and Racial Studies, 30*, 1024–1054.

Whorf, B. (1956). *Language, thought, and reality: Selected writings of Benjamin Lee Whorf* (J. B. Carroll, Ed.). Cambridge: MIT Press.

Wright, S. (2004). *Language policy and language planning: From nationalism to globalisation.* Basingstoke: Palgrave Macmillan.

Young, R. (1995). *Colonial desire.* London: Routledge.

Zammito, J. H., Menges, K., & Menze, E. A. (2010). Johann Gottfried Herder revisited: The revolution in scholarship in the last quarter century. *Journal of the History of Ideas, 71*(4), 661–684.

2 Herder

Blessing or curse for linguistic justice? A contemporary assessment

Helder De Schutter

The world has over seven thousand languages divided into 193 states. Almost all languages are internally marked by diversity in the form of regional, class, or ethnic dialects. In addition, English is today firmly on its way to becoming the lingua franca of mankind. These three facts of linguistic diversity make it clear that multilingualism is the order of the day for all states, cities, and supranational organizations today. In such conditions, countless language policy decisions have to be made: over the question of which language(s) state institutions should function in, which language(s) public education is to be organized in, whether minorities should be granted language rights, whether voting ballots are to be printed in multiple languages, whether each language has a right to equal recognition or whether considerations of efficiency and social cohesion can allow for certain languages or dialects to legitimately gain superior status, etc. And all states where English is not the (sole) official language have to decide whether the spread of English is to be welcomed or resisted, for instance in the public sphere, in schools, and in universities. Everywhere in the world, states are plagued with these challenging and often destabilizing questions over language policy and language rights. In many states, such as Canada, Estonia, India, Rwanda, Spain, South Africa, Sri Lanka, or the United States, and in supranational bodies such as the European Union, language policy issues regularly dominate the political agenda.

Anyone trying to make sense of this situation must at some point give thought to the fact that language identity matters to individuals, as well as to the questions of why this is the case, and whether this fact is compelling enough to normatively warrant measures such as language protection or equal language recognition. Several answers have been worked out in response to these questions, and they are part of today's literature on linguistic justice.

In this literature, the eighteenth-century German philosopher of language Johann Gottfried Herder is a towering figure. His advocacy for the value of language has been immensely influential and is still prominent in contemporary debates. On the Herderian account, languages and life-worlds, shared ways of being, are entwined, such that speakers of a language in relevant ways are and think alike. To destroy such a horizon is to render people anomic, to take away the context within which their activities become meaningful. This argument came to be a key view of a tradition sometimes referred to as the Hamann-Herder-Humboldt view, which also pervades the work of theorists like Martin Heidegger, Hans-Georg Gadamer, and Charles Taylor (Lafont, 1994, p. 13; Taylor, 2016, p. 48). But it has also become influential among language activists arguing for language rights and language recognition: many of these activists argue that language is a protector of culture and of distinct ways of life. Also many advocates of multiculturalism, pluralism, and the politics of recognition today, from Isaiah Berlin (2001) to Charles Taylor (2016) to Will Kymlicka (2001a, 2001b), remain in the grip of this argument for the value of language.

At the same time, Herder is also a controversial figure. While he is heralded as a visionary by theorists like Taylor (2016) or Forster (2018), he has been denounced as a dangerous irrational romanticist by people like Karl Popper (1994, p. 265), Alain Finkielkraut (1987, pp. 112–114), and Paul Cliteur (2005, p. 119). It is certainly true that part of the bad press that Herder receives is due to the direction in which his followers took his nationalism, and as I will show below, Herder in no way approves of nationalist aggression or national favouritism. On the other hand, Herder (2004) is indeed also the father of the idea that the "most natural state is therefore also *one* people, with one national character" (p. 128), he is a fierce critique of multinational states, and, he thinks human beings are essentially monolingual.

Herder is therefore both a blessing and a curse to supporters of linguistic minorities and language rights: he offers the most influential argument that exists for the value of language, but this advocacy is couched in monistic terms. In this contribution I undertake a contemporary assessment of Herder's linguistic nationalism. I analyse the life-world argument and argue that it is successful and should rightly continue to form the philosophical backbone of the pursuit of linguistic justice today. Yet Herder's assumption of a one-to-one relationship between languages, territories, and peoples was and is deeply flawed, back in the eighteenth century and today. It is especially problematic for post-colonial states and for many contemporary instances of linguistic hybridity in Europe and North America. Yet it is possible to peel this monolingual assumption off the life-world account: it is not because individuals and territories can be characterized by linguistic hybridity (such as bilingualism or minorities within minorities) that these hybrid individuals are no longer constitutively embedded in their linguistic life-worlds.

In Section I of this chapter, I reconstruct Herder's famous argument for the value of language. I term it the 'life-world' argument, situate it vis-à-vis other traditions of arguing about language, and I make the case that it can successfully ground a theory of language recognition. In Section II, I show how Herder couches this life-world argument in an "ontology of discreteness", and how this leads to Herder's theory of linguistic nationalism. In Section III, I argue that this argument, and its associated ontology, is still of relevance today, particularly to the school of liberal nationalism. In Section IV, I argue that Herder's life-world account and his monistic concept of language are separable and that we can reground the life-world account in a hybrid conception of language of relevance to multilingual contexts. The result is a form of linguistic pluralism: an argument for language recognition that respects instances of opacity, multiple linguistic identities, and minorities within minorities and does so on the basis of Herder's argument for the value of language.

Section I: the life-world argument

Herder is important for historical reasons because of the major influence he had on later thinkers and movements (see also Forster, 2018, p. 1; Taylor, 2016, pp. 48–50). But he remains also of theoretical importance for understanding linguistic justice today. This is because of his particular argument for the value of language. To grasp the nature of this argument, it helps to oppose it to two other major arguments surrounding the value of language that, like Herder's, are each at the heart of a tradition of thinking about the political value of language in Europe since early modernity.

The first is vernacular humanism: many late fifteenth- and sixteenth-century humanists grounded their thinking about language in the value of dignity and respect. We should not live in humiliation and shame. We are to be proud and esteemed citizens. For this school of thought, this importance of dignity has linguistic preconditions: we should not bow linguistically to other languages, but we should speak and cultivate our own vernacular with confidence and eloquence. We should also avoid loan words and enrich our language with new native words. The people holding this view are sometimes called "vernacular humanists": they included, among others, Pietro Bembo (1967), Lorenzo de Medici (1995), and Joachim du Bellay (1948). This is the tradition that began to actively fight the idea that Latin is to be the language for science. It is responsible for the first vernacular grammars and dictionaries in early modern Europe, and it spurred the development and standardization of national languages such as Italian, Spanish, German, and Dutch. Just as the ancient Romans eloquently used their own mother tongue in politics and when conducting science, so should we today, these humanists argued, also use, develop, and enrich our own vernaculars and speak with dignity (see Gravelle, 1988; Patten, 2006 for overviews).

The second tradition—that of the French Enlightenment—has a radically different take on the political value of language. The late eighteenth-century revolutionary ideologists such as Barère (2002), Grégoire (2002), and Duhamel (1792) were concerned with language and with the role language plays in the thought process. They were convinced that the success of the revolution depended in part on its ability to eradicate vague language and linguistic confusion. Their solution was to purify French and to spread it all over France. The purification project entailed "revolutionizing" French by weeding out synonyms and ambiguous constructions and by producing a transparent spelling, grammar, and dictionary. To spread this new French, they argued for the eradication of linguistic diversity. The *patois* made 30 peoples out of one people, argued l'Abbé Grégoire (2002[1794], p. 337). This is highly problematic, he argues. It leads, for example, to a lack of cohesion and stability. And it is incompatible with the revolutionary ideal of equality because social equality implies linguistic homogeneity: people must be confronted with the same ideas and opportunities, and the best way to ensure these is linguistic unification. In addition, linguistic pluralism is also bad for liberty because it safe-guards the power of local priests over the patois-speaking peasants. For these reasons, France ought to be linguistically unified. These French ideologues did not deny that languages may be sources of local identity. On the contrary, their argument was premised on the belief that languages mattered to identity. Yet, they argued that equality, cohesion, and liberty provide reasons to actively seek to destroy local minority languages. It is because language is a source of identity that we should crush local identity and create one French nation.

Herder is the intellectual trailblazer of a third view of thinking about language policy, one that agrees with vernacular humanists that preserving and protecting language identities is of great value (in contrast to French Enlightenment theo-rists, who sought to destroy local linguistic identities), but for a different reason. Herder believes that languages are valuable not because they provide dignity but because they open a common way of thinking among speakers, a shared "life-world". For Herder, language discloses the world for human beings, as I will now set out to show.

Herder argues that we are brought up in the world as linguistically constituted human beings. But it is not merely *Sprachigkeit* or "linguisticality" that counts: in addition to being constituted by language per se, we are constituted by our particular language, our mother tongue, by *Muttersprachigkeit*. He emphasizes that the world that we experience is the one handed down to us through the par-ticular language spoken by our parents and family. Parents raise their children in their own mother tongue. Children are consequently immersed in the language of their parents and, because of that, in the parents' feelings and experiences that are interwoven with that language. When a child stammers its first words, it merely repeats the feelings of its parents. Both the child's tongue and its soul are impreg-nated by its parents' particular way of life (Herder, 2002, p. 142, 1987, p. 335). Herder says that for the parents, the language of their children is therefore "*a dialect of their own thoughts, a paean to their own deeds*" (Herder, 2002, p. 143, 1987, p. 336).

The languages that the parents speak and inculcate their children with are them-selves influenced by the ethics and customs of the peoples that speak them (as well as by climate and local circumstances). Since the language of the parents is the language of a people, a nation, the children are not just brought up in a familial way but also in a national way of thinking. For Herder, language gives the speaker access to a national way of thinking; it moulds the individual into a national mind-set. Languages are thus repositories of national ways of being. A people has no idea for which it does not have a word (Herder, 1987, p. 309; SW, XIII, p. 357[1]).

Yet it is not the case that people are passive in this process: peoples shape language just as much as language shapes peoples. Languages and peoples stand in a symbiotic relationship. Herder argues that every people speaks as it thinks and thinks as it speaks (SW, II, p. 18). In fact, the genius of a people or nation is nowhere better displayed, says Herder, than in the physiognomy of its language, including in how its language expresses time and person, whether it has an abun-dance of action terms or rather of abstract nouns, etc. (SW, XIII, p. 364). He goes as far as to say that, given this connection between languages and peoples, the best way to compose a history of human understanding would be to write a philosophical comparison of languages (SW, XXIII, p. 363).

This gets us to the heart of the idea of there being a *Volksgeist* [national spirit]: by being inculcated with a language that fits a people like a (tailor-made) shoe fits a foot, we get to experience the world in a similar manner. Language moulds people into a national frame of thinking, enabling them to act in unison. By being inculcated with a language, the child is also inculcated with a specific perspective, with a mental world. "[A]long with words viewpoints got established as shrines for youthful adoration at the same time, so that the world should be regarded from these viewpoints and no others for a whole lifetime!" (Herder, 2002, p. 143, n. 167). Our language gives access to this world: "our mother-tongue was simultaneously the first world that we saw, the first sensations that we felt, the first efficacy and joy that we tasted!" (Herder, 2002, p. 143, 1987, p. 336).

By contrast, if we lose the disposition to think in the language in which we are brought up, we lose ourselves and also the world (SW, XVIII, pp. 336–337). In other words, we perceive the world in linguistic terms, that is, in terms passed on to us by our family and people. Language is one of the things that constitute who we are: an individual's being in the world and worldview is inherently tied up with his language.

This also means that we never acquire direct, culturally unmediated access to things. Already in his early *Fragmente über die neuere Deutsche Litteratur* (1768), Herder mentions that language sets severe limits to human cognition (Herder, 2002, p. 48–49). Herder incessantly stresses that human beings think in words (1987, p. 324). Without words, reason would have remained a mere bare and speculative capacity (SW, XIII, p. 138). He firmly castigates all naive forms of metaphysical enthusiasm that want to break away from our linguistic embeddedness—which he sees at work in Kant and Condillac—and declares them utterly senseless (SW, XIII, p. 361). "Pure reason without language is on earth a utopia [ein utopisches Land]" (SW, XIII, p. 357[2]).

In Herder's *Ideen* this is developed into a full-fledged nominalism, which Herder sees as the result of the imperfect nature of language. This imperfection has two features. The first is the fact that language never expresses things, but only names for our *Merkmale* of things (*Merkmale* can be translated as ideas; literally: "characteristics" or "properties") (SW, XIII, p. 358). There is no essential connection between our sounds for things and these things themselves.

The second nominalist feature is that there is also no essential connection between the sounds with which we clad these ideas (*Merkmale*) and these ideas themselves. For Herder, there is an utterly "arbitrary" connection between sound and thought: humans could have had entirely different sounds for their thoughts and ideas (SW, XIII, p. 359).

In this double distancing (words/things and words/ideas), then, our linguistic condition provides a limit to human cognition. Should we be able to think in things instead of in abstract (words for) ideas (*Merkmale*), and should words express the nature of thoughts instead of being arbitrary sounds, then we would live in the world of universal truth. But that is fiction: we only have *Merkmale* and arbitrary sounds.

Herder connects this explicitly with an account of the frailties of the human condition. He argues that the result of this wide gap between the thing itself and our linguistic representation of it leads to the inevitability of errors and false opinions (SW, XIII, p. 359). These originate, Herder argues, not from any fault of the observer, but from the way in which our ideas are expressed and organized in language. Our *Bildung*, says Herder, is "unavoidably tied to imperfections" (SW, XIII, p. 360).

Yet, we cannot emancipate ourselves from language: we cannot push language aside. In contrast to typically French Enlightenment ideas over language, however, this inability to free ourselves from the limits of linguistic traditions is not something negative, not something we should regret. Herder wholeheartedly embraces linguistic embeddedness as a transcendental feature of the human condition. So, in the same passage that contains his nominalist views, he argues that we should fully accept our embeddedness in language and tradition. We should even thank God for it, since God made human beings alike through language. Human beings "only get to reason through language, and to language through tradition, through belief in the Word of the Father"[3] (SW, XIII, p. 362).

It is certainly true that language is imperfect: because we perceive the world through language, we are inclined to repeat the errors and distortions that our parents and forefathers have made part of the structure of language. Herder argues that errors and prejudices are passed on from generation to generation via the medium of language. Talking about these errors conferred on us through language, he says:

> Here lie rules and laws [commanding people] to think in accordance with the analogy of their fathers and not in accordance with the analogy of nature, to read the images of the universe in the distorting mirror of tradition and not in nature. Here lie the forms of that cave in which the inventors of language and all their followers thought: the plastic shapes of those small worlds from out of which they looked into the great world.
>
> (Herder, 2002, p. 144, n. 167)

We "look into the great world" from the point of view of the "plastic shapes" filled with tradition and its errors. And we should not have the ambition to emancipate ourselves from those errors by destroying tradition (Herder, 2002, p. 144, n. 167).

But that does not mean we are passive. We cannot and should not leave our embeddedness behind, but neither are we passive robots. What we should do is throw ourselves into the vast ocean of traditional truth and errors, to stand in the footsteps of those before us, but also to amend when necessary and, essentially, to add something of our own, based on our own creativity and way of being, adding something new, by applying existing models in our own individual way. As Muthu (2003) notes, for Herder "it is only through the combination of a situated reason and language that any change and improvement occurs in human life" (p. 230).

This role of the notion of "reason" needs clarification, since it is a major theme in Herder's work and crucial to his understanding of the nature of the world-disclosing function of language. Herder strongly believes in the universal progress of reason and of *Humanität* [humanity]. Herder is in no way a relativist: he holds that there is one universal reason at work in humankind which manifests itself through history in the manifold of human beings and human communities.

This may at first sight seem odd given the just-described "world-disclosing" function of language, which makes clear that Herder espouses a strong version of the thesis of the dependence of reason on language. Rather than seeing language as a mere instrument to thoughts formed in the alinguistic functioning mind, Herder puts forward the claim that reason and language are deeply entangled.

But this strong version of the role of language in reasoning does not imply that reason is merely passive. Reason in Herder depends on language, but is not fully determined by it. Reason also plays a crucial role in shaping language. Essential to Herder is an interdependency of reason and language; reason and language develop jointly. Herder (2002, 1987) speaks about the *"progress of language with reason,* and of its *development* out of reason" (pp. 120, 317). In contrast to such contemporaries as Jacobi, Herder never abandons the importance of reason in outlining its linguistic or communal presuppositions (see also Beiser, 1992, 2003; Larmore, 1996, p. 47).

For Herder, universal reason is possible because there is a universally uniform human nature, which is expressed through the central notion of *Humanität* [humanity]. *Humanität* stands for a fundamental force in human beings that manifests itself in all times and all places and provides for a universal progression of reason (SW, XIII, p. 350). With this progression of reason, humanity advances. Herder argues that, despite the immense historical and contemporary variety of individual and national ways of life, there is a single process of advancement of humanity—which is at the same time a progress of reason and a total and perfect realization of all human potentialities—at work in all human beings and peoples (SW, XIII, p. 154). For Herder there is a uniform human nature behind the tremendous diversity of languages, climates, nations, and regions in which individuals are immersed. This central unity underlying the wide diversity which progressively manifests itself on the earth should not be understood as the evolution of all peoples towards a single, perfect way of living. Rather, it should be understood as a process of translation and application: every individual and people is understood as a link within the chain of humanity and reason and has to appropriate the universal humanity by interiorizing and instantiating it within one's own tradition (SW, XVIII, pp. 284–285). For Herder, there are many varieties of human beings and nations, but all fundamentally share the same humanity. While there are many complexions, they are all "different shades of the same great picture which extends through all the ages and all the parts of the globe" (quoted in Fox, 2003, pp. 253–254).

Section II: from the life-world argument to linguistic nationalism

It is the way in which Herder brings his life-world argument to bear on his political philosophy that raises eyebrows today. Both features we just discussed—the role of language in disclosing a situated world and the trust in the progress of reason and humanity—are cornerstones of Herder's political philosophy. This political philosophy finds its central premise in Herder's aversion of processes like mechanization and uniformization. Herder sees these processes at work not only in the many absolutist centralistic regimes of his time, but also in the notion of the social contract as a normative foundation of political community, where individuals join out of self-interest. In both cases, Herder argues, the state turns into an instrumental machine, and social contacts are regulated by lifeless calculation which he deems destructive for the creative energy of the people.

Herder's alternative is a more substantial foundation of political community. This view of the foundation of political order grounds the political community in the nation and its associated shared life-world.[4] What is a nation? A nation or a people (*Volk*)—(Herder uses both concepts interchangeably)—is a cultural entity with distinct characteristics and essentially with a shared language (SW, XIII, pp. 257–258, pp. 363–365). Herder believes that each nation has a specific national character, often called the *Volksgeist*.[5] The national character of the people is embodied in its language (SW, XIII, p. 363). Each people, says Herder, has a distinct language; we can't speak of a people if there is no distinct language. A people without a language, says Herder, is an anomaly (SW, I, p. 147).

In Herder's view, the nation provides for a natural fit between individuals and the state. A people is a plant of nature, just one with more branches (SW, XIII, p. 384). In Herder's work we never encounter any possible form of discomfort with one's embeddedness. We are firmly rooted in our language, in an organic manner. Members of the national people are at the same time recipients of and creative participants to the national language and culture, using reason to improve or change their lifeworld. Based on this organic view, Herder argues that the members of a people are *intrinsically* connected. When he is asked, in 1787, to compile a plan for the creation of an "*Institut für den Allgemeingeist Deutschlands*", he argues that Germany still pays too little attention to the unity of the collective. This unity should be found in a national language. A national language, Herder states, is not something that only grammarians should be concerned with, as is too often believed. Rather, the national language is an essential organ for the social integration of the entire people (SW, XVI, p. 607; Barnard, 1965, p. 58). Herder then contrasts this organic, intrinsic connection to mechanical and multinational associations which can only maintain unity in an *external* and artificial way, by enforcing it from above.

Based on this view of the national language as providing the unity of a state, Herder put forward the principle that national and linguistic communities should be states. It is this principle that has become known as the essence of nationalism.

> Nature raises families; the most natural state is therefore also *one* people, with one national character. . . . Nothing, then, seems to run so obviously

counter to the purpose of governments as the unnatural expansion of states, the wild mixture of all types of races and nations under one scepter. The human scepter is much too weak and small for such contrary parts to be implanted into it; pasted together, they become a fragile machine called the machine of state, without inner life or sympathy of the parts for one another.

(Herder, 2004, p. 128; SW, XIII, pp. 384–385)

Herder's nationalism consists of the idea that languages and nations disclose a world for individuals and that each state best contains one nation and one language. Multilingual and multinational states have no inner, natural sympathy; they need artificial forms of cohesion. Natural states are nation-states; they can rely on the natural bonds between co-nationals. Compatriots are therefore ideally only co-nationals. It is this last passage that arouses much suspicion today, and that makes many inclined to refrain from Herder's nationalism and to denounce it as "premodern" and dangerous. Yet, to justly interpret Herder's nationalism, we need to be fully aware of the following four "moderating" features.

First, Herder's nationalism is not static and does not force subjects to assume a uniform cultural straitjacket. Its organicism is grounded in the importance of growth, variety, spontaneity, and dynamism. Language, culture, and tradition are anything but dead artefacts, entities that are to be respected merely passively by individuals. Rather they are living forces that grow continuously and are susceptible to change (SW, XXXI, p. 27; 1987, pp. 338–339; see also Spencer, 1996, p. 250). Individuals are both recipients *and* active participants: they inherit a tradition and, in doing so, appropriate and shape it, adding to the progress of reason and humanity.

Second, Herder's nationalism is linguistic and cultural in nature and is not couched in racial or ethnic terms (see Fox, 2003, pp. 253–254; Muthu, 2003, pp. 249–250).

Third, Herder's nationalism never assumes an imperialistic or aggressive twist. Herder does approve of linguistic and national patriotism. But even here he only defends a "purified" form of patriotism (*geläuterter Patriotismus*), which he compares to the concern that can be expected of all those on board of a ship to care for the well-being of the collective (SW, XVII, pp. 315–316; SW, XVIII, pp. 270–271). Patriotism is positive for Herder as long as it awakens people to good things and deeds, like Enlightenment, bravery, interest in art and the national language, self-respect, and the will to defend against the imperialism of other peoples and cultures (SW, XVIII, p. 345). But things go astray when patriotism turns into chauvinism and even imperialism. Herder propagates self-defence[6] but forcefully condemns invasions in foreign countries: perhaps cabinets and state machines may engage in deceit and war against each other, but that is not something fatherlands do.

Fatherlands do not move against each other in that way; they lie peacefully beside each other, and support each other as families. *Fatherlands against fatherlands* in a combat of blood [*Blutkampf*] is the worst barbarism in the human language.

(Herder, 2002, p. 379; SW, XVII, p. 319)

This brings us to the fourth and most important qualification of Herder's nationalism: Herder embeds nationalism in a form of cosmopolitanism. To be sure, Herder shows no appreciation whatsoever for people who define themselves as cosmopolitans in the sense that they believe they have nothing to do with the peoples in which they are raised and that they are impartial and impervious to their national background. He therefore finds the primitive man, firmly rooted in his *Volk*, a truer human being than the cultivated cosmopolitan "shadow-man" (SW, XIII, p. 339).

Yet Herder's aversion to cosmopolitanism is merely directed at those views that in exposing love for humankind denounce the importance of national affiliations. While Herder repudiates this sort of cosmopolitanism, we can however correctly characterize his theory as a *cultural cosmopolitanism* that expresses equal respect for the world's cultural diversity, without sacrificing the equal dignity of every individual human being. Kleingeld (1999) has defined "cultural cosmopolitanism" as the view "that humanity expresses itself in a rich variety of cultural forms, that we should recognize different cultures in their particularity, and that attempts to achieve cultural uniformity lead to cultural impoverishment" (p. 515). She finds the German form of cultural cosmopolitanism at the end of the eighteenth century mainly present in the work of Georg Forster. The very same tendency lies at the basis of Herder's nationalism. Indeed, Herder's theory is grounded in an account of *Humantität* which he believes is universally shared. Herder understands humanity as a unity and he sees history as a "chain of humanity" that binds together individuals and nations (SW, XIII, p. 346). He even says that whoever might know all possible variations of the fundamental "human type" behind all peoples and individuals, might reconstruct with a few given features the whole character of a people or an individual (SW, XVIII, p. 250). Thus, he clearly expounds the view that humanity expresses itself in a plurality of cultural forms.[7]

This internationalist cosmopolitanism is most clearly displayed in Herder's important battle against colonialism and imperialism. Herder continuously lashes out against the arrogance of European states, which claim to know how the right way to live looks like and wish to force others—especially African and American peoples—to live according to European norms, often as slaves. Rather than having brought civilization and cultivation to the colonized nations, the European powers have destroyed local cultures and imposed their own (SW, XVIII, pp. 222–223). Apart from European states' colonial ambitions, all past forms of cultural imperialism are fiercely criticized by Herder. Herder has no good word to say about heroes like Alexander or Julius Caesar, who have oppressed many peoples and are responsible for numerous deaths. One of the requisite dispositions that are to be inculcated in people so as to foster universal peace mentioned by Herder in his *Briefe* is called: "reduced respect for heroic glory" (*verminderte Achtung gegen den Heldenruhm*) (SW, XVIII, p. 269). Likewise, he criticizes the crusades which, in his opinion, have only brought death, destruction, and injustice.

It is remarkable here that Herder essentially grounds his moral justification of the nationalistic nation-state model in this aversion to colonialism and imperialism. When condemning Christianity's oppression of foreign peoples, for instance, he says that we should allow each people to thrive on itself, undisturbed and pure (SW, XVIII, p. 222). Herder builds his nation-state model on the premise that peoples possess the right not to be overrun by aggressive others. In his view the world consists of an enormous diversity of peoples who each provide their members with a steady and safe home base. Imperialism—both in the form of the attitude of colonial empires towards other nations and in the imperialism of bureaucratic multinational empires against their internal peoples—is immoral because it oppresses certain peoples and forces them to live by the particular norms and habits of another people. Even in the passage quoted earlier where Herder outlines the nation-state model (with the adage that the most natural state is one people with one character), his defence of it is linked to an aversion to the "unnatural expansion of states" (SW, XIII, pp. 384–385). So, the nation-state model essentially strives towards an international order where every nation is enabled to determine its collective way of life for itself, independently from the inimical interference by others. Just like the duty of humaneness (*Menschlichkeit*) entails not disturbing a child when it develops its forces and pleasures, so should also nations not disturb each other (XVIII: 287). Suitably, he holds the idea, characteristic of the harmonious tendency present throughout his entire work, that the earth is big enough for every people to have its own spot: "Does the earth not have space for us all? Does not one land lie peacefully beside the other?" (Herder, 2002, p. 379; SW, XVII, p. 319). He writes that that is also how God has wanted it, and that the diversity of languages, ethics, and desires was meant (by God) as a stop against the presumptuous assembling of peoples, as a dam against "foreign inundations" (*ein Damm gegen fremde Überschwemmungen*), to enable each people to maintain their own national character (Herder, 2002, p. 385; SW, XVIII, p. 236).

Herder additionally justifies this nationalistic policy to let every nation thrive within its own political borders apart from foreign influence, by arguing that this alone will enable "humanity" and the "progress of reason" to manifest itself. Only if peoples are provided with the means to pass down their own traditions and shape them according to their own beliefs and customs, will this progress occur. There is definitely no one universal "yardstick", and it certainly is not the European way of life that all peoples have to follow. Each culture has its own way of being. The culture of humanity (*Menschheit*) is different: it shoots forth here and there in larger or smaller quantities and eventually blossoms in all of them (SW, XVIII, p. 248). Every nation will develop this culture of humanity and the progress of reason in its own way, according to its own customs: the spirit of history is encouraging and gentle, leaving every people where it is. It does not step in the way of any political constitution (and Herder had also famously argued for non-intervention in the French civil war ensuing the Revolution). Rather, with a friendly hand and as a gentle force it shows man his mistakes and outlines the right route to follow (SW, XVIII, p. 284).

In summary, Herder's nationalism is non-static, non-racist, non-aggressive, and in fact compatible with cosmopolitanism. These cannot be legitimate sources of discomfort with Herder's nationalism. However, there is one crucial respect in which Herder's theory remains wanting today as a moral foundation of linguistic justice. As the preceding passages have shown, Herder operates on an assumption that the world is divided into clearly distinguishable cultural-linguistic units, with members having essentially monolingual identities. The natural state of affairs is for cultures to be separate and to be characterized by clear identities. No mention is ever made in Herder of individuals with two languages of identification. Nor does he ever mention the possibility of there being territorially scattered minorities, who live intermingled on the same territory with other language groups. These do not feature in his ontological framework, which is premised on their being discrete cultural units.

This "discreteness" framework consists of three united assumptions. First, there is an understanding that a language is to be spoken exclusively by speakers with monolingual identities. A unilingual identity structure is therefore taken as the normal case. People may surely be bi- or multilingual, but they have only one "mother tongue".[8] Second, languages are believed to have transparent boundaries, both linguistically and territorially, which give rise to a mosaic picture of our linguistic world, with neatly juxtaposed languages marked off by sharp lines. Third, it is assumed that the members of a linguistic community are undivided with regard to the issue of identity: individual linguistic identity variation is believed to be very low. That is what justifies speaking about a *group's desire* to have its own territory and to maintain its own linguistic context.

It is not Herder's point that we should not be influenced at all by cultural alterity or that intercultural contact might weaken collectives or individuality. At the end of the *Abhandlung*, for example, he explicitly argues that Nature has provided us with the ability to learn from other nations. "We Germans", says Herder, would still, like the native Americans, "live quietly in our forests, or rather still roughly war and be heroes in them", if the "chain of foreign culture" had not influenced us (Herder, 2002, p. 160–161). Likewise, the Romans have received their *Bildung* from Greece, and the Greeks got it from Asia, etc. Thus, he says, the chain has progressed from a first ring and will perhaps one day encircle the entire earth (Herder, 2002, pp. 161, 1987, pp. 353–354). So, it is simply wrong to say that Herder believes that Germans "should sternly resist cultural imports, which can only contaminate the purity of their ancestral culture" (Barry, 2001, p. 260). Herder valued cultural influences. He detested cultural imperialism but he encouraged cultural contact, and he thought it helped the progress of humanity and reason.

Yet at the same time, while there is a lot of scope for the mingling of cultural *content*, there is surprisingly no mention by Herder of a mixing of the cultural *form*, of the structure of culture. The structure of cultures—their boundaries, their territorial concentration, their membership, their monolingual nature, their absence of minority cultures within their remits—remains untouched while the cultural content—the values, ideas, reason, and language—is appropriately influenced by other languages and cultures. As discussed earlier, there is room for all cultures on the earth to live uninhibited by others, and God wanted the diversity of languages and desires as a dam against encroachment by others (SW, XVII, p. 319

and SW, XVIII, p. 236). For Herder, indeed, there is no mixture, not at the level of individuals, nor at the level of societies: the idea of having two mother tongues, or having a bilingual *Volksgeist*—a national spirit spread out over two languages, is foreign to Herder.

The purpose of this section was to show how Herder's life-world account leads to his view that the best state is a monolingual and mononational state. In the final section, I will argue, however, that it is possible to disentangle those: we may not like discreteness but the life-world view is compatible with hybrid situations. But first I want to show the contemporary relevance and popularity of Herder's life-world account, including its discreteness realization and why in today's context this conception is problematic.

Section III: contemporary influence of Herder: Kymlicka and liberal nationalism

Herder grounded his nationalism in an account of the value of language and culture. A similar move is made by contemporary nationalists. Liberal nationalisms often acknowledge their indebtedness to Herder. Tamir (1993) has argued that liberal nationalism "is a direct descendant of the cultural pluralism of Herder" (p. 79). And Charles Taylor, who is sometimes also identified as a liberal nationalist (e.g. by Kymlicka, 2001a, p. 210), mentions Herder as one of his most important intellectual fathers (Tamir, 1993, pp. 135–139). I don't have the space here to comprehensively show the Herderian influence on all exponents of liberal nationalism, but will instead focus on one paradigmatic and influential liberal nationalist, Will Kymlicka and argue how his liberal nationalism is markedly similar to Herder's argument.[9]

Kymlicka's account of the value of language and cultural membership is grounded in the idea that culture is a context of choice. "In deciding how to lead our lives, we do not start *de novo*" (Kymlicka, 1989, p. 164). We reflect upon the values, beliefs, and models offered to us within our culture and language and then choose to uphold or reject particular values from that given choice-set. Culture and language thus function as a *context of choice* (p. 164). Our cultural structure makes us aware of the options available to us, so that we can examine them and select the ones we find valuable. Language and culture are the "media through which we come to an awareness of the options available to us, and their significance; and this is a precondition of making intelligent judgments about how to lead our lives" (p. 165). Without our cultural context of choice, we could not meaningfully exercise our capacity for making autonomous life choices. "Put simply, freedom involves making choices amongst various options, and our societal culture not only provides these options, but also makes them meaningful to us" (Kymlicka, 1995, p. 83).

As we have seen, for Herder, language and culture function as a psychological matrix in which we are raised as social beings. This is similar to describing culture (as Kymlicka does relying on Dworkin) as the "spectacles" through which we experience the world (Kymlicka, 1995, p. 54), or as the "media" that make us aware of options. The phrase that culture "provides options" and "makes them meaningful to us" (p. 83) might have been written by Herder.[10] Both reason that individuals need cultural and linguistic "spectacles" through which they see their world.

Thus Herder (and his romantic followers) have argued that individuals need to have access to their linguistic and national-cultural life-world, which provides them with a "horizon of meaning" that they need in order to fully realize themselves (Taylor, 1993, pp. 46–47). Kymlicka (and his multicultural and liberal-nationalist followers) have argued that individuals need access to their linguistic and national-cultural context of choice, which provides them with shared options from which they can make autonomous and free life choices. Both hold that language and culture help structure what we think and choose in life, *and* that this linguistic and cultural structuring justifies policies that seek to explicitly accommodate linguistic and cultural groups.

Yet, while the freedom argument is grounded in romantic life-world premises, Kymlicka's version of liberal nationalism is not a replica of the romantic tradition. Kymlicka articulates an explicitly *liberal* version of the life-world argument (see De Schutter, 2016). As a liberal, Kymlicka integrates the romantic conception of the value of language and culture into an explicitly liberal framework. This liberalization changes the argument in two ways. First, it means that the life-world argument is made dependent on the validity of liberal premises: language and cultural membership are presented as necessary for the liberal value of freedom. Since liberals care about enabling individual choices, they have a reason to give people access to language and culture.

Second, liberalizing the argument implies imposing liberal limits on what can be tolerated in the name of securing access to linguistic and cultural membership. For example, "internal restrictions", by which a group attempts to silence individuals who seek to change the character of culture, are illegitimate from a liberal point of view (Kymlicka, 1995, pp. 104–105). They are illegitimate because they are freedom-destroying instead of freedom-enhancing. The resulting liberal nationalism can be understood as a nationalism that has been stripped off anything illiberal. Nationalistic politics are not aggressive against other national identities and typically expose a "thin" or open conception of national identity.[11]

So Kymlicka's version of the life-world argument can be characterized as grounded in a liberal romanticism: it gives a distinctively liberal shape to the argument, and it sanitizes romanticism from its illiberal offshoots by formulating liberal limits to what can be demanded in the name of multiculturalism. It would therefore be wrong to see Kymlicka as a romantic theorist *pur sang*. But Kymlicka and Herder (and the Hamann-Herder-Humboldt tradition more generally) *are* united in the account given of the value of cultural membership. This account serves for both as the ground for the political concern for cultural groups. It holds that individuals are not fully formed beings prior to having language and culture: individuals need their situated horizon. Language is not simply a tool for communication; it influences our cognitive constitution and thereby structures our life options. And individuals have a legitimate interest in the protection of their linguistic and cultural life-world. Kymlicka takes this romantic account, liberalizes it, and puts it at the heart of a comprehensive political theory of multiculturalism.

In addition to similarities in the life-world account, the political sociology embedded in Kymlicka's political philosophy has a similar tendency to gloss over instances of cultural mixing and hybridity. Let me explain.[12] The unit within which people are, according to Kymlicka, constitutively embedded—the societal culture—refers in fact to the "cultural structure", which is contrasted with the values or beliefs of a culture (Kymlicka, 1989, pp. 165–167).

> I call it a *societal* culture in order to emphasize that it involves a common language and social institutions, rather than common religious beliefs, family customs, or personal lifestyles. Societal cultures within a modern liberal democracy are inevitably pluralistic. . . . This diversity, however, is balanced and constrained by linguistic and institutional cohesion.
>
> (Kymlicka, 2001a, p. 25)

So, far from postulating the homogeneity of the *values*, the *character,* or the *content* of culture, Kymlicka provides ample room for cultural pluralism and content-based cultural variety. He draws a distinction between the pluralistic *content* and the *form* of culture, the cultural structure which contains the content. That is how Kymlicka can hold that societal cultures are "inevitably pluralistic" while still attributing substance and cohesion to their form, which is manifested in the culture's language and in its institutions.

But this presumption of cohesion in the form of culture is problematic, both in Kymlicka and in Herder. We should cast doubt not only on the homogeneity of the character of culture, but also on the homogeneity of culture as a form or structure. The idea of a "societal culture" is associated with the idea that the culture in question is institutionally complete, clearly distinct from others, and territorially concentrated (Kymlicka, 1995, pp. 76–77, 2001a, pp. 25, 269). There is a very Herderian assumption here: to take as a starting point a picture of the world as a transparent mosaic of discrete cultural and linguistic units, where clear and stable boundaries mark off monolingual cultures.

This assumption is inappropriate. There are many things that do not fit within it and it is, more often than not, untrue. Indeed, the cultural landscape we inhabit is imbued with cultural hybridity and opacity. It is characterized by dual identities, complicated "mother tongue" situations, minorities within minorities, and bi- and multilingualism (for similar critiques, see Benhabib, 2002, pp. 59–67; Carens, 2000, pp. 65–66). Our world is not a patchwork of clearly distinct cultural units. The list of "exceptions" is large, but let me, by way of example, just zoom in on one type: the problem of locating nationality in multinational states like Canada, Bolivia, Belgium, Spain, Ethiopia, or India.

In such states, many people identify with both the state and the sub-state as the context of their national identity. Take for instance Belgium (but very similar remarks can be made in the case of Spain and Canada, see Moreno, 2001, pp. 112–126; Mendelsohn, 2002, respectively). Kymlicka argues that in multinational states like Belgium, Spain, and Canada, citizens share citizenship but not a national identity. For instance, he understands people in Flanders to have Belgian citizenship but only a Flemish national identity (Kymlicka, 2001b, p. 256). However, when probed for their national identity feelings, 38.7% of Flemish respondents in a 2014 survey answered that they self-identified as much with Flanders as with Belgium (Swyngedouw, Abts, Baute, Galle, & Meuleman, 2015, p. 22). And in a study of the national identities of Belgian citizens, the researchers conclude that throughout the whole of Belgium, citizens experience a "dual national identity" (Flemish/Wallonian *and* Belgian) and that in Flanders, the strength of both national identities (Belgian *and* Flemish) are in balance (Maddens, Billiet, & Beerten, 1999).

So these multinational states themselves can be understood to sustain a statewide nation alongside sub-state nations: we can relevantly speak of the existence of a nation at both levels. Citizens may be members of more than one national community at once (such as of the Spanish and of the Catalan nation simultaneously), and different individuals of the same "nation" may be internally divided with regard to which context is the most relevant one. For instance, while as just mentioned 38.7% of Flemish respondents in 2014 self-identified as much with Flanders as with Belgium, 31.1% self-identified as "only Flemish" or as "more Flemish than Belgian", and 29.8% as "Belgian-only" or as "more Belgian than Flemish" (Swyngedouw et al., 2015, p. 22). This shows that people may have more than one national identity at the same time. But it also shows that the members that make up a nation may not be identical in the way they adhere to their culture. Kymlicka and Herder attribute a shared cultural identity (membership of a distinct societal culture) to all the members of a certain group and then base their normative political conclusion on the existence of this identity. But, if the analyses of the just-mentioned surveys are correct, then peoples may consist of members with divergent, and often dual identities.

Section IV: non-discrete life-world rights

In my view, the life-world account, in Herder's or a Herderian (such as Kymlicka's) version, is valuable as a basis for granting protection and recognition to languages and cultures. But the discreteness framework in which it has often been defended is in my view problematic. The life-world account is valuable because it allows us to see that cultures matter to human beings in a way that could, when sufficiently fine-tuned, lead to the foundation for a general right to cultural protection, preservation, and recognition. But the conceptualization of the life-world account by Herder as fit for a world mosaic of communicating but structurally discrete monolingual blocks is problematic for all bilingual identity structures, minorities within minorities, non-territorially concentrated groups, and binational constellations.

Interestingly, 250 years of nation-building have polished away many such cracks in the bastion of the discrete monolingual nation-state. Especially in Europe and North America, much of the linguistic diversity has been weeded out by centuries of standardization and nation-building. These have resulted in a map resembling a painting by Modigliani—as inventively remarked by Gellner in his *Nations and Nationalism* (2006, p. 139)—with ethnographically and linguistically "neat flat surfaces" that are "clearly separated from each other". Gellner contrasted this Modigliani world with one resembling a painting by Kokoshka, marked by many complex relations between individual units in an opaque landscape with fluid boundaries.

The much vaster linguistic diversity in other parts of the world, such as in (but not limited to) Latin America, parts of Africa, and South East Asia, corresponds more closely to such a Kokoshka setting. Putting a Modigliani frame on a Kokoshka situation results in glossing over instances of linguistic hybridity and multilingualism. It also makes it easier to think of solutions based on monolingual premises, such as the "linguistic territoriality principle", which sets out to draw boundaries around language groups, in order to give one language per territory superior official status (see Van Parijs, 2011 for a defence of this principle). This principle is at the heart of the linguistic justice regimes installed in Switzerland and Belgium.

However, it is misguided to centrally theorize linguistic justice on the basis of the linguistic situation in "Modigliani" states with relatively few languages. Issues of linguistic justice typically arise in cases where two or more language groups or identities are present: in situations with no minorities or virtually no linguistic hybridity, like Iceland, for instance, linguistic justice is not a serious concern (exempting the spread of English, a global phenomenon also engulfing Iceland). The hallmark of linguistic justice should thus not be based on an ontological framework befitting a Modigliani situation.

But that does not mean that the life-world account—the essence of the romantic tradition—is to be thrown overboard along with the Modigliani-like discreteness concept. (And even that discreteness concept can work in certain cases; just not in all.) The life-world account shows why language and culture are valuable and why language rights and language recognition ought to be granted. If it is valid, and treating hybrid multilingual settings with discreteness frames is problematic, then we should seek to disentangle the discreteness realization from the life-world account of linguistic justice. That people can be embedded in multiple nations or languages, that many languages are not territorially concentrated, and that some nations are nested within other, larger such nations, are all perfectly compatible with the idea that the members of those nations and the speakers of those languages are constitutively embedded in their life-worlds and that their access to their life-worlds should be officially recognized.

How do we disentangle Herder's life-world account from its discreteness realization? It may sometimes be harder for people to get access to their language and culture if that culture is a territorially scattered minority within a territory dominated by another language or culture, or when its culture is relatively small. Yet, the life-world account might in fact ground an argument in such cases that more expensive efforts are needed to satisfy people's interest to access their language and culture, in schools or with respect to police services, than would be needed in more "simple", discrete cases. For instance, the scale advantages enjoyed by the majority make the per capita cost for the language provisions for the minority larger. The costs of school books in the language, health prevention campaigns, printing voting ballots in the language are all cheaper per capita for the majority language. As a result of this, we may think that minorities should have a right to a greater share of the available resources for language rights than those whose linguistic membership is safely guaranteed.

Frequently, such minority groups have come to embrace elements of the life-world of the larger surrounding culture, for example, certain ideas, loan words, or cultural norms. Their members may even have come to be bilingual. This is certainly also the case for those non-discrete situations where people have bilingual identities, or national identity attachments to both a more local and a larger national-cultural context, as in the cases of multinational states discussed earlier. The life-world in such cases is partly or entirely bilingual, and a proper protection or recognition of life-worlds involves both languages or nations. In such cases, solutions like federalism, or bilingual policies, are in fact first-best solutions, not unfortunate concessions. If Catalans partly realize their life-world interest in Spanish, and if there are Catalans who primarily identify with Spanish rather than Catalan in Catalonia, then the first-best solution for this situation is a form of federalism catering to both Spanish and Catalan forms of political self-government and not independence or Spanish-wide Unitarianism favouring the Spanish nation. This shows that realizing the life-world interest can imply bilingual or federalist policies, rather than ensuring their discrete habitation on the earth's surface by insisting on structural walls between monolingual blocks, as Herder imagined.

Conceptually, the life-world account is independent from the discreteness concept. The life-world account says that individuals need their linguistic and national horizon to fully realize themselves. Discreteness involves neat separation, monolingual identities, and monolingual nations. Since these two concepts do not involve common characteristics, it is possible to defend one without the other. If the life-world argument is valid, non-discrete or hybrid situations are just as protection-worthy.

In short, minorities within minorities are equally in need of a linguistic life-world, and bilingual individuals also deserve access to their linguistic belongings. In some cases, access to their linguistic life-world is harder for such minorities than it is for majority speakers, and we may need to provide extra resources to such minorities, as discussed previously. But in other cases, recognition is easier or cheaper, due to the fact that certain elements of the life-world can be exercised through the larger group, either the dominant language or the larger nationality, in a diglossic fashion. In yet other cases, these two facts may balance each other out and the non-discrete realization of the life-world argument may be equally costly. The point is that, once we endorse Herder's life-world account, it can be followed up equally by:

1   a discreteness concept, as Herder himself assumed, and as is still appropriate for transparent, Iceland-like Modigliani cases, or
2   with a hybridity extension, which is more suitable for multilingual Kokoshka constellations.

So, the suggestion is that in a world imbued with Kokoshka situations, Herder's theory is still useful, when it is uncoupled from its discreteness realization. If people are embedded in linguistic horizons, and if this is seen as important enough to make sure people get access to public support for their language and culture, as Herder argued and as liberal nationalists argue in his wake, then the life-world account can sometimes cash out in Modigliani terms for Iceland-like situations and in other cases in Kokoshka forms of regulation. Both are possible. One should not be ruled out or be substituted for the other. It depends on the shape and content of the life-world, as it actually exists.

Conclusion

Herder was not the first to argue that languages and cultures open worlds of meaning to people. Grégoire and other scholars in the French Enlightenment did so too. But Herder differed from these theorists in arguing that we should respect and protect people's own languages and cultures, rather than seek to assimilate people into other life-worlds. This defence of life-worlds is of continuing relevance to anyone trying to further the cause of minority cultures and language groups in the world today. The problem with Herder's nationalism is not that it is a form of anti-cosmopolitan or belligerent national favouritism—it is not. As discussed earlier, Herder in fact is a cultural cosmopolitan and a believer in universal values and the progress of reason; and his nationalism is no way belligerent or minority-crushing. We should depart from Herder, though, at the point in his theory where he weaves a discreteness ontology of language into the life-world account. As I have argued, contemporary theorists and practitioners of linguistic justice should build their case on Herder's life-world account while extending it for Kokoshka situations, which should not be transformed into Modigliani settings. The result is a form of linguistic pluralism: it safeguards the life-world argument, purifies it (for hybrid cases) from the residues of national-linguistic homogeneity in which Herder dressed it, and makes it compatible with a pluralism of linguistic and national identities. I have shown how doing so is possible, building on Herder's life-world account, but pairing it with a different linguistic ontology.

Notes

1 I will refer to Herder's *Sämtliche Werke* (1877–1913) as "SW" for the rest of the chapter. Volume numbers will be indicated, followed by page numbers.
2 My translation.
3 My translation.
4 There is discussion over the extent to which Herder has a developed political philosophy. Beiser (1992) argues that Herder hasn't developed a full-fledged theory of the state. Part of the reason for this is to be found in his anarchistic sympathies and in his association of the concept of the state with the modern centralized bureaucracies of his time. Forster (2018), however, fundamentally disagrees and devotes a full chapter of his Herder book to Herder's political philosophy: according to Foster, Herder did have a worked-out political philosophy, though not one based on a grand metaphysical theory à la Hegel but in fact on a rejection of such metaphysical idealism.

5   It is interesting to note that Herder himself has never put forward the term *Volksgeist* as a central concept or as an important part of his theory, in contrast to what much secondary literature suggests. I was not been able to find a single passage where Herder uses the term, although I should add that he would endorse the meaning of this term, and that he has used related expressions (like *Charakter eines Volkes, Geist der Völker,* or *Geist der Zeiten*).

6   It is clear that apart from the typically Romantic concern with organicism, self-realization, and authenticity, we can in addition still see a rather "Renaissance" concern with "dignity" and "pride" in Herder. This concern is what underlies, among other things, Herder's justification of the importance of military self-defense. In addition, he appeals to the "glory" and "dignity" of the fatherland and also approves of a new sort of contest between the peoples of Europe, no longer one of physical but rather of mental and artistic forces. In this mental contest, some nations can lead whereas others can lack behind as barbarians and get despised and humiliated (SW, XVII, pp. 311–319).

7   And in his *Briefe*, Herder approvingly quotes Fénelon's adage to love one's family more than oneself, one's fatherland more than one's family, and humanity more than one's fatherland (SW, XVIII, p. 241).

8   The notion of the "native speaker" has been criticized lately by numerous linguists. They have often unravelled the notion by distinguishing between, for instance, language of heritance, language of identification, and language of communication or expertise (see Y. Y. Tan, 2014, for an excellent overview of the debate). I am here using the Herderian understanding of the word.

9   The formulation of this section draws extensively on De Schutter (2016: 52–54).

10 Moreover, for liberal nationalists like Kymlicka, and for Herder alike, we are not just embedded in cultures, but in *national* cultures. Kymlicka uses culture as synonymous with "nation" or "people" (1995, p. 18). Also, Herder interchangeably uses "people" (*Volk*) and "nation", understanding the nation as a cultural entity with a shared language as its essential feature (SW, XIII, pp. 257–258, 363–365).

11 Herder is not generally seen as a central theorist of liberalism. At the same time, Herder upholds the importance of the rights and interests of individuals. Herders' nationalism can also be called liberal in the sense of moderate. As we saw, it is not based on racial or ethnic criteria but on linguistic and cultural ones. And both Herder's and Kymlicka's versions of nationalism grant group-differentiated rights such as self-government rights to national minorities, instead of seeking to assimilate minorities within a statewide nationalism. It is a common criticism that romantic political theories tend to limit the moral community to the national community and thus ignore the moral duties they have to individuals of other nations (see Larmore, 1996, pp. 54–56). But this characterization does not apply to Herder, who systematically grounds his nationalism in the universal moral equality of individuals and their shared *Humanität* (e.g. SW, XIII, p. 346), and who is a firm defender of minority nations. For an account of Herder's liberal credentials, see Patten (2010).

12 For the formulation of this argument, I draw extensively on my earlier work (De Schutter, 2011).

References

Barère, B. (2002 [1794]). Rapport du comité de salut public sur les idiomes [Report of the committee of public safety on the languages]. In M. de Certeau, D. Julia, & J. Revel (Eds.), *Une politique de la langue. La Révolution française et les patois: L'enquête de Grégoire [A politics of language. The French revolution and the Patois: The survey of Grégoire]* (pp. 323–331). Paris: Gallimard.

Barnard, B. (1965). *Herder's social and political thought: From enlightenment to nationalism.* Oxford: Clarendon Press.

Barry, B. (2001). *Culture and equality*. Cambridge, MA: Polity Press.

Beiser, F. (1992). *The genesis of modern German political thought*. Cambridge, MA: Harvard University Press.

Beiser, F. (2003). *The romantic imperative: The concept of early German romanticism*. Cambridge, MA: Harvard University Press.

Bembo, P. (1967 [1525]). *Prose della volgar lingua [Discussions of the vernacular language]* (M. Marti, Ed.). Padova: Liviana.

Benhabib, S. (2002). *The claims of culture: Equality and diversity in a global era*. Princeton, NJ: Princeton University Press.

Berlin, I. (2001). *The roots of romanticism*. Princeton, NJ: Princeton University Press.

Carens, J. (2000). *Culture, citizenship and community: A contextual exploration of justice as evenhandedness*. Oxford: Oxford University Press.

Cliteur, P. (2005). Neoromantiek en multiculturalisme [Neoromantics and multiculturalism]. In B. van Leeuwen & R. Tinnevelt (Eds.), *De multiculturele samenleving in conflict [The multicultural society in conflict]* (pp. 113–124). Leuven: Acco.

de' Medici, L. (1995 [1473–1478?]). *The autobiography of Lorenzo de' Medici the magnificent: A commentary on my sonnets* (J. W. Cook, Ed. & Trans.). Binghamton, NY: The State University of New York.

De Schutter, H. (2011). Federalism as fairness. *The Journal of Political Philosophy, 19*(2), 167–189.

De Schutter, H. (2016). The liberal linguistic turn: Kymlicka's freedom account revisited. *Dve domovini/Two Homelands, 44*, 51–65.

du Bellay, J. (1948). *La défense et illustration de la langue francoyse [Defense and illustration of the French language]*. (H. Chamard, Ed.). Paris: Marcel Didier.

Duhamel, J. (1792). *Essai analytique sur cette question: Quelle est l'Instruction nécessaire au Citoyen Français? [Analytical essay on the question 'what is the necessary instruction to the French citizen?]* Paris: Imprimerie de l'Institution Nationale des Sourds-Muets.

Finkielkraut, A. (1987). *La défaite de la pensée [The defeat of the mind]*. Paris: Gallimard.

Forster, M. N. (2018). *Herder's philosophy*. Oxford: Oxford University Press.

Fox, R. A. (2003). J. G. Herder on language and the metaphysics of national community. *Review of Politics, 65*(2), 237–262. https://doi.org/10.1017/S0034670500049950

Gellner, E. (2006). *Nations and nationalism*. Oxford: Blackwell.

Gravelle, S. S. (1988). The Latin-vernacular question and humanist theory of language and culture. *Journal of the History of Ideas, 49*(3), 367–386. https://doi.org/10.2307/2709483

Grégoire, H. (2002 [1794]). Rapport sur la nécessité et les moyens d'anéantir les patois et d'universaliser l'usage de la langue française [Report on the necessity and means of eradicating the *patois* and of universalizing the use of the French language]. In M. de Certeau, D. Julia, & J. Revel (Eds.), *Une politique de la langue: La Révolution française et les patois: L'enquête de Grégoire [A politics of language: The French revolution and the patois: The survey of Grégoire]* (pp. 331–351). Paris: Gallimard.

Herder, J. G. (1877–1913). *Sämmtliche Werke [Complete works]* (B. Suphan, Ed., vol. 1–33). Berlin: Weidmann Verlag.

Herder, J. G. (1987). Abhandlung über den Ursprung der Sprache [Treatise on the origin of language]. In W. Pross (Ed.), *Werke [Works]* (vol. II, pp. 251–399). Munich: Carl Hanser Verlag.

Herder, J. G. (2002). *Philosophical writings* (M. N. Forster, Ed. & Trans.). Cambridge: Cambridge University Press.

Herder, J. G. (2004). *Another philosophy of history and selected political writings* (I. D. Evrigenis and D. Pellerin, Ed. & Trans.). Indianapolis/Cambridge: Hackett.

Kleingeld, P. (1999). Six varieties of cosmopolitanism in late eighteenth-century Germany. *Journal of the History of Ideas, 60*(3), 505–524.

Kymlicka, W. (1989). *Liberalism, community and culture.* Oxford: Oxford University Press.

Kymlicka, W. (1995). *Multicultural citizenship: A liberal theory of minority rights.* Oxford: Oxford University Press.

Kymlicka, W. (2001a). *Politics in the vernacular: Nationalism, multiculturalism and citizenship.* Oxford: Oxford University Press.

Kymlicka, W. (2001b). Territorial boundaries: A liberal egalitarian perspective. In D. Miller & S. H. Hashmi (Eds.), *Boundaries and justice: Diverse ethical perspectives* (pp. 249–275). Princeton, NJ: Princeton University Press.

Lafont, C. (1994). *Sprache und Welterschliessung: Zur linguistischen Wende der Hermeneutik Heideggers* [*Language and world disclosure: On the linguistic turn of Heidegger's hermeneutics*]. Frankfurt am Main: Suhrkamp.

Larmore, C. (1996). *The romantic legacy.* New York: Columbia University Press.

Maddens, B., Billiet, J., & Beerten, R. (1999). De (sub)nationale identiteit en de houding tegenover vreemdelingen in Vlaanderen en Wallonië [(Sub)national identity and the attitude toward foreigners in Flanders and Wallonia]. In K. Deprez & L. Vos (Eds.), *Nationalisme in België: Identiteiten in beweging 1780–2000* [*Nationalism in Belgium: Idetnitities in movement 1780–2000*] (pp. 298–313). Basingstoke: Palgrave Macmillan.

Mendelsohn, M. (2002). Measuring national identity and patterns of attachment: Quebec and nationalist mobilization. *Nationalism and Ethnic Politics, 8*(3), 72–94. https://doi.org/10.1080/13537110208428670

Moreno, L. (2001). *The federalization of Spain.* London: Frank Cass.

Muthu, S. (2003). *Enlightenment against empire.* Princeton, NJ: Princeton University Press.

Patten, A. (2006). The humanist roots of linguistic nationalism. *History of Political Thought, 27*(2), 223–262.

Patten, A. (2010). "The most natural state": Herder and nationalism. *History of Political Thought, 51*(4), 657–689.

Popper, K. (1994). *The open society and its enemies.* Princeton, NJ: Princeton University Press.

Spencer, V. (1996). Towards an ontology of holistic individualism: Herder's theory of identity, culture and community. *History of European Ideas, 22,* 245–260.

Swyngedouw, M., Abts, K., Baute, S., Galle, J., & Meuleman, B. (2015). *Het communautaire in de verkiezingen van 25 mei 2014* [*The communautarian issue in the election of 25 May 2014*]. CeSO/ISPO/2015-1. Retrieved from https://soc.kuleuven.be/ceso/ispo/projects/

Tamir, Y. (1993). *Liberal Nationalism.* Princeton, NJ: Princeton University Press.

Tan, Y. Y. (2014). English as a "mother tongue" in Singapore. *World Englishes, 33*(3), 319–339.

Taylor, C. (1993). *Reconciling the solitudes: Essays on Canadian federalism and nationalism* (G. Laforest, Ed.). London: McGill-Queen's University Press.

Taylor, C. (2016). *The language animal: The full shape of the human linguistic capacity.* Cambridge: Belknap Press.

Van Parijs, P. (2011). *Linguistic justice for Europe and the world.* Oxford: Oxford University Press.

3 Rethinking the principle of linguistic homogeneity in the age of superdiversity

Stephen May

> If, despite the evidence of our senses, we accept the premise that we or our forebears created the state, then we must also accept its entailment: that we or our forebears could have created the state in some other form, if we had chosen; perhaps, too, that we could change it if we collectively so decided.
>
> J. M Coetzee: *Diary of a Bad Year* (2007, p. 3)

Participation in modern political and social life—the rise of globalization notwithstanding—remains primarily defined by the demands of national citizenship, of what it means to be a citizen of a particular nation-state. A key ongoing requirement of national citizenship is commitment to a national language (or, more rarely, a number of national languages) as a visible and ongoing demonstration of both political and social integration by its members. In effect, citizenship in modern nation-states is invariably linked to at least some knowledge of, and facility in, the requisite national language(s) as a key indicator or proxy of one's wider civic and national commitment (Bauman & Briggs, 2003; May, 2017a). This apparently ineluctable connection between national languages, national identities, and national citizenship has thus become a leitmotif of modern political organization.

And yet, we also know that this valorization of national languages, most often via public monolingualism, is a relatively recent historical development (Gramling, 2016; May, 2012). It arose only within the last few centuries, from the politics of nationalism and the modern nation-state system to which it gave rise. The extent to which national languages have subsequently become normalized as a key entailment of citizenship can therefore also be brought into question, or at least, be scrutinized more critically. This is what I aim to accomplish in this chapter. I will first discuss the principle of linguistic homogeneity, arising from the politics of nationalism that underpins the apparent normativity and ascendancy of national languages and, in doing so, trace Herder's initial influence on these developments. I will then explore how current trends amplified by globalization, most notably changes in migration and transmigration, might provide a useful basis for rethinking this preoccupation with public linguistic homogeneity. In particular, I will examine Vertovec's (2007) notion of "superdiversity" and Kraus's (2012) concept of "complex diversity" with respect to their potential to provide an alternative, more pluralistic conception of linguistic citizenship in this late modern world.

From this, I will argue that only by accepting the principle of greater linguistic pluralism can we begin to remediate the long-standing, and often negative, positioning of linguistic minorities in modern nation-states. These minorities, more often than not, find themselves consigned to the social, economic, and political margins of national life, despite (or rather, *because of*) the rhetoric of social inclusion underpinning the advocacy of the principle of linguistic homogeneity.

Linguistic homogeneity and the nation-state system

Herder and the German Romantics

The initial veneration of national languages in the age of nationalism is most often associated with the late eighteenth-century triumvirate of Herder, Humboldt, and Fichte—the "German Romantics" as they have come to be known. Johann Gottfried Herder (1744–1803) argued, for example, for the divine inspiration of the nation as a natural form of human organization: "A nation is as natural as a plant, as a family, only with more branches" (1969, p. 324). Herder developed this position philosophically from a view of language that Taylor (1979, 1995) has usefully described as *expressivism*. Herder rejected a designative view of language as a mere instrument of communication—exemplified by the works of Locke and Hobbes, for example—and emphasized, rather, the constitutive role of language in human cognition (Spencer, 2012). Language, for Herder, is not solely referential but fundamentally expressive—not only for the individual but also for the (language) community, or *volk*, to which they belong. As Taylor (1979) summarizes Herder's position on language:

> [For Herder,] words have meaning not simply because they come to be used to point or refer to certain things in the world or in the mind, but more fundamentally because they express or embody a certain kind of consciousness of ourselves and things. . . . Language is seen not just as a set of signs but as the medium of expression of a certain way of seeing and experiencing. . . . Hence, there can be no thought without language, and indeed the languages of different people reflect their different visions of things.
>
> (pp. 17–18)

In Herder's view, then,

> languages not only embody the consciousness of a people but also constitute their thoughts and identity in an interactive relationship. Individual languages are, therefore, intrinsic to the identity of a community and its way of life, as well as to the consciousness of its individual members.
>
> (Spencer, 2012, p. 67)

It is from this understanding of language that Herder and Humboldt, and subsequently Fichte, were to advocate an *organic* or *linguistic* nationalism where culture—and particularly, language—was viewed as central to the essence or character (*Volksgeist*) of the nation. In this perspective, language came to be the *most* important distinguishing characteristic of nationhood—indeed, its very soul.

The interrelationship between language and the soul or spirit of the nation is most clearly stated by Wilhelm von Humboldt (1767–1835): "[The nation's] language is its spirit and its spirit is its language" (see Cowan, 1963, p. 277). Or, as he observes elsewhere: "From every language we can infer backwards to the national character" (Humboldt, 1988[1836], p. 154). Indeed, as a result, Humboldt is credited with the development of the twin theories of linguistic determinism and linguistic relativism—that language plays a significant role in determining culture, and that each language has a different way of "looking at the world" (Joseph, 2004). As Kedourie (1960) observes of the German Romantics, language was seen as "an outward sign of a group's particular identity and a significant means of ensuring its continuation" (p. 71). Or, put another way, the continuing existence of a nation was inconceivable without its own language. Without a language, Herder argued, a *Volk* is an absurdity (*Unding*), a contradiction in terms (see Barnard, 1965, p. 57).

Fichte was subsequently to extrapolate this essentialist principle of language distinctiveness into the wider sociocultural and political arena (Kedourie, 1960). Thus, for Fichte (1968[1807]), "it is beyond doubt that, wherever a separate language can be found, there a separate nation exists, which has the right to take charge of its independent affairs and govern itself" (p. 184). Kedourie (1960) succinctly summarizes the logic of this process of extrapolation as follows: "A group speaking the same language is known as a nation, and a nation ought to constitute a state" (p. 68).

The arguments of the German Romantics provide us, then, with a puzzling contradiction. On the one hand, their organic linking of language to national identity, along with the linguistic relativism to which it gave rise, has since been widely repudiated as essentialist by academic commentators on nationalism (see, e.g. Bauman & Briggs, 2003). Indeed, such advocacy is now heard only in the often-hyperbolic political rhetoric of nationalists themselves. On the other hand, the subsequent establishment and ascendancy of national languages in the wider political imagination has continued unimpeded into the current era. The latter can thus be explained, more adequately, by *modernist* accounts of nationalism that link its rise to the specific historical and social developments of modernization and its concomitants—industrialization, political democracy, and universal literacy—in eighteenth- and nineteenth-century Europe, along with the role of language therein.

Modernist accounts of nationalism and language

Prior to the rise of nationalism, the feudal, dynastic, and largely agrarian societies of the day had little notion of national sentiment—those feelings of collective "national" belonging—that characterize the modern nation (Anderson, 1991; Gellner, 1983). For modernist commentators on nationalism, the important distinctions between premodern and modern nations can thus be summarized as follows. First, modern nations tend to be equated directly with their political representation in the nation-state and its formal administrative territory. In other words, modern nations are seen as "mass" nations, based on the notion of

universal enfranchisement and with the specific goal of administrative and political representation in the form of the nation-state (Smith, 1995). Second, and
relatedly, the term "nation" in its modern sense embodies two interrelated meanings—the "nation" as the people living *within* a nation-state and the "nation" as
the nation-state (Billig, 1995). Accordingly, the modern nation is viewed as both
a "historical culture-community" and a "legal-political" one (Smith, 1995), with
the latter invariably taking precedence over the former. These two dimensions,
and their coalescence in the institutionalized nation-state, are again products of
the ideology of political nationalism. Thus, nationalism legitimates the construction of a particular sense of national identity for those historical culture-commu-
nities that are said to inhabit their own nation-state. This involves the exercise of
internal political and legal jurisdiction over its citizens and the construction (or
attempted construction) of a homogeneous national culture in which political and
ethnic boundaries are seen to coincide (Gellner, 1983).

Third, the link between the modern nation and its institutional embodiment in
the nation-state is further predicated on the rise of a bureaucratic state organization, a capitalist economy, and a "high" literate and scientific culture; the latter is
based, usually, on a single and distinctive vernacular (national) language. In contrast, previous cultural communities tended to be localized, largely illiterate, and
culturally and linguistically heterogeneous (Anderson, 1991; Hutchinson, 1994).
Indeed, as Gellner (1983) argues in his influential account of the rise of nationalism, prior to industrialization, political forms of organization required neither the
demarcation of clear territorial boundaries nor the fostering of internal integration
and homogeneity. Feudal elites, for example, controlled wide territories but exercised little centralized control. Empires, larger in scale again, demanded political
loyalty from their diverse people groups and acceptance of one's place in the
social/political hierarchy, but made few, if any, demands for cultural and linguistic homogeneity (Grillo, 1998; May, 2016). As long as due honour was given to
Caesar and taxes were paid, all was well.

In contrast, the modern industrialized society—with its literate, mobile,
and occupationally specialized division of labour—required cultural and
linguistic continuity and, where possible, cultural and linguistic homogeneity
in order to function effectively. To this end, the development of a standardized,
context-free, and unitary national language becomes crucial, with this in turn
facilitating and reflecting the development of a "high" literate and, crucially, a
perceived *common*, culture. As Gellner (1983) asserts, "whereas in the past the
connection [between state and culture] was thin, fortuitous, varied, loose and
often minimal . . . now it [became] unavoidable. That is what nationalism is all
about" (p. 38). The result was the emergence of the current nation-state model
in which cultural and political, as well as linguistic, boundaries are seen to
conveniently converge. Nationalism has flourished, Gellner concludes, because
"well-defined . . . and unified cultures" (p. 55), as he puts it, offer a path to
modernity, a basis of political legitimacy, and a means of shared cultural and
linguistic identity.

The pre-eminence of national languages in this history of nationalism and in the related construction of national identities is also highlighted by Benedict Anderson (1991):

> What the eye is to the lover—that particular, ordinary eye he or she is born with—language—whatever language history has made his or her mother tongue—is to the patriot. Through that language, encountered at mother's knee and parted only at the grave, pasts are restored, fellowships are imagined, and futures dreamed.
>
> (p. 154)

Anderson is not suggesting here that national languages are somehow primordial, à la the German Romantics. Rather, Anderson is attempting to explain why national languages, which *are* clearly constructed out of the politics of nationalism, nonetheless can invoke such passion and commitment from their speakers. In this sense, a key aspect of language is "its capacity for generating imagined communities, building in effect *particular solidarities*" [emphasis appeared in the original text] (p. 133). The sociolinguist, Monica Heller (1987), makes a similar point when she discusses the interrelationship between language and ethnic identity in a French immersion school in Toronto, Canada.

> Language use is . . . involved in the formation of ethnic identity in two ways. First, it constrains access to participation in activities and to formation of social relationships. *Thus, at a basic level language use is central to the formation of group boundaries* [emphasis added]. Second, as children spend more and more time together they share experience, and language is a central means of making sense out of that shared experience.
>
> (p. 199)

Language, as a communally shared good, then, serves an important boundary-marking function (Bucholtz & Hall, 2004; Tabouret-Keller, 1997). This also helps to explain why, despite their historical recency, national languages and related notions of cultural and linguistic homogeneity have continued to be so closely associated with the idea of, and sociopolitical obligations attendant upon, national citizenship.

Entrenching national languages; marginalizing other languages

Modernist accounts of nationalism usefully explain the preoccupation with establishing national—and, by extension, linguistic—homogeneity in modern nation-states via the notion of *nation-state congruence*. Nation-state congruence holds that the boundaries of political and national identity should coincide. The view here is that people who are citizens of a particular state should also, ideally, be members of the same national collectivity. And if they are to be the same nationality, they should also, by extension, speak the same *national* language. The end result of modern nationalism, in this view, is the establishment of the ethnically exclusive and culturally homogeneous nation-state, represented ideally by one national language to which all must subscribe.

How this is most often achieved is via the twin processes of *legitimation* and *institutionalization* (May, 2012; Nelde, Strubell, & Williams, 1996). Legitimation is understood here to mean the formal recognition accorded to a language by the nation-state—usually, by the constitutional and/or legislative benediction of official status. As Bourdieu (1982) observes of this in relation to France, for example: "la langue officielle a partie liée avec l'État" [the legitimate (or standard) language becomes an arm of the state] (p. 27). Institutionalization, perhaps the more important dimension, refers to the process by which the language comes to be accepted, or "taken for granted" in a wide range of social, cultural, and linguistic domains or contexts, both formal and informal.

The combination of legitimation and institutionalization achieves not only the central goal of linguistic homogeneity but also its inevitable corollary—the devaluing, diminution, and exclusion of other (competing) language varieties. These latter language varieties are, in effect, *positioned* by modern nation-states as languages of lesser political worth and value. As Bourdieu (1991) observes of this process, again in relation to France, "measured de facto against the single standard of the 'common' language, they are found wanting and cast into the outer darkness of *regionalisms*" [emphasis appeared in the original text] (p. 54). Consequently, national languages have come to be associated inextricably with modernity and progress, while their less fortunate counterparts have become associated (conveniently) with tradition and obsolescence. More often than not, the latter are also specifically constructed as *obstacles* to the political project of nation-building—as threats to the *unity* of the state.

This state-led "ideology of contempt" (Grillo, 1989) toward other language varieties thus constructs them as having little linguistic, social, or utilitarian value—as relics or vestiges of antediluvian, premodern forms of communalism, in effect. Such language varieties might perhaps be tolerated in an ongoing way (only) in the private/familial domain but certainly not as public languages and/or languages of wider communication. Not surprisingly perhaps, speakers of these socially and politically *minoritized* language varieties have thus inevitably shifted over time to the dominant language(s), given the latter's apparent association with modernization, civic inclusion, and social mobility. As Nancy Dorian (1998) summarizes it, "it is the concept of the nation-state coupled with its official standard language . . . that has in modern times posed the keenest threat to both the identities and the languages of small [minority] communities" (p. 18). Florian Coulmas (1998) observes, even more succinctly, that "the nation-state as it has evolved since the French Revolution is the natural enemy of minorities" (p. 67). In short, these processes ensured that both national and minority languages were literally *created* out of the politics of European state-making and not, as we often assume, the other way around (Billig, 1995).

Problematizing linguistic homogeneity

I began this chapter with the quote from Coetzee's novel, *Diary of a Bad Year*, because it usefully highlights the potential to review and rethink the principle of linguistic homogeneity in this late modern, increasingly globalized era and the principle of nation-state congruence on which it is based. This is particularly important, as I will proceed to argue, given the ongoing deleterious effects of modern nation-state organization on minority language speakers. In its stead, I will offer an alternative, more linguistically pluralized conception of the nation-state model, drawing on the concepts of superdiversity (Vertovec, 2007) and complex diversity (Kraus, 2012).

Why is such a review and revision necessary? Primarily, because, of course, the idea of a homogeneous nation-state is actually a social and political fiction. As Walker Connor (1993) highlights, for example, in 40% of all states, there are at least five or more statistically and/or politically significant ethnic groups while in nearly one-third of all states (31%), the largest national group is not even the majority. These groups comprise national and Indigenous minorities in countries across the world. Examples include, among others, the Irish, Scots, and Welsh in Britain; Hawaiians and Native Americans in the United States; Québécois and Aboriginal peoples/Native Canadians in Canada; Kurds in Turkey, Iran, Iraq, and Syria; Tibetans in China; Sámi in "Sápmi" (which includes areas of Russia, Finland, Norway, and Sweden); Ainu in Japan; and Māori in Aotearoa New Zealand.

All these national contexts also invariably include a wide variety of immigrant groups. The result is that most states are multinational (comprising a number of national minorities) and/or polyethnic (comprising a range of immigrant groups). Indeed, most countries in the world have been historically, and remain today, a combination of the two (Kymlicka, 1995, 2001, 2007). We can thus surely still agree with Anthias and Yuval-Davis (1992) that

> [t]oday there is virtually nowhere in the world in which . . . a pure nation-state exists, if it ever did, and therefore there are always settled residents (and usually citizens as well) who are not members of the dominant national collectivity in the society.
>
> (p. 21)

As they conclude, the fact that the notion of nation-state congruence remains so powerful is an "expression of the naturalising effect of the hegemony of one collectivity and its access to ideological apparatuses of both state and civil society. This constructs minorities into assumed deviants from the 'normal' and excludes them from important power resources" (pp. 21–22).

If nation-states are more ethnically diverse than nation-state congruence would allow, they are similarly far more linguistically diverse than the apparently ineluctable link between national languages and civic participation would suggest. This is despite the long-standing attempts to marginalize other languages, and their speakers, in modern nation-states. While these historical processes have clearly been successful in achieving the dominance of national languages over the last few centuries, most often at the specific expense of other competing (minoritized) languages, individual multilingualism remains an ongoing characteristic of the majority of the world's population. And this individual multilingualism is increasingly apparent in the changing patterns of migration and transmigration that have come to be termed *superdiversity*.

Superdiversity: a riposte to monolingualism?

The notion of superdiversity was first coined by the British sociologist, Steven Vertovec (2007), to describe the rapid diversification of many national populations as the result of increased migration and transmigration, particularly to major urban centres in the West. Vertovec's initial study focused on London as an exemplar of these trends, with a key point of focus in his study being the increased visibility and complexity of the multilingualism of its population. Not surprisingly, perhaps, superdiversity has since been taken up enthusiastically in the fields of sociolinguistics and applied linguistics as an explanatory framework for the analysis of contemporary multilingualism. Vertovec's work highlights the complex, fluid multilingual repertoires of individuals in their local (usually, urban and superdiverse) contexts and how these differ significantly from more narrow conceptions of "languages" (read: standardized language varieties) in the public domain or civic realm. Such repertoires have been described by Makoni and Pennycook (2012), for example, as "lingua franca multilingualism", where "languages are so deeply intertwined and fused into each other that the level of fluidity renders it difficult to determine any boundaries that may indicate that there are different languages involved" (p. 447). Other comparable terms include Pennycook's (2010) "metrolingualism", Rampton's (2011) "contemporary urban vernaculars", Creese and Blackledge's (2011) "flexible bilingualism", Canagarajah's (2013) "translingual practice", and García and Wei's (2014) "translanguaging", to name but a few.

The terminological proliferation notwithstanding, these developments have been important in usefully foregrounding multilingualism, rather than monolingualism, as the new norm of applied linguistic and sociolinguistic analysis. This "multilingual turn" (May, 2014a) has also highlighted the need for more nuanced ethnographic understandings of the complex multilingual repertoires of speakers in urban environments, along with their locatedness, scale (Blommaert, 2010), flow, and circulation (Heller, 2011) in an increasingly globalized world. As Makoni and Pennycook (2012) summarize it in their recent discussion of the allied notion of *metrolingualism*, the aim of this new, critical, urban applied linguistics is to describe "the ways in which people of different and mixed backgrounds use, play with and negotiate identities through language" (p. 449).

Given these developments, superdiversity can be seen as a potentially useful counterpoint to the codification of national languages and the related notion of linguistic homogeneity underpinning the nation-state system, along with the still predominantly monolingual language policies by which it takes effect (see, e.g.

Arnaut, Blommaert, Rampton, & Spotti, 2016; Blommaert, 2013; Pennycook & Otsuji, 2015). Indeed, a key trope of current sociolinguistic work, influenced directly by superdiversity, is the specific repudiation of named languages, "the desirous and quixotic dream" (Gramling, 2016, p. 9) of the nationalism of the last few centuries. As proponents of sociolinguistic superdiversity argue, the notion of the "well-designed" language (Chomsky, 2009, p. 75)—the idea of a discrete, bounded, and readily identifiable language variety—still holds much power as an ideological artifact of modern governmentality. Nonetheless, as Blommaert and Rampton (2016) argue:

> [I]t is far more productive *analytically* [emphasis appeared in the original text] to focus on the very variable ways in which individual linguistic features with identifiable social and cultural associations get clustered together when people communicate. . . . [From this], a much more differentiated account of the organization of communicative practice emerges.
>
> (p. 25)

These theoretical developments in sociolinguistics have also seen the rejection of related concepts associated with named languages. Notions of distinct "speech communities" and "ethnolinguistic groups" have begun to be replaced by the more fluid and mobile notions of "communities of practice", "institutions", and "networks", while the related concepts of "mother tongue" and "native speaker" have been replaced by an increasing focus on individual multilingual repertoires (Blommaert & Rampton, 2016, p. 25).

Superdiversity and its explanatory limits

Superdiversity as a potential framework for (re)analysing the complex multilingual language practices of migrants and transmigrants in this late modern, globalized world thus appears to hold considerable promise as an alternative conceptualization to the monolingual nation-state model. It certainly brings into sharp relief the increasing disjuncture between the still predominantly monolingual state language and education policies and the burgeoning ethnic and linguistic diversification of constituent national populations. But while superdiversity "troubles" the inherent monolingualism of national language policies, there are also some potential shortcomings to the use of superdiversity as an explanatory framework.

The first is a historical one. While the focus on multilingualism is a welcome one, the presumption that this is a *new* phenomenon is historically elliptical. With regard to a point previously made, empires, which largely predated the modern nation-state system, were, for the most part, more overtly multilingual, not only at the individual level but also, crucially, in their administrative policies. For example, multilingual administration was the norm in the ancient Persian, Ptolemaic, and Carthaginian empires (see, e.g. the biblical book of Esther 1:22 in relation to Persia). Similarly, in the Roman Empire, the Romans were remarkably unconcerned with imposing Latin on their subject peoples. Where it was spoken, it was almost always in conjunction with other languages rather than in their stead, an approach underpinned by the principle *per pacem societatis* [through a pact of society] (Rochette, 2011). Of course, Latin remained important for administrative purposes—it was the dominant language of the Roman governors, the army, and the law courts. Accordingly, the preferred Roman strategy of co-opting local elites into imperial administration saw them schooled in Classical Latin and often also Greek, while administering on behalf of the empire predominantly through vulgar Latin (Mufwene, 2004). However, these local elites simultaneously maintained their own languages, while there were no restrictions imposed on the local populations with respect to their ongoing multilingual language use (Rochette, 2011).

But perhaps the clearest and most historically significant example of an imperial policy that formally protected the multilingualism of its population is that of the Ottoman Empire (c. 1300–1923). Under Mehmet II, a formal system of *millets* (nations) was established in the Ottoman Empire in the fifteenth century in order to accommodate the religious, cultural, and linguistic diversity of peoples within its borders. These millets were first established on the basis of the maintenance of religious freedom for the Empire's non-Muslims. However, over time, the millet system came to foreground the latter's linguistic protections as well, a development that was further bolstered in the nineteenth and twentieth centuries by various forms of multilingual education (Dorian, 1998). In combination, the millet system specifically fostered and sustained regional multilingualism within the Ottoman Empire for nearly half a millennium (Gawrych, 1983; Strauss, 2011). As Gawrych (1983) concludes, "this regional multilingualism remained a significant force for fostering an atmosphere of tolerance toward both religious and cultural diversity into the twentieth century" (pp. 520–521).

I note these examples to highlight both the normalcy and historical longevity of multilingual language use—not just in terms of the complex individual multilingual repertoires that sociolinguistic superdiversity foregrounds but also in relation to collective sociopolitical administration, at least prior to modern nation-state formation, which superdiversity accounts continue to largely ignore. The relentless focus on migrants and transmigrants in urban contexts in superdiversity accounts could also do with a less elliptical historical analysis. In this brave new world, multilingual urban repertoires are constructed as dynamic and cosmopolitan, while supposedly local, often rural, language varieties—particularly Indigenous language varieties—are dismissed as static and ossified (see, e.g. Edwards, 2010; Makoni, 2012). This is an unnecessary, as well as a historically inaccurate, bifurcation (May, 2014b).

Indigenous communities, for example, have exhibited their own long-standing, dynamic, and complex multilingualism over time, including the interaction of local and global language ecologies (Canagarajah, 2005), elsewhere explored as "translocal" language and literacy practices (Brandt & Clinton, 2002), the overlaps and fissures among different generations of speakers (McCarty, 2014), and the simultaneity of transmigration and rootedness (Levitt & Glick Schiller, 2008; Warriner & Wyman, 2013). These dialectics, in turn, are situated within, and expand upon, a long history of colonization for many Indigenous peoples that has included regular displacement and/or forced migration, significant social, cultural, economic, and linguistic inequalities, alongside complex and evolving multilingual interactions with their colonizers over time. As Patrick (2012) observes, for example, the multilingual practices in which Indigenous communities engaged in early contact situations with their colonizers, often in remote and rural contexts, "included the use of multilingual interpreters, lingua francas and trade jargons, and [bilingual] mixed languages" (p. 35). Ironically, it is these same attributes that are now ascribed to "new" urban language varieties that are of such interest to advocates of sociolinguistic superdiversity.

The mention of Indigenous peoples also highlights another lacuna of sociolinguistic superdiverse accounts—their relentless focus on new migrants, and their individual communicative practices, ignores other long-standing or established minority language speakers within modern nation-states, along with their associated group-based language rights' claims for greater recognition in the public sphere. These latter minorities include national minorities and Indigenous peoples—minority language groups who have been historically associated with a particular territory but, because of colonization, confederation, or conflict, or a combination of all three, have come to be marginalized socially, politically, economically, and, more often than not, also linguistically, within those same territories (Kymlicka, 1995; May, 2012). If and when these minority language speakers are ever accorded (limited) recognition in sociolinguistic accounts of superdiversity, they are treated only as individual multilingual speakers, since the theoretical tenets of superdiversity necessarily preclude the recognition of distinct language groups. As a result, any language rights' claims by these minority groups are also rejected on the basis that they simply reinforce narrow, reified conceptions of language that do not match the actual complexities and fluidity of individual multilingualism (see, e.g. Makoni, 2012; Park & Wee, 2017; Wee, 2010).

I have argued elsewhere (May, 2017b) that the result of this increasingly de rigueur rejection of *any* group-based language claims in sociolinguistic analyses of superdiversity is simply to endorse a post hoc validation of *existing* language "hierarchies of prestige" (Liddicoat, 2013) that underpin the dominance of national languages vis-à-vis national minority and/or Indigenous languages in modern nation-states. As Blommaert (1999) has earlier observed, a sociolinguistic approach that fails to take cognizance of these wider sociopolitical and sociohistorical factors takes no account of human agency, political intervention, power, and authority in the formation of particular (national) language ideologies. Nor, by definition, is it able to identify the establishment and maintenance of majority languages as a specific "form of practice, historically contingent and socially embedded" (p. 7).

Meanwhile, the foregrounding of transmigration and globalization in superdiverse accounts, important though it is, also leads to the, at times, overstated assumption that the nation-state model is somehow in permanent decline in this "new", linguistically pluralized (at least at the individual level), globalized world (Park & Wee, 2017). And yet, nation-states—for all their limitations, not least those discussed in this chapter—still remain the *primary* social, political, *and linguistic* frame of reference for our everyday *public* lives. What is needed, then, is not the un-reflexive, de rigueur, dismissal of the nation-state model and associated languages (whether majority or minority), but rather the urgent requirement to *rethink* nation-states in more linguistically plural and inclusive ways *in the public realm*.

Complex diversity: a useful complement (and counterpoint) to superdiversity?

Superdiversity's preoccupation with the linguistic hybridity of new migrants in (predominantly) urban contexts almost entirely ignores existing national and regional minority language speakers. The current sociolinguistic accounts of superdiversity thus continue to entrench a long-standing fissure between the study of national minority and Indigenous languages on the one hand, and migrant languages on the other. This disjuncture was highlighted nearly 20 years ago by Extra and Gorter (2001).

> Despite the possibilities and challenges of comparing the status of regional minority and immigrant minority languages, amazingly few connections have been made in the sociolinguistic, educational and political domains. . . . Contacts between researchers and policy makers working with different types of minority groups are still scarce. . . . Overall, we see disjointed research paradigms and circles of researchers which have very little or no contact, although they could learn a lot from each other.
>
> (pp. 3–4)

Similarly, the emphasis in superdiverse accounts on individual complex multilingualism militates against the recognition of any broader, group-affiliated language rights. Both delimit the possibilities of reconfiguring nation-states in more linguistically pluralist ways, via the greater recognition of minority language rights (May, 2012). This is where Kraus's (2012) associated notion of *complex diversity* might provide a useful complement, as well as a potential counterpoint, to sociolinguistic superdiversity. Kraus's elaboration of complex diversity is helpful because it specifically addresses and incorporates the three key language constituencies in any given national language context—majority language speakers, "old" national (or regional) minority speakers, and "new" migrant speakers. Kraus argues that we must attend directly to "majority" language speakers, precisely because the constructedness of their language, and its elision with national identity, has been both normalized and invisibilized by its "institutional entrenchment" (p. 9). For national minority and indigenous language speakers, their historical marginalization and/or exclusion from state language policies provides the basis for arguments for greater linguistic (and, by extension, sociopolitical) autonomy within those states, including, centrally, the right to revitalize and maintain their languages via state institutions, such as education (see May, 2012, for an extended discussion). Meanwhile, for migrant speakers, the primary focus is on state acknowledgement and, where possible, incorporation of their languages (via bilingual provision, for example), as a mean of gaining greater social and economic equality, and inclusion within nation-states over time.

Kraus (2012) proceeds to argue that the interspersion of these various layers of linguistic identity, and their dynamic and complex articulation in nation-states, both challenge and subvert linear and reductionist notions that continue to dominate in contemporary discussions of (linguistic) diversity. These include the reduction of diversity to a demographic scale—moving from less diverse to more diverse in this late modern age. It also includes the focus on (individual) migrants as a distinct analytical category, without due regard for other language speakers. Both of these notions, ironically, continue to underpin sociolinguistic accounts of superdiversity. In contrast, "complex diversity" is constructed as fluid and multidimensional, while simultaneously bringing "into focus the importance of recognition in struggles over what equality means, and how it has to be achieved" (p. 13). In doing so, the individual or group nexus is also revisited, with Kraus arguing that, while all cultural and linguistic identities are necessarily constructed and malleable, they also clearly remain *situated* within their social, cultural, and political contexts. Accordingly, "we will realise that complex diversity is not equal to exuberant hybridity. To the extent that cultures are holistic, their potential for 'hybridization' is not unlimited" (p. 18).

Following from this, the notion of complex diversity allows for a *non-essentialist* approach to language that does not recognize groups, as such, but rather culturally grounded *contexts of praxis*, as embodied by different language speakers, their differential positioning within modern nation-states, and their related language claims. In this way, complex diversity also offers a useful bridge between the rampant individualism and hybridization of linguistic practices evident in sociolinguistic accounts of superdiversity and the parallel discussions of language rights, which necessarily contextualize multilingual language practices within their broader social, cultural, and political contexts (including, but not limited to, relevant group affiliations).

Conclusion

Coetzee's protagonist in *Diary of a Bad Year* provides us with an elegant riposte to the politics of linguistic homogeneity which constitutes both the foundation of modern nation-state formation and the continuing sociopolitical imperative that underpins it. In this chapter, I have outlined how the politics of linguistic homogeneity emerged initially from the arguments of Herder and his fellow German Romantics but became effectively instantiated by more modernist conceptions of nationalism and the nation-state system to which it gave rise. I have also outlined here the sociopolitical consequences of these developments for linguistic minorities—both historically and contemporaneously—almost always to their relative disadvantage in relation to majority (national) language speakers.

Finally, I have explored how recent sociolinguistic accounts of superdiversity ostensibly provide a basis for both challenging linguistic homogeneity and normalizing multilingualism, via their focus on the increasingly hybridized language practices of new migrants/transmigrants in urban contexts worldwide. While sociolinguistic superdiversity has much to offer—not least, its welcomed analytical focus on contemporary multilingualism—its preoccupation with individual multilingualism, new migrants, and the related ignoring of other language speakers in modern nation-states, limits, in the end, its usefulness as a basis for reconceptualizing nation-states in more culturally and linguistically pluralist ways.

The notion of complex diversity, however, does provide a potential basis for doing so. Complex diversity draws on both the normalcy and dynamism of multilingualism, while also attending to the situatedness of different language speakers within nation-states. On this basis, it potentially provides for a more egalitarian, inclusive, and linguistically pluralist reconceptualization of modern nation-states. Indeed, returning to Herder's conception of the significance of language to both individual and collective identities, one could even argue that this more pluralist conception of language within nation-states is a more accurate reflection—or, at least, a useful extension—of Herder's own philosophy of language.

References

Anderson, B. (1991). *Imagined communities: Reflections on the origin and spread of nationalism* (rev. ed.). London: Verso.

Anthias, F., & Yuval-Davis, N. (1992). *Racialized boundaries: Race, nation, gender, colour and class and the anti-racist struggle*. London: Routledge.

Arnaut, K., Blommaert, J., Rampton, B., & Spotti, M. (2016). *Language and superdiversity*. London: Routledge.

Barnard, F. (1965). *Herder's social and political thought: From enlightenment to nationalism*. Oxford: Clarendon Press.

Bauman, R., & Briggs, C. (2003). *Voices of modernity: Language ideologies and the politics of inequality*. Cambridge: Cambridge University Press.

Billig, M. (1995). *Banal nationalism*. London: Sage.

Blommaert, J. (1999). The debate is open. In J. Blommaert (Ed.), *Language ideological debates* (pp. 1–38). Berlin: Mouton de Gruyter.

Blommaert, J. (2010). *The sociolinguistics of globalization*. Cambridge: Cambridge University Press.

Blommaert, J. (2013). *Ethnography, superdiversity and linguistic landscapes*. Bristol: Multilingual Matters.

Blommaert, J., & Rampton, B. (2016). Language and superdiversity. In K. Arnaut, J. Blommaert, B. Rampton, & M. Spotti (Eds.), *Language and superdiversity* (pp. 21–48). London: Routledge.

Bourdieu, P. (1982). *Ce que parler veut dire: L'économie des échanges linguistiques* [*The economics of linguistic exchanges*]. Paris: Arthème Fayard.

Bourdieu, P. (1991). *Language and symbolic power*. Cambridge: Polity Press.

Brandt, D., & Clinton, K. (2002). Limits of the local: Expanding perspectives on literacy as a social practice. *Journal of Literacy Research, 34*(3), 337–356.

Bucholtz, M., & Hall, K. (2004). Language and identity. In A. Duranti (Ed.), *A companion to linguistic anthropology* (pp. 369–394). Oxford: Blackwell.

Canagarajah, A. S. (Ed.). (2005). *Reclaiming the local in language policy and practice.* Mahwah, NJ: Lawrence Erlbaum.

Canagarajah, A. S. (2013). *Translingual practice: Global Englishes and cosmopolitan relations.* London: Routledge.

Chomsky, N. (2009). *Cartesian linguistics: A chapter in the history of rationalist thought* (3rd ed.). Cambridge: Cambridge University Press.

Connor, W. (1993). Beyond reason: The nature of the ethnonational bond. *Ethnic and Racial Studies, 16,* 374–389.

Coulmas, F. (1998). Language rights: Interests of states, language groups and the individual. *Language Sciences, 20,* 63–72.

Cowan, M. (1963). *Humanist without portfolio: An anthology of the writings of Wilhelm von Humboldt.* Detroit, IL: Wayne State University Press.

Creese, A., & Blackledge, A. (2011). Separate and flexible bilingualism in complementary schools: Multiple language practices in interrelationship. *Journal of Pragmatics, 43*(5), 1196–1208.

Dorian, N. (1998). Western language ideologies and small-language prospects. In L. Grenoble & L. Whaley (Eds.), *Endangered languages: Language loss and community response* (pp. 3–21). Cambridge: Cambridge University Press.

Edwards, J. (2010). *Minority languages and group identity: Cases and categories.* Amsterdam: John Benjamins.

Extra, G., & Gorter, D. (Eds.). (2001). *The other languages of Europe: Demographic, sociolinguistic and educational perspectives.* Bristol: Multilingual Matters.

Fichte, J. G. (1968 [1807]). *Addresses to the German nation.* New York: Harper and Row.

García, O., & Wei, L. (2014). *Translanguaging: Language, bilingualism and education.* New York: Palgrave Macmillan.

Gawrych, G. (1983). Tolerant dimensions of cultural pluralism in the Ottoman empire: The Albanian community, 1800–1912. *International Journal of Middle East Studies, 15,* 519–536.

Gellner, E. (1983). *Nations and nationalism: New perspectives on the past.* Oxford: Blackwell.

Gramling, D. (2016). *The invention of monolingualism.* New York: Bloomsbury Academic.

Grillo, R. (1989). *Dominant languages: Language and hierarchy in Britain and France.* Cambridge: Cambridge University Press.

Grillo, R. (1998). *Pluralism and the politics of difference: State, culture, and ethnicity in comparative perspective.* Oxford: Oxford University Press.

Heller, M. (1987). The role of language in the formation of ethnic identity. In J. Phinney & M. Rotheram (Eds.), *Children's ethnic socialisation: Pluralism and development* (pp. 180–200). Newbury Park, CA: Sage.

Heller, M. (2011). *Paths to post-nationalism: A critical ethnography of language and identity.* Oxford: Oxford University Press.

Herder, J. (1969). *J. G. Herder on social and political culture* (F. Barnard, Ed. & Trans.). Cambridge: Cambridge University Press.

Hutchinson, J. (1994). *Modern nationalism.* London: Fontana.

Joseph, J. (2004). *Language and identity: National, ethnic, religious.* Basingstoke: Palgrave Macmillan.

Kedourie, E. (1960). *Nationalism.* London: Hutchinson.

Kraus, P. (2012). The politics of complex diversity: A European perspective. *Ethnicities, 12*(1), 3–25.

Kymlicka, W. (1995). *Multicultural citizenship: A liberal theory of minority rights.* Oxford: Clarendon Press.

Kymlicka, W. (2001). *Politics in the vernacular: Nationalism, multiculturalism, citizenship*. Oxford: Oxford University Press.

Kymlicka, W. (2007). *Multicultural odysseys: Navigating the new international politics of diversity*. Oxford: Oxford University Press.

Levitt, P., & Glick Schiller, N. (2008). Conceptualizing simultaneity: A transnational social field perspective on society. In S. Khagram & P. Levitt (Eds.), *The transnational studies reader: Intersections and innovations* (pp. 284–294). London: Routledge.

Liddicoat, A. (2013). *Language-in-education policies: The discursive construction of intercultural relations*. Bristol: Multilingual Matters.

Makoni, S. (2012). Language and human rights discourses: Lessons from the African experience. *Journal of Multicultural Discourses, 7*(1), 1–20.

Makoni, S., & Pennycook, A. (2012). Disinventing multilingualism: From monological multilingualism to multilingua francas. In M. Martin-Jones, A. Creese, & A. Blackledge (Eds.), *The Routledge handbook of multilingualism* (pp. 439–453). London: Routledge.

May, S. (2012). *Language and minority rights: Ethnicity, nationalism and the politics of language* (2nd ed.). London: Routledge.

May, S. (Ed.). (2014a). *The multilingual turn: Implications for SLA, TESOL and bilingual education*. London: Routledge.

May, S. (2014b). Contesting metro-normativity: Exploring indigenous language dynamism across the urban—rural divide. *Journal of Language, Identity and Education, 13*, 229–235.

May, S. (2016). Language, imperialism and the modern nation-state system: Implications for language rights. In O. García & N. Flores (Eds.), *Oxford handbook on language and society* (pp. 35–53). Oxford: Oxford University Press.

May, S. (2017a). Language education, pluralism and citizenship. In T. McCarty & S. May (Eds.), *Language policy and political issues in education: Encyclopedia of language and education* (3rd ed., pp. 31–45). Cham: Springer.

May, S. (2017b). National and ethnic minorities: Language rights and recognition. In S. Canagarajah (Ed.), *Routledge handbook of migration and language* (pp. 149–167). London: Routledge.

McCarty, T. (2014). Negotiating sociolinguistic borderlands: Native youth language practices in space, time, and place. *Journal of Language, Identity and Education, 13*(4), 254–267.

Mufwene, S. (2004). Language birth and death. *Annual Review of Anthropology, 33*, 201–222.

Nelde, P., Strubell, M., & Williams, G. (1996). *Euromosaic: The production and reproduction of the minority language groups in the European Union*. Luxemburg: Office for Official Publications of the European Communities.

Park, J., & Wee, L. (2017). Nation-state, transnationalism, and language. In S. Canagarajah (Ed.), *Routledge handbook of language and migration* (pp. 47–62). London: Routledge.

Patrick, D. (2012). Indigenous contexts. In M. Martin-Jones, A. Blackledge, & A. Creese (Eds.), *Routledge handbook on multilingualism* (pp. 29–48). London: Routledge.

Pennycook, A. (2010). *Language as a local practice*. London: Routledge.

Pennycook, A., & Otsuji, E. (2015). *Metrolingualism: Language and the city*. London: Routledge.

Rampton, B. (2011). Style contrasts, migration and social class. *Journal of Pragmatics, 43*(5), 1236–1250.

Rochette, B. (2011). Language policies in the Roman republic and empire. In J. Clackson (Ed.), *A companion to the Latin language* (pp. 549–563). Oxford: Blackwell.

Smith, A. (1995). *Nations and nationalism in a global era*. Cambridge: Polity Press.

Spencer, V. (2012). *Herder's political thought: A study of language, culture, and community*. New York: University of Toronto Press.

Strauss, J. (2011). Linguistic diversity and everyday life in the Ottoman cities of the Eastern Mediterranean and the Balkans (late 19th—early 20th century). *The History of the Family, 16*, 126–141.

Tabouret-Keller, A. (1997). Language and identity. In F. Coulmas (Ed.), *The handbook of sociolinguistics* (pp. 315–326). Oxford: Blackwell.

Taylor, C. (1979). *Hegel and modern society*. Cambridge: Cambridge University Press.

Taylor, C. (1995). *Philosophical arguments*. Cambridge: Harvard University Press.

Vertovec, S. (2007). Super-diversity and its implications. *Ethnic and Racial Studies, 30*, 1024–1054.

von Humboldt, W. (1988 [1836]). *On language: The diversity of human language structure and its influence on the mental development of mankind* (P. Heath, Trans.). Cambridge: Cambridge University Press.

Warriner, D. S., & Wyman, L. T. (2013). Experiences of simultaneity in complex linguistic ecologies: Implications for theory, method, and practices. *International Multilingual Research Journal, 7*(1), 1–14.

Wee, L. (2010). *Language without rights*. Oxford: Oxford University Press.

4 From cultural difference to monoglossia

Herder's language trap

Tony Crowley

In this essay, I want to consider the legacy of Herder's thinking on language by considering the case of Ireland. Specifically, I will discuss the way in which the principles expounded in Herder's philosophy of language underpinned the development of a form of Irish cultural nationalism. I will argue that, grounded in a belief in the importance of cultural difference as the basis of national identity, Herder's account, and its extension in the work of German idealists such as Schlegel, Fichte, and Humboldt, provided the means by which Irish linguistic and cultural nationalism could be used as a weapon in the struggle against British colonialism. In this regard, I will propose that in the context of anti-colonialism, Herder's language theory was a progressive tool. I will also argue, however, that once Ireland had achieved independence in 1921, Herder's abstract account of the ineluctable relation between language and national identity became a cultural and political trap whose effects remain problematic. I will conclude by considering why this was the case.

Herder's cultural anti-colonialism

It is important to start with Herder's standing as an anti-imperialist, anti-colonialist thinker. Consider for example his denunciation of European colonial practice in his *Letters for the Advancement of Humanity* (1793–1797):

> Let the land be named to which Europeans have come without having sinned against defenceless, trusting humanity, perhaps for all aeons to come, through injurious acts, through unjust wars, greed, deceit, oppression, through diseases and harmful gifts! Our part of the world must be called, not the wise, but the *presumptuous*, *pushing*, *tricking*, part of the earth; it has not cultivated but destroyed the shoots of people's own cultures wherever and however it could.
>
> (Herder, 2002, pp. 381–382)

The emphasis on cultural destruction is significant, and it is reiterated in *This Too a Philosophy of History for the Formation of Humanity* (1774), in which the ironic contempt is savage.

> *Whither* do European colonies not *reach*, and whither *will* they not reach! Everywhere the savages, the more they become fond of our brandy and

luxury, become *ripe* for our *conversion* too! Everywhere approach, especially through brandy and luxury, *our culture*. Will soon, God help us!, all be human beings *like us!—good, strong, happy human beings!*

(Herder, 2002, p. 325)

Notably, the critique covers not simply European colonialism in the New Worlds, but colonialism within Europe, as the scorn is extended: "Shame for *England* that *Ireland* for so long remained savage and barbarous; [though now] it is *civilly administered* and *happy*" (Herder, 2002, p. 325). Indeed, the depth of Herder's anti-colonialism is such that in "This Too a Philosophy", he prophesizes the historical reversal whereby colonialism will be undone.

We Europeans invent *means* and *tools* to subjugate, to deceive, and to plunder you other parts of the world. . . . Perhaps it will one day be precisely your turn to *triumph*! We affix chains with which *you* will pull *us*; the *inverted pyramids* of our constitutions will turn *upright* on your ground.

(Herder, 2002, p. 352)

In *Letters*, it is clear that the basis for Herder's anti-colonial stance is his rejection of European cultural universalism: "Least of all, therefore, can our European culture be the measure of universal human goodness and human value; it is no yardstick, or a false one" (Herder, 2002, p. 396). For what, he argued, "is a measuring of all peoples by the measure of us Europeans supposed to be at all? Where is the means of comparison? That nation which you call savage or barbaric is in essentials much more humane than you" (Herder, 2002, p. 386). Yet although the rejection of universalism is reiterated in Herder's work, it is important to recall the grounds on which it rested: the recognition of the historical, political, and indeed moral significance of cultural difference.

In his *Enquiry Concerning Human Understanding* (1748), David Hume claimed that it is universally acknowledged that there is a great uniformity among the actions of men, in all nations and ages, and that human nature remains still the same, in its principles and operations. . . . Mankind are so much the same, in all times and places, that history informs us of nothing new or strange in this particular (Hume, 1975[1748], p. 83). Herder's philosophy could not be more opposed to this doctrine in its emphasis on the radical differences between human beings who inhabit distinct cultures and indeed historical periods. In *Letters*, for example, he asserts that *"manner of living* (habitus) is what defines a kind; in our diverse humanity it is extremely various" (Herder, 2002, p. 396). This diversity in "manners of living" (or as it was later defined, "culture as a way of life"), ordained by Nature, was precisely the guarantee of specific identities that were threatened by the depredations of colonialism.

The diversity of languages, ethics, inclinations, and ways of life was destined to become a bar against the presumptuous *linking together* of the peoples, a dam against foreign inundations—for the steward of the world was concerned that for the security of the whole each people and race preserved *its* impress, *its* character; peoples should live *beside* each other, not mixed up with and top of each other oppressing each other.

(Herder, 2002, p. 385)

If culture was the guarantor of identity, then at the heart of culture lay language itself, and it is the articulation of this link that is perhaps Herder's most significant legacy, specifically in relation to the foundation of nationality. His most famous proclamation on this topic appears in "Dialogue after the Death of Emperor Joseph II" and concerns the imposition of German as the language of administration in the Hapsburg Empire after 1784 (it should be recalled that the dominant languages in Germany until the mid- to late eighteenth century were Latin and French). The text is rarely referenced in the original, but it is worth citing in full (my translation).

Hat wohl ein Volk, zumal ein uncultivirtes volk etwas Lieberes, als die sprache seiner Fäter? In ihr wohnet sein ganzer Gedankenreichthum an Tradition, Geschichte, Religion und Grundsäken des Lebens, alle sein herz und Seele. Einem solchen Volk seine Sprache nehmen oder herabwürdigen, heisst ihm sein einziges unsterbliches Gigenthum nehmen, das von Altern auf Kinder fortgeht. [Does a people, especially an uncultivated people, have anything dearer than the language of its ancestors? In it resides their entire wealth of ideas on Tradition, History, Religion and the Principles of Life, all their heart and soul. To take away or despise the language of such a people means to confiscate its immortal property, that which is passed on from parents to children.]

(Herder, 1888, p. 58)

It continues:

Die beste Cultur eines Volkes ist nicht schnell; sie lässt sich durch eine fremde Sprache nicht erzwingen; am schönsten, und ich möchte sagenn, einzig gedeihet sie auf dem eignen Boden der Nation, in ihrer ererbten und sich forterbenden Mundart. Mit der Sprache erbeutet man das Herz des Volks. [The best culture of a people does not develop quickly; it cannot be forced through a foreign language; it is at its most beautiful, and I might say, exclusively so, only on the soil of its own nation, in its inherited and eternal dialect. Language captures the heart of a people.]

(Herder, 1888, p. 59)

Language, culture, nationalism

Herder's identification of language as the key to understanding the radical difference of distinct cultural, and therefore national formations, was historically significant in two ways. First, as Williams (1977) points out, it was an important part of the shift away from a singular definition of "culture" to a recognition of "cultures" (p. 17). Second, it was taken up by Herder's successors in the German tradition and became a key component of European nationalist thought.

In his *Addresses to the German Nation* (1968[1808]), for example, J. G. Fichte, writing in the period of Napoleonic imperialism, adopted Herder's account of one original human language that had developed historically as different languages in distinct areas of the globe. Following Herder's linkage of language and identity, this led Fichte to the bold declaration that "we give the name of people to men whose organs of speech are influenced by the same external conditions, who live together, and who develop their language in continuous communication with each other" (p. 49). It was a belief taken up and propagated by Wilhelm von Humboldt in *The Diversity of Human Language-Structure and its Influence on the Mental Development of Mankind* (1836)—a title which conveys its relativist emphasis. Humboldt (1988[1836]) notes that "since the development in man of his human nature depends on that of his language, the very concept of the nation is thereby directly given as that of a body of men who form language in a particular way" (p. 153). This led to the further belief, already articulated by Herder, concerning the necessary link between language and national character.

> But the individualities to be found in the same nation fall within the *national uniformity*, which again distinguishes each particular turn of thought from those that resemble it in another people. From this uniformity, and that of the special stimulus peculiar to every language, the *character* of that language arises. Every language receives a specific individuality through that of the nation, and has on the latter a uniformly determining reverse effect.
>
> (Humboldt, 1988[1836], p. 152)

The consequences of the insistence on the radical separateness of distinct languages, cultures, and nations could have been restricted to the important achievement of anthropological respect and the deflation of European cultural universalism. But at a political level, the implications were more direct and practical. They were made explicit by Fichte (1968[1808]): "It is beyond doubt that, wherever a separate language is found, there a separate nation exists, which has the right to take charge of its independent affairs and to govern itself" (p. 184). The step from an acknowledgement of the equivalence of cultural difference to the right to self-determination was crucial and had far-reaching effects both within Europe in the nineteenth century and then later in anti-colonial struggles. Within Europe the lesson was understood and taken up, to name but a few, in Germany, Poland, Hungary, Italy, Switzerland, and of course, Ireland.

In fact, Ireland was no stranger to the concatenation of language and national and cultural identity, as centuries before Herder and his philosophers theorized the links, English colonialism had made them explicit through the policy of Anglicization. In response to the fact that English colonialism in Ireland was an uncertain, costly, and politically treacherous project, the English Crown decided in the mid-sixteenth century to depart from previous policy by attempting to make the

Irish English-speaking. Thus in 1537, Henry VIII passed the Act for the English Order, Habit and Language of 1537, which was based on a crucial presupposition:

> There is again nothing which doth more contain and keep many of his subjects of this his said land [Ireland], in a certain savage and wild kind and manner of living, than the diversity that is betwixt them in tongue, language, order and habit, which by the eye deceiveth the multitude, and persuadeth unto them, that they should be as it were of sundry sorts, or rather of sundry countries, where indeed they be wholly together one body, whereof his highness is the only head under God.
>
> (*Statutes* 28 H 8. c. xv)

As with Herder, cultural difference, including linguistic difference, was considered to be a powerful force by the Crown. But whereas Herder heralded cultural diversity for its capacity to distinguish between people and preserve identity, colonialism wanted to banish cultural diversity for the very same reason. That is, from the colonial perspective, the differences of "language, order and habit" between the Irish and English, meant that the King's Irish subjects were "persuaded" that they and the English belonged to "sundry countries" (with distinct political allegiances), rather than being united under the King's authority. The political threat was considered so serious that the legislation focused on culture as the means to enforce colonial hegemony. Cultural conformity was ordained by edict in understated but menacing terms.

> His Majesty doth hereby intimate unto all his said subjects of this land, of all degrees, that whosoever shall, for any respect, at any time, decline from the order and purpose of this law, touching the increase of the English tongue, habit, and order, or shall suffer any within his family or rule, to use the Irish habit, or not to use themselves to the English tongue, his Majesty will repute them in his noble heart . . . whatsoever they shall at other times pretend in words and countenance, to be persons of another sort and inclination than becometh true and faithful subjects.
>
> (*Statutes* 28 H 8. c. xv)

The political significance of cultural difference was also noted later in the seventeenth century by the major English poet and colonial servant, Edmund Spenser in *A View of the State of Ireland* (1596): "The speach being Irish, the heart must needes bee Irish" (Spenser, 1633, p. 48). It was an observation which led Spenser (1633) to recommend brutal measures, since "it hath ever beene the use of the Conquerour, to despise the language of the conquered, and to force him by all meanes to learne his" (p. 47). Such thinking may have reflected not simply awareness of the dangers of cultural difference, but anxieties about English national identity at this significant moment in the emergence of the English nation-state. But whatever the cause, there was certainly an understanding of the link between language and national identity. Indeed in a comment in his *Itinerary*

(1617) that pre-empts Herder and his followers some two centuries later, Fynes Moryson, an English colonial adventurer, noted that "communion or difference of language, hath alwayes been observed, a spetial motive to unite or allienate the myndes of all nations". "In generall", he added, "all nations have thought nothing more powerfull to unite myndes then the Community of language" (Moryson, 1903[1617], p. 213).

Language and cultural nationalism in Ireland

In his *Projects for Re-Establishing the Internal Peace and Tranquility of Ireland* (1799), written just after the 1798 Rebellion that led directly to the incorpora- tion of Ireland into the United Kingdom, Whitley Stokes, a nationalist Fellow of Trinity College, noted in passing that "it is easier to alter the religion of a people than their language" (Stokes, 1799, p. 45). His observation was no doubt based on the fact that although Anglicization had been the colonial policy since the mid-sixteenth century, a significant portion of the population remained stubbornly Irish-speaking at the turn of the nineteenth century. It was not that the policy had been neglected, since there had been various legal attempts to eradicate or at least control the use of Irish. The legislation included An Act for the Uniformity of Common Prayer and Service in the Church of 1560; An Act for the Erection of Free Schools of 1570; An Act for the Explaining of some Doubts Arising upon an Act Entitled, An Act for the Better Execution of his Majesty's Gracious Settle- ments of his Majesty's Kingdom of Ireland of 1665 (this law sought to Anglicize the names of "towns, land and places"); An Act to Restrain Foreign Education of 1695; and His Majesty's Royal Charter for Erecting English Protestant Schools in the Kingdom of Ireland of 1733. Nevertheless, Stokes (1799) himself claimed that of a population of some four and a half million, "at least eight hundred thou- sand of our countrymen speak Irish only, and there are at least twice as many who speak it in preference" (p. 45).

And yet, if at the end of the eighteenth century more than half the population con- sisted of Gaelic monoglots or spoke the language by choice, then that situation was soon to change as a result of a number of factors. These included the extension of the British state apparatus throughout Ireland after 1801; the decision of the Catholic Church to adopt English; the effect of the British State's economic policies— particularly industrialization and the growth of the cities; the introduction of the Anglicized National Schools system after 1831; the Famine and its impact on the predominantly Irish-speaking rural areas; and, from the mid-century, the consoli- dation of the cultural hegemony of English at the expense of Irish. The impact of this combination of issues was stark. In the 1851 census, 1,524,286 people were recorded as Irish speakers (23.3% of the population), of whom 319,602 were Irish monoglots. This was already a significant fall from the beginning of the cen- tury, but the situation pejorated significantly. The 1911 census registered 582,446 Irish speakers (13.3% of the population), of whom only 16,873 were monoglot (less than 3% of Irish speakers). Stokes was proven wrong in the nineteenth century; in Ireland it was easier to alter the language rather than the religion.

In the midst of this calamitous decline in the use of Irish, a group of radical nationalists (the Young Irelanders) emerged in the 1840s gathered around the *Nation* journal. The main figure in the group was Thomas Davis, who was influenced by the type of European cultural nationalism outlined earlier (Davis visited Germany in 1839–40). Thus, seizing on the articulation between language and nationality that Herder and his successors had proposed, Davis composed a seminal essay titled "Our National Language" in 1843. In the piece, he echoed Fichte's rhetoric (specifically the emphasis on bodily constitution, space, culture, and history), in his declaration that

> [t]he language which grows up with a people is conformed to their organs, descriptive of their climate, constitution and manners, mingled inseparably with their history and their soil, fitted beyond any other language to express their prevalent thoughts in the most natural and efficient way.
>
> (Davis, 1914, p. 97)

This led to an assertion that became the founding principle of Irish cultural nationalism: "A people without a language of its own is only half a nation. A nation should guard its language more than its territories—'tis a surer barrier, and more important frontier, than fortress or river" (Davis, 1914, p. 98). Encoded within this statement is the belief that was to divide cultural and political nationalism in the late nineteenth century: that an Ireland without Irish would never be a fully independent nation.

Davis followed his German forebears in rejecting the damage that the forced acquisition of a foreign language engendered and again the resemblance is clear in the use of common rhetorical tropes. Here is Fichte (1968[1808]) on a people who have lost their own language and speak the language of another nationality.

> They receive the flat and dead history of a foreign culture, but not in any way a culture of their own. They get symbols which . . . must seem to them entirely as arbitrary as the sensuous part of the language. For them this advent of history . . . makes the language dead and closed in respect of its whole sphere of imagery and its continuous flow is broken off.
>
> (p. 54)

And here is Davis (1914):

> To impose another language on a people is to send their history adrift among the accidents of translation—'tis to tear their identity from all places—'tis to substitute arbitrary signs for picturesque and suggestive names—'tis to cut off the entail of feelings and separate the people from their forefathers by a deep gulf.
>
> (pp. 97–98)

There is also an echo here of Herder's (1888) protest against the rupturing of tradition—the "immortal property" (p. 58) passed from generation to generation.

For Davis (1914) it followed therefore that "nothing can make us believe that it is natural or honourable for the Irish to speak the language of the alien, the invader, the Sassenagh tyrant, and to abandon the language of our kings and heroes" (p. 101).

Davis died in 1845 (aged 30) and his political influence was limited within his lifetime. Later in the century, however, Charles Gavin Duffy, an important figure in the nineteenth-century Irish nationalist politics, reflected on the significance of Davis's work. To it, Duffy (1896) argued, "may be traced, as to their fountain-head, many of the opinions now universally current among the Irish people" (p. v). Those opinions included the cultural nationalism that played an important role in the anti-colonial struggle.

Language against colonialism

As noted earlier, the position of the Irish language in Ireland towards the end of the nineteenth century was precarious. Even in the areas where Irish was spoken as a community language, typically amongst the poorest of the rural poor, the preference for English was becoming marked. Indeed, after the terror of the Famine, Irish parents were forthright in their wishes, as a school inspector on the isolated islands makes clear: "It is natural to inquire how this strong passion for education could have possessed a people who are themselves utterly illiterate. Their passion may be traced to one predominant desire—the desire to speak English" (Keenan, 1858, p. xx). Such was the strength of feeling that Irish-speaking parents fully complied with the English-only regime ordered by the schoolmasters.

> He makes it a cause of punishment to speak Irish in the school, and he has instituted a sort of police among the parents to see that in their intercourse with one another the children speak nothing but English at home. The parents are so very eager for the English, they exhibit no reluctance to inform the master of every detected breach of the school law.
>
> (Keenan, 1858, p. xx)

The 1882 report of the Society for the Preservation of the Irish Language (the society's title is revealing) indicates the scale of the problem.

> The chief obstacle is caused by the indifference, or apathy of the people generally as to the necessity of preserving the National Language. . . . Our success can be deemed but partial until the parents heartily desire that their children should be familiar with their native tongue and cherish and promote its cultivation, by regarding it as an essential part of their children's education.
>
> (Society for the Preservation of the Irish Language, 1884, p. 1)

Such an outcome seemed a long way off in the 1880s, and most mainstream commentators not only foresaw the demise of the Irish language, they welcomed it. But the current of ideas runs underground at times, and it can emerge unexpectedly and with force. This was the fate of an idea that had first been articulated, ironically, by the colonizers, and then reiterated in the work of the cultural nationalists around Young Ireland: that the Irish language and Irish identity were ineluctably linked. Given the developments within Irish political nationalism at the end of the nineteenth century, it is perhaps in retrospect unsurprising (though the idea would have been astounding to most observers of the time) that language and culture were to become driving forces in the struggle to overthrow British rule. The late nineteenth-century cultural nationalists took Fichte's claim about language, nationality, and the right to self-determination (Fichte, 1968[1808], p, 184) very seriously indeed.

One of the prime, albeit unlikely, propagandists for the revival and preservation of the Irish language was Douglas Hyde, the son of a rector in the (Anglicized, Protestant minority) Church of Ireland. In "The Necessity for De-anglicising Ireland" '(1892), an address to the Irish Literary Society that was met with derision, Hyde issued the manifesto that was to underpin Irish cultural nationalism's most effective and powerful organization, *Conradh na Gaeilge* (the Gaelic League). As justification, it drew attention to the apparent historical irony facing Ireland: At precisely the point that the country seemed likely to gain Home Rule, and thus a significant measure of political independence, it was losing what Herder (1888) called its "immortal property" (p. 58).

> What the battleaxe of the Dane, the sword of the Norman, the wile of the Saxon were unable to perform, we have accomplished ourselves. We have at last broken the continuity of Irish life, and just at the moment when the Celtic race is presumably just about to largely recover possession of its own country, it finds itself deprived and stript of its Celtic characteristics, cut off from the past, yet scarcely in touch with the present.
>
> (Hyde, 1986, p. 157)

Hyde's (1986) aim was simple: "to show the folly of neglecting what is Irish, and hastening to adopt, pell-mell and indiscriminatingly, everything that is English, simply because it *is* English" (p. 153).

The issue, of course, was "what is Irish?", or to put it in clearer terms, what constitutes Irishness? For cultural nationalists, the answer was simple: Irish national identity resides in Irish culture, at the core of which lies the Irish language. For Hyde (1986), it followed that

> [e]very Irish-feeling Irishman, who hates the reproach of West-Britonism, should set himself to encourage the efforts which are being made to keep alive our once national tongue. The losing of it is our greatest blow, and the sorest stroke that the rapid Anglicisation of Ireland has inflicted upon us. In order to de-Anglicise ourselves we must at once arrest the decay of the language.
>
> (p. 160)

As it became increasingly likely that 700 years of colonial rule would finally be thrown off, the danger was that colonialism's cruellest trick would be to reduce the Irish to West Britons (English-speaking Irish men and women, Irish in name only). Hyde's essay, and the Gaelic League movement that it inspired, aimed to avoid that national peril.

In the mid-eighteenth century, Andrew Donlevy claimed (inaccurately) that Irish was "now on the Brink of utter Decay", "to the great Dishonour and Shame of the *Natives*, who shall pass everywhere for *Irish-Men*. Although *Irish-Men* without *Irish* is an incongruity, and a great Bull" (Donlevy, 1742, pp. 506–507). It is testimony to the achievement of the late nineteenth-century Gaelic revivalists that they made this sentiment a national reflex: The loss of Irish became thought of as a shameful national disgrace which risked the forfeiture of Irish identity. Such was the success of their project that cultural nationalists were confident enough to warn political nationalists that "political weapons are not to be despised, nor can they be well dispensed with; but we must not forget that politics are but a means to an end, and that end is nationhood" (O'Farrelly, 1901, p. 3). What was nationhood? The answer was couched in terms that could have been taken directly from the German tradition.

> A people's language tells us what they were even better than their history. So true is this that even if the people had perished and their history had been lost, we might still learn from their language—and in language I include literature—to what intellectual stature they had attained, what was the extent of their moral development, and what their general worthiness.
>
> (Kavanagh, 1902, p. 1)

"Tír gan teanga, tír gan anam" ("A nation without a language is a nation without a soul") and "tír agus teanga" ("nation and language") became the slogans of a cultural nationalist movement that was a significant element amongst the nationalist forces pitted against imperial arrogance and might. Indeed, reflecting on the origins of that movement, Pádraig Pearse, one of the leaders of the 1916 Rebellion against British rule, declared that the founders of the Gaelic League in 1893 had started "not a revolt, but a revolution" (Pearse, 1952, p. 95).

Language and identity

Having made cultural difference the radical foundation of the movement to gain independence for Ireland, it followed that once independence had been gained, the new nation-state would take measures to recognize and protect its distinctive features, not least the Irish language. Thus, reflecting on the past and the future, Michael Collins, a leader of the Republican forces in the Irish War of Independence, commented:

> We only succeeded after we had begun to get back our Irish ways, after we had made a serious effort to speak our own language, after we had striven

again to govern ourselves. How can we express our most subtle thoughts and finest feelings in a foreign tongue? Irish will scarcely be our language in this generation, nor even perhaps in the next. But until we have it again on our tongues and in our minds, we are not free.

(Collins, 1922, p. 100)

Despite Collins's recognition that the struggle to create an "Irish Ireland" (another slogan of cultural nationalism) would be long-lasting, Dáil Éireann, the government of Ireland, set about the task with despatch after independence. The Constitution of the Irish Free State of 1922 declared Irish to be the national language and made allowance for special provisions for its maintenance. But the key to the linguistic and cultural transformation of Ireland was not to be legislation, but education. For as W. T. Cosgrave, President of the Executive Council (effectively prime minister), asked rhetorically: "Must we not look to the Minister of Education to mark the Gaelicisation . . . of our whole culture . . . to make our nation separate and distinct and something to be thought of" (Lee, 1989, p. 132).

Measures were immediately stipulated with regard to the use of Irish in schools, including a deeply controversial plan to educate all infants entirely in Irish, whatever the home language of the parents, or indeed the competence of teachers in the language (the proposal was soon amended, though still with the overall aim of achieving Irish-medium education). Further steps included the creation of teacher-training for Irish teachers; extra payment for teachers of the language; extra marks for pupils who answered in school exams in Irish; grants for schools that taught the language; and the requirement for a pass in Irish in the leaving certificate. This last innovation, together with the practice of reserving certain public service jobs for Irish speakers, became known as "compulsory Irish". Taken together, this set of measures were defensible in terms of making education the linchpin of the attempt to revive and disseminate the Irish language as a way of preserving cultural and national identity. And yet this policy failed for two practical reasons.

First, within education, the measures became increasingly controversial. One issue was that the various policies designed to foster Irish in effect favoured one section of the community (Irish speakers) over another (those who spoke only English or whose Irish was substandard). Another major problem was that the *Revised programme of Primary Instruction* (which was held from 1934 to 1971) decreased the considerable pressures on schools and their teachers by reducing the requirements in English, science, and maths. The predictable result was dismay on the part of parents, as a report commissioned by the teachers' national organization found:

Parents generally are opposed to a method for the Irish revival which would tend to lower the educational standard of their children according to their values. . . . Many examples were cited of parents who endeavoured to teach their children at home through English, subjects that the same children were being taught in school through Irish, while it was repeatedly urged that complaints from the parents on the low standard of their children's education were widespread.

(Irish National Teachers Organisation, 1941, p. 60)

Taken together, the sense that the favouring of Irish was divisive and unfair, and the concerns about educational standards, led to ambivalence at best, cynicism and hostility at worst, towards the stated desire for a monoglot Ireland.

The second reason for the failure of the measures intended to promote Irish was the lack of support in even those areas in which the language had survived as a native, community vernacular—known from the 1920s as the Gaeltacht. The Gaeltacht was central to revival efforts, as Cosgrave noted in 1922:

We recognise also that the future of the Irish language and its part in the future of the Irish nation depend, more than anything else, on its continuing in an unbroken tradition as the language of Irish homes. . . . For this reason the Irish people rightly value as a national asset their "Gaeltacht", the scattered range of districts in which Irish is the home language.

(Ó Cuív, 1951, p. 7)

Yet as the Gaeltach Commission report on these areas observed in 1926, they continued to be blighted by the conditions that had been imposed under British rule.

The area in which the language persisted came to be reduced to one in which the economic problem was so acute that the surplus population had continually to look for a living outside, while those who remained at home lived in grinding poverty. The economic conditions then became an important and a growing factor in the decline of the language. We are now in the full tide of that destructive effect.

(Rialtas na hÉireann, 1926, p. 371)

Such was the deprivation that those closest to the Irish-speaking community reported hostility to the language. One teacher from Acaill commented that:

[i]f it could be brought home to the parents that their children stand to gain something by their speaking Irish to them you might have a remedy. As it is they are opposed to Irish. They see people with English getting all the jobs. . . . It is just a question of bread and butter.

(Walsh, 2002, p. 60)

Another teacher from An Clochán called it "mockery" to say to Irish speakers: "Don't speak English, or emigrate: Speak Irish, stay at home and starve, cry out yearly for doles, and send your children picking winkles instead of being at school" (Walsh, 2002, p. 101).

It was not as though the problem was not recognized, as is clear again from the Commission's report:

> It is necessary to show the people who still speak Irish traditionally, that not only does the State recognise the Irish language as the National language, but that it is determined to redress the disabilities which that language has suffered, and to restore it to its position and prestige. Much propaganda of an educative kind will be necessary before a large number of them will be convinced that it is no longer despised.
>
> (Walsh, 2002, p. 85)

The difficulty was that in practice more emphasis was placed on trying to persuade native Irish speakers that their language was not despised, than on the radical social and economic transformation of the poorest areas that would have been required to provide the conditions by which the language could have been sustained. And as it was, those measures that were taken to promote Irish, were, as noted earlier, nationally divisive and otherwise problematic. The long-term result was a situation that had been forecast in 1924 by Eoin MacNeill, Gaelic Leaguer and Minister of Education in the first independent government: "Purely bureaucratic and official favouring of Irish in the absence of a strongly favourable public attitude, would lead to no desirable result, nothing more than barren conformity" (Ó Huallacháin, 1994, p. 88).

Though Ireland managed the post-colonial transition successfully and became a stable, if deeply conservative, democratic state, the means by which it had done so inflicted considerable costs. Not always through its own making, in the first 50 years of independence, Ireland developed into a relatively poor, insular, sectarian state in which emigration was a perennial tragedy that affected the young and the old. Where did that leave the language revival, the core of the project to preserve national identity along Herderian lines? By the 1960s, the plan to create a monoglot Ireland was in serious difficulty and the "compulsory Irish" policy was abandoned. As one commentator later put it, "Irish had become identified in the popular mind with trouble at school, irregular verbs and tight-faced schoolteachers" (Kiberd, 1981, p. 5). The language had become the focus of anger from all sides of the political debate and was enveloped in the crisis around the nature of Irish national identity that developed from the 1960s through to the 1980s. By the 1960s, however, for many of those on the receiving end of "compulsory Irish", the language had become associated, not always accurately or fairly, with the narrow conception of the nation promoted by the dominant reactionary forces in post-independence Ireland (principally the Catholic Church and a deeply conservative State). The result was a disaster for both the language and the nation: a failed revivalist movement linked to an abstract, idealized, homogeneous, and backward-looking mode of national identity.

Herder's trap

The question that arises from the history set out earlier is this: How did the Irish language, the repository and guarantor of national identity in the Herderian model, change from being a radical weapon in the fight against imperialism and colonialism, to a tool that served the ends of reactionary forces in post-independence Ireland? The answer to that question has implications that range far beyond Ireland and lead to more general questions about cultural nationalism itself.

The core of the difficulty lies in the fact that the language-nation equation was, from the very start, a rhetorical abstraction that belied the realities of linguistic and cultural difference by privileging monoglossia over heteroglossia. In other words, in the face of the realities of linguistic variation, one specific form of language was taken to be the central, determinate (national) form, at the expense of other forms. Given that, it is perhaps surprising that Herder reveals himself to be acutely aware of the heteroglot nature of language. In the *Essay on the Origin of Language* (1772), for example, in the section concerned with the "third natural law" (of the "formation of different national languages"), Herder (2002) issues the caveat that because of the differences of language, "in the real metaphysical sense, it is already never possible for there to be a single language between man and wife, father and son, child and old man" (p. 147). At the level of pronunciation, for example, there is individual variation even within one language.

> As little as there can be two human beings who share exactly the same form and facial traits, just as little can there be two languages in the mouths of two human beings which would in fact still be only one language, even merely *in terms of pronunciation.*
>
> (Herder, 2002, p. 148)

And again, at the level of lexis and meaning, variation was key: "but *words* themselves, *sense*, the *soul* of language—what an endless field of differences" (Herder, 2002, p. 148). Even synonyms, Herder (2002) asserts, develop differently:

> [T]his one became familiar to the one person, that one to the other person, more appropriate to his viewpoint, more original for his circle of sensation, more frequently occurring in the course of his life . . . then there arose *favourite words, words of one's own idioms, linguistic idiom.*
>
> (p. 148)

Indeed, Herder (2002) highlights the historical variability of language in terms that pre-empt the emphasis that Mikhail Bakhtin placed on heteroglossia in his highly influential work on language and culture (Bakhtin, 1981).

> For the former person that word became extinguished, this word remained. That word got bent away from the main subject through a secondary viewpoint; here the spirit of the main concept itself changed with the passage of time. There hence arose distinctive bendings, diversions, changes, *promotions* and *additions* and *transpositions* and *removals, of whole and half* meanings—a new idiom!
>
> (p. 148)

Given this awareness of the heteroglot nature of language, the puzzle is why Herder insisted on identifying language as the key to national identity, since for language to operate in such a role, it would have to possess an abstract, stable, determinate nature that would fly in the face of the type of heteroglossia that he identifies. After all, it is not that Herder was not aware of the dangers of rhetorical abstraction. When challenging European universalism, for example, in the *Letters for the Advancement of Humanity*, he stated quite simply that "European culture is an abstracted concept, a name. 'Where does it exist entirely? With which people? In which times?'" (Herder, 2002, p. 396). The objection is well made. But these telling questions could also be posed to the concept of the "immortal property" of the national language, passed on from generation to generation as the guarantor of the nation's identity. Where does it exist entirely? With which people? In which times?

In a sense, Herder's de facto denial of heteroglossia, through the invocation of the national language, is revealingly similar to Saussure's later denial of difference in linguistic practice when it came to the definition of "the language" (a static, synchronic system). In the *Course in General Linguistics*, Saussure (1983[1916]) claims that "an absolute state is defined by lack of change. But since languages are always changing, however minimally, studying a linguistic state amounts in practice to ignoring unimportant changes" (p. 100).

What both Herder and Saussure achieve in their elision of difference (heteroglossia in the case of Herder, linguistic change through time for Saussure) is the rhetorical construction of that self-same abstract object that both claim to have discovered—the national language in the case of Herder, language for Saussure. Which is to say that they both claim to have found the means of identifying what is already presumed to exist. Another way of putting this point is to say that for Herder, cultural difference, embodied in language, is what constitutes the nation, but in reality, the nation can only appear at the cost of the eradication of the everyday cultural differences of heteroglossia. What appears to be foundational, the basis of a form of identity, turns out to be rhetorical. It is an abstraction away from the complex realities of cultural practice in given spaces and times which is then reified and taken to "prove" the existence of the nation.

Perhaps the most significant lesson to be learned from Herder's rhetorical construction is that recognition of cultural difference is not necessarily radical. Cultural difference is at once lived, practical, a historically variable reality, and a discursive construct, and what makes it progressive, or not, is its use in specific historical contexts in relation to the formation of power. This is why the language-nation link, which is, essentially, a claim about cultural difference, can be radical—as in its use in the struggle against imperialism and colonialism in Ireland and elsewhere. But it is also why the language-nation link can be reactionary— as in its use by the state to forge a form of cultural hegemony based on a monoglot notion of "real Irishness" in post-independence Ireland. Herder's trap, into which he, like many of his followers, fell, is that although the language-nation link was, historically, a bold and radical call for the recognition of cultural difference, it is in reality based precisely on a failure to respect the complex actuality of cultural difference. In other words, the identification of "the national language" as the key to "national identity" is based on an elision of the cultural differences within the nation. In short, both "the language" and "the nation" can be radical concepts in some historical circumstances, but they can be reductive and dangerous elisions in other contexts. Like nationalism itself, cultural nationalism can go right or left; its political tendency will depend on the historical conjuncture in which it is deployed.

References

Bakhtin, M. (1981). *The dialogic imagination: Four essays* (M. Holquist, Ed.). Austin: University of Texas Press.

Collins, M. (1922). *The path to freedom*. Dublin: Talbot Press.

Davis, T. (1914). *Essays literary and historical*. Dundalk: Dundalga.

de Saussure, F. (1983 [1916]). *Course in general linguistics* (C. Bally & A. Sechehaye, eds., R. Harris, Trans.). London: Duckworth.

Donlevy, A. (1742). *An Teagsag Críosduidhe do réir ceasda agus freagartha: The catechism, or Christian doctrine by way of question and answer*. Paris: Guerin.

Duffy, C. G. (1896). *Young Ireland, 1840–1850*. London: Cassell.

Fichte, J. G. (1968 [1808]). *Addresses to the German nation* (G. A. Kelly, Ed.). New York: Harper and Row.

Herder, J. G. (1888). *Herders sämmtliche Werke [Complete works]* (vol. 17). Weidmannsche Buchhandlung.

Herder, J. G. (2002). *Philosophical writings* (M. N. Forster, Ed.). Cambridge: Cambridge University Press.

Hume, D. (1975 [1748]). *Enquiries concerning human understanding and concerning the principles of morals* (L. A. Selby-Bigge & P. H. Nidditch, Eds.). Oxford: Oxford University Press.

Hyde, D. (1986). *Language, lore and lyrics: Essays and lectures of Douglas Hyde* (B. Ó Conaire, Ed.). Dublin: Irish Academic Press.

Irish National Teachers Organisation (1941). *Report of the committee of inquiry into the use of Irish as a teaching medium to children whose home language is English*. Dublin: Cahill.

Kavanagh, P. F. (1902). *Ireland's defence—her language*. Dublin: Gaelic League.

Keenan, P. J. (1858). *Twenty-second report of the commissioners of national education in Ireland* (vol. ii, p. 75, pt 2, p. 81). House of Commons Papers.

Kiberd, D. (1981). Editorial: The Irish language. *The Crane Bag, 5*(2), 4–6.

Lee, J. (1989). *Ireland 1912–1985: Politics and society*. Cambridge: Cambridge University Press.

Moryson, F. (1903 [1617]). *Shakespeare's Europe: Unpublished chapters of Fynes Moryson's Itinerary* (C. Hughes, Ed.). London: Sherratt and Hughes.

Ó Cuív, B. (1951). *Irish dialects and Irish-speaking districts*. Dublin: Institute for Advanced Studies.

O'Farrelly, A. (1901). *The reign of humbug*. Dublin: Gaelic League.

Ó Huallacháin, F. C. (1994). *The Irish and Irish—a sociolinguistic analysis of the relationship between a people and their language*. Dublin: Irish Franciscan Office.

Pearse, P. (1952). *Political writings and speeches*. Dublin: Talbot.

Rialtas na hÉireann. (1926). *Gaeltacht commission: Report*. Béarla: Oifig an tSoláthair.

Society for the Preservation of the Irish Language (1884). *Proceedings of the congress held in Dublin 1882.*

Spenser, E. (1633). A view of the state of Ireland in Ware, Sir James. In *The historie of Ireland collected by three learned authors.* Society of Stationers.

The statutes at large passed in the parliaments held in Ireland (1786–1801). (vol. 20). Grierson.

Stokes, W. (1799). *Projects for re-establishing the internal peace and tranquility of Ireland.* Dublin: Moore.

von Humboldt, W. (1988 [1836]). *On language: The diversity of human language-structure and its influence on the mental development of mankind* (P. Heatth, Trans.). Cambridge: Cambridge University Press.

Walsh, J. (2002). *Díchoimisiúnú Teanga: Coimisiún na Gaeltachta.* Dublin: Cois Life.

Williams, R. (1977). *Marxism and literature.* Oxford: Oxford University Press.

5 Multilingualism in the United States

The long history of official translations

Rosina Lozano

There is no single language in the United States. English has predominated politically even without the U.S. Congress designating it as the official language of the nation; yet state law and the country's residents tell a more dynamic story of multilingualism. In 2011, the number of people who spoke a language other than English at home hovered at just over one-fifth of the population—but this is no recent development (Ryan, 2013, p. 2). In 1790, non-native English speakers made up almost one-quarter of the United States' population (Lepore, 2003, p. 28). This long-standing multilingual reality meant that the United States could and did implement a variety of language policies that provided translations for those who spoke languages other than English at the state and local levels. As the United States added new states and territories, it endorsed and courted a broad multilingual settler base as part of an effort to create a culturally accepted—European—settler community in the burgeoning nation.[1]

As others have explained elsewhere in this volume, the philosophy of Johann Gottfried Herder looms large over theoretical conceptions of language and government. His strongly held beliefs about the all-encompassing unity of *Volksgeist*, a commonality of culture, lifestyle, and fatherland, would suggest an insurmountable disconnect when considering the United States (Berlin, 2009, p. 30; Pagden, 1994, pp. 141–142). The country was formed through the removal of Indigenous populations from the land of their ancestors. The new settler state took away the place names, languages, and history of the land, along with exterminating a large number of its Indigenous people. Most accounts of the language of government in the United States place English as the "native" language, erasing the Native languages that better correlated with Herder's understanding of a language's ties to nation and fatherland.

Unable to supplant the Native population solely with English speakers, the United States encouraged the growth of their nation by recruiting and offering land to a broad swath of immigrants who did not speak English. Senators preferred white settlers who they did not require to become citizens to obtain land. As Democratic Senator Thomas Hart Benton of Missouri explained in 1850, settlers "conquered [the land] in every sense of the word, and they are entitled to its gain" (Frymer, 2017, p. 138). The nation expanded its immigrant population by over five million between 1820 and 1860 (Frymer, 2017, p. 134). Land grabs that contributed to the nation's expansion were a continual national theme of the nineteenth century.

Between 1830 and 1930, the U.S. Congress created 20 incorporated territories that eventually came to make up the nation's current 50 states. It also admitted 24 states over the century. The nation grew far beyond the original 13 colonies on the Eastern Atlantic seaboard to encompass the entire continent, Alaska, and Hawaii. In 1898, the nation also added noncontiguous territories like Guam, Puerto Rico, and the Philippines. These territories are more like colonies and had a very different relationship to language, one which is not included in this chapter. The nation's fast expansion created a tiered system of citizenship and rights based on whether an individual resided in a state, a position that gave them full rights as citizens, or a territory.

Territorial governments did not have as much autonomy as states. The presidents of the United States could choose the territorial governor, secretary of the territory, and territorial judges. While territorial citizens elected their own legislature, Congress reserved the right to review and intervene on any laws it disagreed with, though they rarely overturned territorial laws. A final federal restriction on U.S. citizens living in territories was that they were not permitted to vote for the president who chose their executive and judicial officials. Territorial residents aspired to petition to Congress for statehood in large part so that they could exercise their full rights as citizens.[2]

For Herder, the U.S. political system that allowed non-English speakers into its new nation would likely be a nightmare. After all, he could see "nothing . . . more manifestly contrary to the purpose of political government than the unnatural enlargement of states, the wild mixing of various races and nationalities under one sceptre" (Bauman & Briggs, 2003, p. 179). Yet this form of political government is precisely what emerged in the United States. The strength the nation gained from immigrant settlers and the enslavement of African people allowed the federal government and capitalists to make the most of the rich resources on vast Native lands, which contributed to the subsequent rise of the nation's global, political, and cultural power. The mixed languages and cultures which make up the United States clash with Herder's views. He was opposed to this sort of immigrant settlement creating a nation (Bauman & Briggs, 2003, p. 180).

The United States became a nation where English, the native language of England, presumed political dominance. It did so despite the perpetual resistance of Native peoples whose language and culture remained tied to the lands being taken over, alongside the continued entry of large numbers of immigrants who spoke other languages.[3] These immigrants joined a larger European colonial legacy that included British, Dutch, French, and Spanish settlers. One of the reasons for the success of English as the major political language was due to the adoption of a language policy that was anathema to Herder's conceptions of "one people, one fatherland, one language", but which at times supported what some have characterized as his belief that "government should be based on consent rather than coercion" (Bauman & Briggs, 2003, pp. 188, 193). Whether intentionally or through neglect, the nation avoided any all-encompassing laws that would have required

English in political settings and thus allowed people who spoke European languages to initially participate in their adopted nation in their native languages. The young nation was so successful at incorporating immigrants that few remember any of the translation laws at the state and local level that allowed for this political participation.

While the English spoken in the United States varies to some degree from what is spoken or written in England, it is unlikely that Herder would have designated it as the "new language" he required for "each new nation" (Pagden, 1994, p. 144). Moving beyond Herder's theories is required to understand how language rights and nation-building intertwined during the expansion and settlement of the continental United States. Instead of only serving English-speaking citizens, the United States contended with dozens of languages that coexisted across the nation's territory. The languages heard across the growing nation ranged from Indigenous languages to the immigrant languages of arriving Europeans, Asians, and Latin Americans. It also included multiple colonial languages—English, Spanish, French, etc.—that were spoken and used in governing the first European settlers who took over Indigenous lands prior to the creation of the United States.[4] The final language group was made up of languages originally spoken by African slaves who were forced onto the land and stripped of all language rights. Each of these languages had a different political strength and relevance. Speakers of non-English languages had varied levels of access to translations through state and local laws, which permitted specific language groups to experience greater inclusion in the political and electoral systems of the United States than others.

The multilingualism encountered socially and politically during the colonial and early republic eras did little to displace English as the language of the majority of the new nation or as the language used federally. A distant second to English was providing official translations for speakers of other European languages. The supremacy the federal and state governments held for European languages over others is apparent in the almost complete exclusion of Native, African, and Asian languages from state and territorial laws, while hundreds of laws endorsed at least a dozen European languages. Over 25 states and territories mentioned at least one of the following languages specifically: German, French, Dutch, Norwegian, Spanish, Swedish, "Holland", Welsh, Scandinavian, Chinese, Bohemian, and Italian.[5] Non-European languages also did not appear in the state and territorial laws as an accepted language of instruction for children. Multilingual Indigenous communities were almost completely stripped of their language rights even on reservations where their children were forced into boarding and day schools that prohibited the use of their Native languages.[6]

English has predominated in political and legal settings since the founding of the United States. The dominant language narrative of the United States privileges and uses English-language sources almost exclusively, especially at the federal level, with little recognition of the nation as anything but monolingual. This chapter turns towards other language communities within the United States and specifically highlights federal, state, and territorial laws that promised them translations of official documents.

The crux of this chapter uses state and territorial legislative session laws from 1830 to 1930 to analyse the ways that translations in languages other than English corresponded with the nation's continental expansion and how language was tied to the extension of U.S. citizenship to immigrants. The study ends with the decade following World War I, a period that historians have identified as a high point for national English-only policies. The laws protecting English in the late-1910s and early 1920s led to a drastic decrease in the use and instruction of the German language nationally.[7] These language restrictions proved to be a distinct pivot in language policy after decades of state and territorial laws that supported the translation of German and other languages.

The legislatures of states and territories had the right to offer translations of official documents for their residents. The proliferation of these laws demonstrates how language tolerance was an important tool of settlement and nation-building. The HeinOnline database, a subscription-based legal database, created a platform in the 2010s that facilitates the recovery and systemic study of these language-based state and territorial laws. The database offers the opportunity to search for session laws in every state and territory in the country. Searching HeinOnline for the term "language" in each state's session laws yielded thousands of hits over the identified decades. This robust database has ensured that there are no false positives in this chapter's findings, because the laws related to translations come from scans of these session laws. But the sheer number of session laws searched and the reality of imperfect scanning recognition technology render the conclusions incomplete. Future scholars may encounter more laws by expanding the search to other terms, but for the purposes of this chapter, the search was a cursory one. Still, even this preliminary search encountered enough evidence to push back against views of the United States as a nation with just a single language and permits an analysis of what the presence of these official translations tells us about the inclusion of certain immigrant communities into the nation.

English predominates in federal discourse

Early decisions concerning federal language use suggest a preliminary acceptance of multilingualism. During the Revolutionary War (1775–83), the Continental Congress paid for translations into both German (1774–79) and French (1774–77) (Kloss, 1998, pp. 27–28). This early practice did not set a precedent, as no further government-sponsored translations emerged during the 1780s. The early multilingual reality was viewed by contemporary authors as a serious impediment to nation-building. Building on a comparison made by Jill Lepore (2003), in 1790, Thomas Paine noted the difficult, if not impossible, task of uniting people who shared different languages, government, and culture in the *Rights of Man*. A "union of such a people", he declared, "was impracticable" (Paine, 1998, p. 218). John Jay, a statesman and so-called founding father of the nation, supported an image of one nation, one language, in the *Federalist Papers* by praising the new nation for its common language (Jay, 2008, p. 12). The co-author Alexander Hamilton also saw language as a key unifier for the nation (2008, p. 63). While these opinions do not explain the federal choice to use only English, they do highlight the prevailing sentiment of some of the era's key statesmen in texts that continue to be read as foundational to the nation.

English served without any real debate as the language of the young federal government. Officially supported translations unified the nation during the Revolutionary War, but once the urgency of war was gone, federally supported translations largely disappeared as more pressing state-building concerns took precedence over multilingualism. The young United States privileged English through exclusive reliance on that language in printings of the constitution, federal reports, laws, court decisions, presidential addresses, legislative journals, and many other official government publications. They did so with little debate or discussion, further cementing the place of English.

The federal use of a single language did not reflect the on-the-ground linguistic experience of citizens. Non-English-speaking American Indians, African slaves, and early European settlers and immigrants could easily be shut out of all spheres of the U.S. government without translations. Congress fielded requests for translations of federal documents for mostly European-based language communities and refused to support any until after the U.S.-Mexican War (1846–48) (Baron, 1990, p. 91; Kloss, 1998, pp. 29–35). For example, in 1794 and 1795, Congress recorded requests to publish congressional reports in German. Although not discussed in 1794, in 1795, the petition failed to pass by just one vote (Kloss, 1998, pp. 29–30). In 1810, Michigan territorial residents requested a French translation of federal and territorial laws, which was denied (Kloss, 1998, p. 214). Requests for translations of the President's address occurred each year between 1843 and 1847. Congress rejected each of the petitions (Kloss, 1998, pp. 31–32).

The change in federal support after the U.S.-Mexican War came out of necessity. The United States took Mexico's North to make its current Southwest. The vast land acquisition included portions of what would become California, Nevada, Arizona, Colorado, and New Mexico. The War also clarified U.S. claims to the state of Texas and its border. The former Mexican citizens who lived on the newly ceded land almost universally spoke Spanish. For example, over 90 percent of the territory of New Mexico spoke Spanish and the vast majority of legislators in the first decades after the United States took over the land came from this Spanish-speaking population. In 1853, Congress allowed for the payment of legislative translators in New Mexico and then paid for the translation of legislative journals and session laws into English. The majority of laws passed by the New Mexico legislature before 1874 were originally written in Spanish, which meant English-speaking congressional representatives and other government officials could not have understood them without paying for translations. Precinct officials recorded New Mexico's elections in Spanish, and it was common to hear bilingual political campaign speeches in Spanish. The United States acceded to the use of Spanish in New Mexico because its residents had settled in the region and formed alliances with local Native people like the Pueblos, which helped the nation secure the land from autonomous Indigenous nations like the Apache or Comanche, who regularly raided the territory and threatened U.S. settlement.[8]

The federal government's financial support for translations of New Mexico's official documents into Spanish set no precedent. Congress rejected a request to support Spanish-language territorial translations in Colorado (Lozano, 2018, pp. 58–59). In 1861, Congress supported a request for translations of official documents—the only other known federal case of support for federal translations in the period—when German-language supporters successfully appealed to print the Secretary of Agriculture's report in their native language. The motion passed due to sectional politics. The absence of Southern delegates during the Civil War increased the weight of representatives from the Midwest who were more sympathetic to the request for German translations, because these states more regularly translated government documents for its citizens and residents. Perhaps predictably, given the general trend against support for federal translations and the fact that the Civil War was beginning, Congress repealed its approval of the German-language translation due to concerns over the cost of translation and printing (Kloss, 1998, p. 33).

Although translations remained absent at the federal level, most government documents in a federalist system do not come from the federal government. The Constitution of the United States dictates the powers of the federal government and extends all other governance to state governments. The federal government almost exclusively chose English at the federal level, but due to federalism, Congress did little to halt individual states or local municipalities from supporting their own multilingual citizens with translations of official documents. Specifically, it was a state or territory's choice to pay for any official support of a language other than English.

Congress could have proactively taken a very different stance on language in the United States by declaring English as the official language of the nation or by making English a requirement for territories to secure statehood. It did not. Instead, the reigning federal response throughout the nineteenth century remained one of tolerance for local and state language policies that accepted and supported multilingual translations and interpreters.

There are many plausible reasons for the relative silence of U.S. federal officials on language rights during the nineteenth century. Securing the nation's land claims stands out as the most pressing one. By supporting European immigrant settlers in their takeover of Indigenous lands, the federal government encouraged settlement by those who could begin reinventing the land in ways that federal officials and American cultural expectations deemed acceptable.[9] By creating federal policy that extended settlement to European immigrants from various linguistic communities, the federal government, unwittingly perhaps, opened the door to states and territories supporting multilingual translations, and at times, even to bilingual territorial and state legislative proceedings and elections (or, more likely, local communities where political participation was dominated by settlers in a language other than English). Lax federal immigration policies also ensured the growing political strength of these immigrant communities.

Settlers govern multilingually

Speakers of European immigrant languages benefitted from federalism and the control it offered local officials to govern their communities. Immigrant settlers who spoke limited or no English often chose to live in communities where others spoke their language, which increased their political strength and their likelihood of receiving translations funded by state governments or their local municipality or county.[10] Their political relevance or attractiveness as desirable settlers could garner the attention needed to pass laws supporting publicly funded translations.

States and territories as distinct as Minnesota, Michigan, and Arkansas recruited and encouraged immigrant settlement in their states in the middle decades of the nineteenth century by advertising with pamphlets they paid to have translated and distributed internationally (1879 Minnesota Laws 76–77; 1849 Michigan Laws 364; 1873 Arkansas Laws 279–280). State and territorial legislators targeted specific language groups in these recruiting tactics. It follows then that when a state or territory was successful in drawing their targeted settler community, the legislature would be willing to offer language translations as a way to encourage the new settlers to remain in their territory or state.

The inclusion of laws relating to translations in session laws extends back to the nation's founding. There was one region where these laws served far more than just translations for an immigrant population and instead demonstrated how languages other than English also served as a language of government along with English. In the Southwest, after the U.S.-Mexican War, territorial and state officials included substantial numbers of Spanish speakers who represented long-standing Spanish-speaking settlers. The Treaty of Guadalupe Hidalgo, which ended the War, promised the Mexican settlers in these territories U.S. citizenship. These new "treaty citizens" made up the majority of settlers in most of the Southwest, with the exception of California where the gold rush had resulted in a huge influx of miners from across the country and the world. Due to the demographic reality of this new Spanish-speaking citizenry, in California, Colorado, and New Mexico, the legislature allowed for and funded Spanish-language translations along with translators in the legislative chamber for Spanish-speaking legislative members (Lozano, 2018, pp. 43–61, 89–110).

The significant power yielded by settlers of European descent led to distinct language policies for states than what was found at the federal level. At least 24 states between 1830 and 1930 recognized the language rights and needs of some of its non-English-speaking citizens through translations promised by the legislature. These states included: Arizona, California, Colorado, Connecticut, Delaware, Illinois, Indiana, Iowa, Kentucky, Louisiana, Maine, Maryland, Michigan, Minnesota, Missouri, Nebraska, New Jersey, New Mexico, New York, Ohio, Pennsylvania, Tennessee, Texas, and Wisconsin.[11] These varied and localized translations were approached and determined on a state-by-state basis. States approved and paid for translations of official documents and reports, aided non-English speakers in elections, and provided official notices (often in newspapers) in immigrant and colonial languages (1859 Ind. Acts 122; 1855 La. Acts 413;

1877 NY Sess. Laws 292 (v.2), 390–391 (v.1); 1879 Ind. Acts 298; 1873 Mo. Laws 56; 1868 Iowa Acts 227). States and municipalities permitted some of these languages to have a future in the region by allowing for the instruction of school children in those languages.

The large number and scattered passage of these various laws, along with their impermanence (many translations were passed for specific years and not in perpetuity), have made it exceedingly difficult for historians to make broad statements or conclusions about the nation's use of languages other than English in official capacities. As linguist Joshua Fishman explained, "American laws are—in the long run—neither mandatory with respect to English nor prohibitory with respect to other languages" (Baron, 1990, p. 14). Language provisions occurred outside of the national spotlight at the state and local level and have received little recognition because of this reality.

Most of the state and territorial laws related to translations in other languages occurred in the first decades of settlement and during the initial set-up of the territorial or state government. The state laws that mention specific languages largely disappeared in the first decades of the twentieth century. By then, Congress had incorporated the vast majority of the continental United States as states and early immigrants had resided in the United States long enough to speak English, which weakened the power of arriving settlers and negated their key role in expanding the nation and laying claim to its territory. The state and territorial laws allowing official translations into another language were largely replaced by laws that explicitly mention English as the language required for the publication of official documents and notices, and more broadly, as the language of operation for office holders, courts, and juries (1911 Neb. Laws 549; 1915 Utah Laws 199; 1908–1909 Nev. Stat. 276; 1919 S.D. Sess. Laws 296; 1915 Mich. Pub. Act 314 30, 37, 46; 1909 Kan. Sess. Laws, 380).

This protection of English contrasts with the different types of translations sponsored by state and territorial legislatures for their non-English-speaking residents. While this chapter does not examine the translations themselves or their reception, efficacy, or completeness, by uncovering the rich number of legislatively approved translations, it is possible to analyse these acts as a symbol of political power and influence. Governmentally supported translations included real-time simultaneous translations of proceedings, as well as published translations of materials prepared in English. Either of these translations entailed a considerable amount of political lobbying for them to become state law. Legislated language concessions required states to locate a translator and typesetter in each language and then pay for both the translation and the publication of these translations. The resulting published translations involved a significant financial investment, especially for fledgling western territories with few inexpensive options for printing. Due to the exorbitant costs, many of the approved translations never reached publication due to a lack of funds. Often, it was the cost rather than any specific opposition to publishing in a language other than English that led to a negative vote. Despite the costs, states offered a broad range of translations on official notices, election material, legislative journals, and state laws in the mid- to late-nineteenth century. These official translations stand in stark contrast to more contemporary state views of language. By 2010, 29 states had passed legislation protecting English as their official language (Maurais, 2010, p. 167). For more on current "language acts" that protect English, see Riera Gil (2016, pp. 100–109).

The types of translations that states and territories supported varied and changed annually. These translations can be divided into two major categories: translations that were required by elected officials and voters for the state to operate versus translations that merely recognized the presence of a specific language community in the state or territory and were offered as a way of including the members of that community into the political life of the state.[12] In the former, there were usually multiple translations required by the state at all tiers of government and for most types of official documents. For example, New Mexico offered the most extensive language translations and translated its session laws, legislative journals, ballots, and constitution, among other official documents (Lozano, 2018, pp. 38–66, 89–111). For the latter, there may have only been the mention of translating one document in a year or a decade. These translations appeared in seemingly random years for official documents such as governor's addresses, tax notices, session laws, or reports (1869 Ill. Pub. Laws 418; 1865 Mich. Pub. Acts 813; 1866 Iowa Acts 93, 101; 1853 Wis. Sess. Laws 127;1879 Minn. Laws 179,194; 1868 Kan. Sess. Laws 988; 1867 Neb. Laws 128; 1870 Iowa Acts 146–147; 1844 Ohio Laws 383; 1853 Tex. Gen. Laws 86; 1878 Ky. Acts 213–214; 1875 Ind. Acts 75; 1856 MO. Laws 675). In these more minor instances of translation, speakers of non-English languages received insufficient officially sponsored translations to effectively use the state government to learn about state or territorial laws or the U.S. political system more broadly. (It is possible that newspapers or local community contacts could help fill these gaps.) Without states and local communities offering extensive translations, some non-English-speaking individuals would not have been able to participate in the political process as full citizens. Regardless of the quantity of available translations, the reality of both categories of translations supports the conclusion that language minority communities had a sufficient level of political weight and recognition to secure the translations at all.

Translations serve as a measure of the power of specific ethnic groups in a state or territory. Language concessions rarely became permanent in state policy and members of language minority communities, or their representatives, had to remain vigilant to renew them. The passage of translations did not always mean that they would be printed and distributed. The lack of follow-through on printing suggests that translations served more as a marker of non-English-speaking settlers' presence and collective power, rather than as a necessity in their day-to-day lives.

At best, these annually negotiated translations demonstrated a tacit acceptance of the language reality in the state. Their disappearance from most states' session laws in the twentieth century demonstrates the dominance of English as the language of politics and government in the state. Or at the very least, it demonstrates a desire to protect English and expand its role in governance. The loss of translations in languages other than English could go to the extreme with the adoption of official English policies at the state level that precluded the use of other languages. Illinois, for example, passed one such law in 1923 where it "established the American language as the official language of the State of Illinois" (1923 Ill. Laws 7–8).

There are two regions of the country that stand out for having more laws that state or territorial legislatures have approved that supported languages other than English: the U.S. Midwest and the U.S. Southwest. The Midwest had few European settlers prior to U.S. expansion into the territory, but the Southwest had a significant pre-existing Spanish-speaking settler population. By comparing a region where settlement preceded U.S. control with a region settled by European immigrants after U.S. claims to the land, this chapter draws conclusions about how translations funded by state and territorial laws differed depending on demographic, regional, and territorial status.

The most logical language to serve as a case study in the Midwest is German. German-language speakers received translations in 25 states, including the Midwest states of Michigan, Illinois, Ohio, Indiana, Minnesota, Wisconsin, Iowa, Missouri, Kansas, Nebraska, and South Dakota. German was by far the most explicitly mentioned in laws that discussed officially supported translations. Many of the German language concessions that would be considered necessary to participate in the electorate, purchase land, or learn a language other than English in public schools were focused on specific towns and counties. The teaching of the German language in particular was explicitly mentioned in a broad array of states.[13] The states themselves had no real robust demonstrations of support for German. Instead, the most common translations granted by Midwest states and territories included the governor's annual messages, state session laws, court translators, legal notices required in a language other than English, and aid with elections.

None of the Midwest laws that mention translations suggested that the state legislature required these translations to operate and were generally more fleeting language rights. Spanish, by contrast, served as a "language of politics" in several states and territories after the U.S.-Mexican War. As was already discussed, the U.S. Congress financially supported translations in New Mexico, but the states of California and Colorado also privileged Spanish language translations. The state constitutions of California, New Mexico, and Colorado initially required language concessions for all official documents in Spanish—the only states encountered that offered early constitutional language protections. (Lozano, 2018, pp. 46–48, 60, 154). In Colorado, the 1876 constitution (XVIII, §8) also protected German translations alongside Spanish until 1900. The only other contiguous state to guarantee language translations was Louisiana. It did so in its second constitution in 1845, but removed most of the translation provisions for French by 1914 (Baron, 1990, pp. 83–87).

In the Southwest, state and territorial legislators supported a full range of translations that territories like New Mexico required to operate their territorial government. In some counties of California, Colorado, Arizona, and New Mexico, jurors heard cases argued in Spanish. Each of these states required a translator in the state legislature itself in at least one session and all but Arizona translated certain editions of their session laws and legislative journals into Spanish. Rather than serving as the language of an immigrant community, Spanish operated as a colonial language in the Southwest and persisted as a language of politics and government for decades (Lozano, 2018, pp. 38–66).

Not all states made up of former Mexican land had the same experience. The state of Texas joined the Union in 1845 with 10 times as many Anglos as former Mexican citizens. After decades of very few laws that supported Spanish, it passed more laws that explicitly mention the language, most likely in response to the growing immigrant population. In 1927, a law (1927 Tex. Laws 267) was passed that allowed Spanish to again serve as a language of instruction in certain counties of the state, a rare move at a time when most states explicitly limited instruction to English (Ramsey, 2010, p. 156). Spanish speakers' ability to participate in the political system depended on where—which town, county, territory, or state—an individual lived.

The extension of robust and long-standing language rights for Spanish speakers in parts of the Southwest could lead to the conclusion that Spanish speakers were colonized and second-class citizens set apart from the rest of the country. Instead, the proliferation of very significant uses of Spanish in government settings supports a different conclusion. States, territories, and the federal government strengthened the persistence of Spanish in these communities by accepting its use in so many facets of its government. By doing so, local, state, and federal officials included Spanish speakers as citizens and statesmen who were crucial to the political processes in the Southwest. The nation initially required these long-standing Spanish speakers who were the demographic majority in New Mexico, southern Colorado, and Southern California to adopt and participate in U.S. political institutions. Making these settlers invested in the United States strengthened the nation's claim on the land (Lozano, 2018, pp. 38–66, 89–110).

This brief discussion of how Midwest and Southwest states and territories used language translations demonstrates how officials varied in their acknowledgement of speakers of languages other than English. Language should be considered a key marker of how immigrants and new citizens learned about, or at the very least, came to feel welcomed, into the nation. The existence of so many different officially supported translations and other acts that mention language provide the evidence that explains how the nation incorporated different immigrants into the political system of an English-speaking nation. Language offers a rich avenue for research in the United States once we look beyond the federal government.

While the passage of officially supported translations challenges the idea that the United States has always chosen English-only policies, the general trend in the late nineteenth and early twentieth centuries was towards that of formalizing the place of English in politics (Baron, 1990). This language preference was adopted slower than most would expect and federally permissive policies allowed a wide variety of translations across the country in the nineteenth century.

The presence of substantial numbers of newspapers in languages other than English by the end of the nineteenth century offers a plausible reason why state-supported translations may have declined or altered at the state level at the dawn of the twentieth century. Did language minority communities refrain from using their political capital on officially sanctioned translations because newspapers increasingly published laws and official notices? Did the immigrant groups even want this information? Early studies of the immigrant European presses suggest newspapers had more of an ardent nationalism for their fatherland rather than a U.S.-based political focus. It is however important to note that this outward-facing reporting is not at all the focus of content in Spanish-language newspapers in New Mexico and Colorado, which focus heavily on U.S. politics and news (Park, 1922, pp. 49, 88; Meléndez, 1997, pp. 101–186). European settler newspapers that published laws and state legislative activity would provide ample evidence of a high level of acceptance and engagement by non-English-speaking immigrants in the nation's political and legal system. Or, did states pass laws to encourage the publication of their laws and proceedings to draw the political interest of communities that preferred reading about political affairs in their country of origin? The proliferation of newspapers in the late nineteenth century (over 1,000 newspapers) makes answering these questions a challenge (Park, 1922, p. 318). The session laws provide evidence that the political weight of the language groups was such that states honoured some requests for language translations. Perusing state and territorial legislative journals would provide the opportunity to observe all of the rejected requests for language concessions. Unfortunately, at this point, no database exists that would allow for a systematic search of these journals.

Considering that only certain language communities received state and territory-sanctioned translations, this political power was also tied to race. Some may wonder why in that case there was so much support for the Spanish language, since Mexican Americans have faced significant xenophobia and discrimination in the United States. Former Mexican citizens not only became citizens in 1848, but were also categorized as "white" in the federal census and other official documents. Mexican Americans hold a unique place in the United States and therefore it is not anomalous to use racial difference to explain the excluded language groups. For example, in 1900, California had a total of 82,326 "colored" residents. This census designation included "negro, Chinese, Japanese, and Indians", but not Mexican Americans, who were legally designated white (1853 Cal. Laws 82–83; Native 1901, 491). Other non-European immigrant groups—like the Chinese, who made up 56% of California's census designated "colored" population by 1900—received no concessions except for the translation of xenophobic laws that informed them of their undesirability. There were no explicit mentions of Native American languages in the laws of the Midwest and Southwest either, despite large populations of Indigenous peoples in states like New Mexico, Arizona, and the Dakotas.

Translations were limited to those who were permitted some political power locally. Both Asians born in Asia and Indigenous peoples were largely excluded from citizenship through the entire century between 1830 and 1930. The Indian Citizenship Act of 1924 was the first to federally extend U.S. citizenship to Native peoples, though not all desired the status and many continued to push for sovereignty (Dunbar-Ortiz, 2014, p. 169). Chinese immigrants could not be naturalized due to the 1791 Naturalization Act that made being a white person a requirement to become a naturalized citizen of the United States. This exclusion was reinforced in *Ozawa v. United States* (1922) (Haney Lopez, 2006, pp. 56–61).

Concluding remarks

States and territories throughout the United States were familiar with extending legislatively supported translations to their non-English-speaking residents. The multifaceted ways that states and territories acknowledged multilingualism over various decades during the mid- to late-nineteenth century make it extremely difficult to recover all instances of official support for translations into languages other than English. Yet it is also clear that when the lens of analysis turns to states, territories, and local communities, the existence of these translations makes it impossible to view the United States as exclusively supporting the English language.

The reality of these various officially supported translations or uses of languages other than English in official political settings paints a much more diverse language landscape than is usually considered of the United States. Large swaths of the nation accepted and invited immigrant communities to settle within their borders, which helped to extend the nation. The federalist system permits state variation, and each state's language choices remind us that being an "American" looked and sounded different depending on where an immigrant chose to settle.

It is important to consider *why* the long multilingual history of the United States has been forgotten along with the reality of dozens of state-supported translation laws. The omission of this history from the popular national perception has led to an almost universal view of the United States as being solely an English-speaking country. Herder's *Volksgeist* offers a compelling reason for the predominance of English in the historical narrative. By claiming one culture, one lifestyle, and one fatherland, the popular narrative of the United States can claim its place as a nation in Herder's eyes. In doing so however, the national popular narrative erases its Indigenous, slave, and imperial past in favour of an English-speaking settler narrative that can be written as complete and eternal. It can view the nation as one with a common language, which needs to protect itself from other language speakers.

By keeping this national popular narrative, the United States has forgotten its own process of becoming an English-speaking nation and how it did so by extending translations in new territories and states as the nation was being settled and then by refusing and ignoring the language rights of other language speakers in the early twentieth century once it was settled. This view of the English language as the only language in the United States also provides the rationale for continuing to deny these language rights to new immigrants and citizens who do not speak English today, a population of limited-English speakers estimated to include 5.5 million potential voters (Salame, 2018).

Notes

1 For scholarship on the idea of settler colonialism, see Veracini (2010), Hixson (2013), and Wolfe (2006).
2 For more on territorial status, see Pomeroy (1947) and Frymer (2017).
3 For more on Native languages during the colonial era, see Lepore (1999), Harvey (2015), and Rivett (2017).
4 The categories of Indigenous, immigrant, and colonial languages come from a discussion in Macías (2001, pp. 333–334).
5 Compiled from the HeinOnline collection of State Laws.
6 For an overview of federally funded Native American schools, see Adams (1995).
7 For more, see Ross (1994) and Gordin (2015).
8 For the history of the politics of Spanish in the Southwest, see Lozano (2018, pp. 21–66, 89–110).
9 See McCoy (1996, pp. 121–126, 197–201).
10 Histories of individual ethnic groups in specific locations abound, for example, Ostergren (1988) and Kamphoefner (1987). For a general history of immigration to the United States and Great Plains, see Dinnerstein, Nichols, and Reimers (2009) and Luebke (1980).
11 Compiled through an examination of HeinOnline Session Laws Library.
12 Kloss (1998, pp. 51, 99) has a similar breakdown that he names Tolerance-Oriented Rights and Promotion-Oriented Nationality Rights. I do not use his categories, because they are too narrow when including the extensive use of the Spanish language in the Southwest.
13 For examples of laws allowing languages of instruction besides English, see 1884 NM Laws 153; 1867 Colo. Sess. Laws 580; 1898 Md. Laws 738; 1838 Ohio Laws 65; 1869 Ill. Laws 493 (v. III); 1849 Mo. Laws 347; 1868 Kan. Sess. Laws 925.

References

Adams, D. W. (1995). *Education for extinction: American Indians and the boarding school experience, 1875–1928*. Lawrence, KS: University Press of Kansas.
Baron, D. (1990). *The English-only question: An official language for Americans*. New Haven, CT: Yale University Press.
Bauman, R., & Briggs, C. L. (2003). *Voices of modernity: Language ideologies and the politics of inequality*. Cambridge: Cambridge University Press.
Berlin, I. (2009). Return of the volksgeist. *New Perspectives Quarterly, 26*(4), 29–39.
Dinnerstein, L., Nichols, R. L., & Reimers, D. M. (2009). *Natives and strangers: A history of ethnic Americans*. Oxford: Oxford University Press.
Dunbar-Ortiz, R. (2014). *An Indigenous peoples' history of the United States*. Boston, MA: Beacon Press.
Frymer, P. (2017). *Building an American empire: The era of territorial and political expansion*. Princeton, NJ: Princeton University Press.
Gordin, M. (2015). *Scientific Babel: How science was done before and after global English*. Chicago, IL: University of Chicago Press.
Hamilton, A. (2008). Federalist #12. In L. Goldman (Ed.), *The federalist papers*. Oxford: Oxford University Press.
Haney Lopez, I. (2006). *White by law: The legal construction of race*. New York: New York University Press.
Harvey, S. F. (2015). *Native tongues: Colonialism and race from encounter to the reservation*. Cambridge, MA: Harvard University Press.

Hixson, W. (2013). *American settler colonialism: A history.* New York: Palgrave Macmillan.

Jay, J. (2008). Federalist #2. In L. Goldman (Ed.), *The federalist papers.* Oxford: Oxford University Press.

Kamphoefner, W. (1987). *The Westfalians: From Germany to Missouri.* Princeton, NJ: Princeton University Press.

Kloss, H. (1998). *The American bilingual tradition: Language in education.* Washington, DC and McHenry, IL: Center for Applied Linguistics.

Lepore, J. (1999). *The name of war: King Philip's War and the origins of American identity.* New York: Vintage.

Lepore, J. (2003). *A is for American.* New York: Vintage.

Lozano, R. (2018). *An American language: A history of Spanish in the United States.* Oakland, CA: University of California Press.

Luebke, F. (Ed.). (1980). *Ethnicity on the great plains.* Lincoln, NE: University of Nebraska Press.

Macías, R. (2001). Minority languages in the United States, with a focus on Spanish in California. In G. Extra & D. Gorter (Eds.), *The other languages of Europe: Demographic, sociolinguistic, and educational perspectives* (pp. 331–354). Celevedon: Multilingual Matters.

Maurais, J. (2010). The language issue in the United States, Canada, and Quebec: Some comparative aspects. In M.A. Morris (Ed.), *Canadian language politics in comparative perspective* (pp. 57–87). Canada and Kingston: McGill-Queen's University Press.

McCoy, D. (1996). *The elusive republic: Political economy in Jeffersonian America.* Chapel Hill, NC: University of North Carolina Press.

Meléndez, A. G. (1997). *So all is not lost: The poetics of print in Nuevomexicano communities, 1834–1958.* Albuquerque, NM: University of New Mexico Press.

Native and foreign born and white and colored population, classified by sex, by states and territories: 1900 (1901). *Table 16 in census reports: Twelfth census of the United States* (vol. 1, pp. 490–491). Suitland, MD: US Census Office.

Ostergren, R. (1988). *A community transplanted: The trans-Atlantic experience of a Swedish immigrant settlement in the Upper Middle West, 1835–1915.* Madison, WI: University of Wisconsin Press.

Pagden, A. (1994). The effacement of difference: Colonialism and the origins of nationalism in Diderot and Herder. In G. Prakash (Ed.), *After colonialism: Imperial histories and postcolonial displacements* (pp. 129–152). Princeton, NJ: Princeton University Press.

Paine, T. (1998). *Rights of man, common sense, and other political writings* (M. Philp, Ed.). Oxford: Oxford University Press.

Park, R. (1922). *The immigrant press and its control.* London: Harper and Row.

Pomeroy, E. (1947). *The territories and the United States, 1861–1890.* Philadelphia, PA: University of Pennsylvania Press.

Ramsey, P. (2010). *Bilingual public schooling in the United States: A history of America's "polyglot boardinghouse".* New York: Palgrave Macmillan.

Riera Gil, E. (2016). *Why languages matter to people: Communication, identity, and justice in Western democracies: The case of mixed societies.* Barcelona: Generalitat de Catalunya, Institut d'Estudis de l'Autogovern.

Rivett, S. (2017). *Unscripted America: Indigenous languages and the origins of a literary nation.* Oxford: Oxford University Press.

Ross, W. (1994). *Forging new freedoms: Nativism, education, and the Constitution, 1917–1927.* Lincoln, NE: University of Nebraska Press.

Ryan, C. (2013). *Language use in the United States: 2011: American community survey reports.* US Census Bureau. Retrieved from https://www2.census.gov/library/publications/2013/acs/acs-22/acs-22.pdf

Salame, R. (2018, November 5). Vote aquí? Limited-English-proficiency voters could help determine congress: A joint investigative fund—nation exposé shows that language accommodation for voting (or the lack thereof) could swing 20 congressional elections. *The Nation.* Retrieved from www.thenation.com/article/limited-english-voters-investigation-election/

Veracini, L. (2010). *Settler colonialism: A theoretical overview.* Houndmills: Palgrave Macmillan.

Wolfe, P. (2006). Settler colonialism and the elimination of the native. *Journal of Genocide Research, 8,* 387–409.

6 A noble dream?

Hindustani and Indian nationalism in the early twentieth century

Pritipuspa Mishra

The title of this chapter comes from Peter Novick's (1988) book, *That Noble Dream: The "Objectivity Question" and the American Historical Profession*, a study of the career of objectivity in American historiography. Novick claims that while there has been a consistent desire for objectivity, its meaning and execution has shifted radically over time. However, Novick argues, as the historian's access to the "truth" of the past is limited due to myriad reasons, objectivity serves as a guiding *myth* in the historical profession rather than a discretely definable and achievable aim. It is this mythical role of objectivity as a guiding principle in historical writing that I would like to borrow to describe the role of Herderian monolingualism in nationalist thinking in post-colonial India.

Like objectivity in historical writing, monolingualism in nationalism can often serve as an unachievable aim in new multilingual nations. Through a reading of literary and anthropological scholarship, Novick has described the work that myths do in society. Myths serve us by enabling the understanding of both the past and the present of a community. By providing a creation or origin narrative, myths tell the story of how a community "began to be" (Novick, 1988, p. 3). For the present, myths serve as "pragmatic charters of social institutions" (p. 3), ensure solidarity by undermining existing social contradictions, and provide a shared view of the future. Effectively, myths are essential for the creation of a normative view of the community. In the case of nationalism, Herder's argument about a common national language that held within it the very specific world view of the community of speakers serves as the site for such a mythic unity. The history of the language and its speakers provided the origin myth of the national community even as its use in the present provides the much-needed common ground for the citizens of the nation. Herder's injunction that a nation should have a common language has become the normative myth that founds the contemporary understanding of the connection between nationalism and language. However, while this injunction provides the origin myth of modern nation-state and enables its continued rationale for the nation-states, the Herderian model does not reflect the linguistic realities of post-colonial multilingual nation-states. How do such nation-states then relate to the Herderian model as the norm-making myth of modern nationalism? In this paper, I use the example of India to show how the Herderian model is engaged with precisely as an unreal myth that performs crucial nation-building work even as any approximation to the model is repeatedly abandoned.

In India, the myth of common national language held a particular allure as the people of India were divided on a number of different vectors—religion, caste, class, and region. At the centre of this myth building is a language called Hindustani. Rather than being a discrete and recognizable language, Hindustani has been a remarkably plastic idea in the late colonial and early post-colonial India. The name Hindustani meant different things to different people. Since the early years of British colonialism in India Hindustani has had a chimeral existence. The earliest British mention of Hindustani can be found in George Hadley's grammar of the "vulgar dialect of the *Indostan* language" in 1772. In later years, the name came to signify a number of different linguistic realities that the new rulers encountered in their early years (Rai, 2005, p. 140).[1] The name Hindustani simply signified the language of Hindustan or India (Rai, 2005). By the 1930s and early 1940s, the question of Hindustani animated nationalist discussions about the linguistic, legal, and educational future of India. Mohandas Karamchand Gandhi argued for the institution of a two-tiered language system in India with Hindustani as the lingua franca and the regional languages like Bengali, Marathi, and Tamil as the regional mother tongues that would serve as the official languages of the provinces. Jawaharlal Nehru, who was to be the first prime minister of independent India, made a case for Basic Hindustani (modelled on Basic English) as a means to resolve the political and administrative problems posed by the irreducible multilingualism in India. Organizations like the Hindustani Prachar Sabha worked towards identifying Hindustani as the "largest common factor of languages spoken in Northern India" (Gandhi, 1937) and attempted to build a compact vocabulary of the language by drawing on words from Hindi and Urdu.[2] However, we see that this language-in-making gradually disappeared from official documents as it failed to appear in the list of official languages in the Eighth Schedule of the Indian constitution in 1950 and was ultimately dropped from the Indian census in 1971 (Lelyveld, 1993, pp. 679–680). Hindustani succumbed to two crucial obstacles to its institution as the national language; it was seen as an instance of North Indian hegemony over the Dravidian speaking South, and it was viewed as a concession to Muslim political presence in India on the eve of violent Hindu–Muslim strife during the partition. Even as Hindustani disappeared, the other half of Gandhi's linguistic imaginary—the provincial mother tongues—came to dominate the subsequent structure of the post-colonial nation. By 1960, much of India was organized into linguistically defined provinces, each with its own official mother tongue.

What does this history of thwarted nationalist desire for a lingua franca tell us about multilingualism and its relationship with Indian nationalism in the twentieth century? I would suggest that reflecting on this nationalist detour through the quest for a pan-Indian language allows valuable insight into the influence of the Herderian model of linguistic nationalism in a colonized context. Herder's arguments about the fundamental plurality of national cultures helped shape a compelling case against colonialism. If each nation has a constitutive culture which was housed in the national language, folk narratives, and everyday idiomatic speech then the imposition of the culture, power, and language of an imperial nation was unacceptable and could not last in the long term. Such imposition would inevitably lead to revolution. Furthermore, his rejection of the western universalism and his defence of cultural plurality and particularity allowed colonized actors to celebrate their difference from the West without having to see such difference as an instance of inferiority or cultural inability to approximate to Western standards. In India, Gandhi's arguments about the need to preserve and use regional mother tongues and the need to renounce English in favour of an Indian lingua franca often drew on Herderian ideas of linguistic heritage. More broadly, the legacy of Herder's ideas on language and self-determination can be seen in the way in which language is cited as one of the central markers of self-determination during the interwar period in the twentieth century. When we look at discussions about franchise and representation in late colonial India, we find references to Woodrow Wilson's claims that self-determination required that people be ruled by states that functioned in the people's language (Manela, 2007).

While it can be argued that the Herderian ideal of one nation-one language had greatly influenced nationalism and linguistic politics in India, we need to consider how far this influence was able to shape the linguistic reality of post-colonial India. In this paper I would like to present the colonial linguistic landscape of the nation. I will illustrate how the colonial administration and regional linguistic politics effectively transformed the Indian population into monolingual language groups. As a conclusion, I will also explore one of the most detailed expositions of the case for Hindustani, and that is Suniti Kumar Chatterji's *Indo-Aryan and Hindi* first published in 1942, to show why using Hindustani as a national language to unite the nation was impossible.

Languages of India during the empire

The linguistic history of twentieth-century India needs to be contextualized within a longer history of language in India. In his work on the South Asian vernacular millennium, Pollock (2000) notes that in Indian languages there is no term that could serve as a literal translation of "vernacular".[3] In the economy between vehicular Sanskrit and local Prakrit languages, these languages were called *deshi* languages or languages of place. Other terms used to denote these major Prakrit languages were "loka bhasha" (language of the people or language of the world) or "apabhramsha" (corrupt languages). Scholars have illustrated how each of these terms was a symptom of the prevailing relationship between Sanskrit and its allied Prakrit languages at different moments. In the earliest reference to what we would call Sanskrit, the language is simply called *bhasha* (language) or *samskrta* meaning "refined language". The distinction between Sanskrit and Prakrit seems to appear around the beginning of the Christian era. About this time, roughly 100 BCE, we find that the Prakrit languages were outstripping Sanskrit in popular usage. The Brahmanical reaction to this competition was to pose Sanskrit as the grammatically correct language of dharma, while the Prakrits were posed as corrupt, worldly languages. Sanskrit came to be seen as an eternal language of grammatical finitude and the Prakrit languages were seen to be constantly evolving and "degenerating" away from their pure Sanskrit origins. This suggests that in this period the relationship between Sanskrit and Prakrit was overturned. While the earlier use of the term "refined language" suggests that Sanskrit was the product of the refinement of more colloquial but original Prakrits, the idea of degeneration points to a relationship where the Prakrits are the product of an uninformed misuse of an originary and pure Sanskrit. It is the latter relationship between Sanskrit and Prakrit languages that became dominant in the subsequent centuries (Sawhney, 2009, pp. 6–7).

Between the twelfth century ACE and the sixteenth century ACE, the life of Prakrit languages in India underwent a significant shift. As this period saw the rise of regional polities, literature in *deshi* languages were used to demarcate the spatial boundaries of regional political praxis. The term *deshi* or of-place was used by local intelligentsia to mark out their regional spheres of influence from the world of *marga* (literally "path", "way") or vehicular languages like Sanskrit and Persian. This period witnessed the efflorescence of literary production in most regional languages such as Tamil, Telugu, Brajbhasha, Oriya, Bengali, Kannada, Gujarati, and Marathi. However, as Pollock (2000) insists, this literization was not accompanied by affective discourses of "maternal generation" (p. 612). As he notes, "the notion of mother tongue itself . . . has no conceptual status whatever in Pre-European South Asia" (Pollock, 2000, p. 612). Furthermore, contrary to what we would expect, the regional states did not impose language regimes by law. Despite the emerging influence of these regional languages, royal courts issued royal inscriptions and patronized literature in multiple languages. For instance, the King of what is today Karnataka issued royal inscriptions in Kannada, Marathi, and Tamil while his court featured songs in an even broader variety of languages—"Avadhi, Bihari, Bengali, Oriya and Madhyadeshiya" (Pollock, 2000, p. 614). Therefore, this first moment of vernacularization [I use this term with some discomfort] did not entail exclusive monolingualism.

The monolingualism that would be familiar to us today emerged with the growth of colonial governmentality in India in the last 250 years. The writings of early philologists like William Jones and administrators such as Thomas Macaulay suggest that languages in India were classified into classical languages (Sanskrit and Persian) and vernaculars (Prakrit languages and the languages of the indigenous peoples of India). From comments like "some languages not vernacular among them", we can infer that in the late eighteenth and early nineteenth centuries "vernacular" simply meant language commonly spoken by the people (Zastoupil & Moir, 1999, p. 236). However, the shift in the relationship between language, place, and people had already begun with this usage. As Pollock (2000) has argued, in the pre-colonial period, language was not linked to people but to place. In Europe, on the other hand, "origins of languages and people, morphing into chronologies and histories of kingdoms-and-peoples, can fairly be called an obsession . . . in the first half of the vernacular millennium" (Pollock, 2000, p. 612). The history of colonial and comparative philology in India suggests that a trace of this European legacy carried into the colonial linguistic policy. Using the example of C. P. Brown, a scholar of nineteenth-century Telugu, Rama Sundari Mantena has illustrated how colonial philology saw languages as having "progressive histories" that would foreshadow later debates about modernization of Indian languages (Mantena, 2005). In later years, regional linguistic activism would conflate the progress of the speakers with the progress of the language. For instance in the late 1930s, Tamil nationalists argued that the prosperity of Mother Tamil or Tamiltay would entail the prosperity of Tamil speakers—"If Tamiltay prospers, so will Tamilians and so will Tamilnadu" (Ramaswamy, 1993, pp. 691–692). Language, people, and place now shared a common destiny.

The most influential aspect of colonial philology, however, was the inflection of biological relationships in the categorization of Indian languages. By discussing languages in terms such as "descent", "family trees", "ancestors", and "genetic relations", colonial philology embodied global languages in gendered terms (Errington, 2008, p. 59). The notion of an Indo-European language family invoked a sisterhood of major root languages across the globe as William Jones repeatedly referred to Sanskrit as a beautiful sister of Latin and Greek. Sanskrit in turn was posed as the *mother* of Prakrit languages who were sisters among themselves. The notion of Sanskrit as a mother language first appears in colonial rhetoric, where it is posed as the root language that could make up for the colonial official's inability to understand local tongues. This view endures as we see that delegates in the Constituent Assembly speak of Sanskrit as "mother of all languages in the world" and the "fountain head of our mother tongues" (Ramaswamy, 1999, pp. 346–357). The matrilineal relationship between Indian languages is then consolidated with references to the sisterhood of Indian languages. Charu Gupta has illustrated how Hindi nationalists deploy this rhetoric of sister to suggest that other Indian languages are merely filial versions of Hindi (Gupta, 2001, p. 206).

With the publication of the Dravidian proof by Francis Whyte Ellis in 1856 and Robert Caldwell's thesis that the languages of the indigenous peoples of India formed a separate language family from the northern Indo-European languages and the southern Dravidian languages, a new racial theory of Indian civilization emerged with a hierarchy of languages from Sanskrit down to the languages spoken by the indigenous peoples (Trautmann, 2005). The notion of language communities as *jati*, a term also used to denote caste, came to gain ground in India. The conflation of language and community selfhood in subsequent linguistic activism across India in the twentieth century attests to the emerging categorization of the Indian populace into parallel language communities (Mitchell, 2005).

Not simply an academic exercise, colonial philology was implicated in the mechanics of colonial rule. The conflation of language and community selfhood came to be inscribed in the colonial state's regimes of legal justice and primary education. Colonial concerns that "just" and "liberal" government could only be carried out through popularly understood languages, resulted in the use of regional languages in judicial and revenue matters. To this end, Act no.29 of 1837 decreed that in the Bengal presidency Bengali, Oriya, and Hindustani would replace Persian as the language of law courts (Mishra, 2020, pp. 34–36).

In 1856, reforms in primary education introduced the stipulation that "vernacular" languages be used as the medium of primary education throughout India. This decision led to debates within the government and local pressure groups about the actual geographical domain of Indian languages. For instance, during the 1860s and 1870s, a rather acrimonious debate involving colonial officials and the Oriya- and Bengali-speaking elite dealt with the question of whether Oriya or Bengali should be taught in the schools of Oriya-speaking areas in the Bengal presidency. Thus, even institutionally, the contours of language communities were increasingly solidified into monolingual communities as the engagement between the individual colonized subject and the colonial state was mediated by local "mother tongues". Ultimately, by the late nineteenth century, languages had come to define communities both historically and in everyday life, and the colonial state apprehended its subjects as members of discrete language communities.

While the colonial language regime produced parallel mother tongue communities, it also crafted a narrative of linguistic lack. Even as regional languages were being increasingly incorporated into the everyday life of colonial rule, the discourse about the inability of these languages to express modern thoughts and realities pervaded colonial discussions about translation, literature, and administration. For instance, through a history of translation at Delhi College, Dodson (2005) illustrates how Urdu was considered "extremely deficient in compass, in precision, and generally in its power of expression for what we propose to teach by its means" (Dodson, 2005, p. 821). English on the other hand was seen as the quintessentially modern language that could carry the burden of modern scientific knowledge. Consequently, the Delhi College undertook to "improve" Urdu so that it could serve more contemporary educational purposes. There are two implications of this ascription of lack. First, unlike the pre-colonial understanding of "vernacular" languages as constantly evolving, even "degenerating" languages of the world, this colonial narrative of lack sees them as finite languages unable to absorb changes imposed by Western modernity. In this sense, colonial vernacularization transforms them into a-historical patois. The second implication of this narrative of lack is the emergence of a native translational guilt that doubles upon itself. As Spivak (2000) suggests, translation to and from the mother tongue invokes guilt as one is forced to see the mother tongue as simply one among many languages. In such translations, each language "is assumed to be or to possess the generality of a semiotic that can appropriate the singularity of the other's idiom by way of conscientious approximations" (Spivak, 2000, p. 15). However, in the translational economy between Urdu and English, there is an assumption of inequality. In this relationship there is no general semiotic that can enable conscientious approximation. With the discovery of the Indo-European connection between Sanskrit and European languages, early Orientalists posed Indian culture as a culture in decline from a more golden past and focused on recuperating the lost "ancient constitution" of India (Trautmann, 2004). This narrative of decline was internalized into Indian cultural politics of the nineteenth and twentieth centuries.

Indian responses to the creation of parallel mother tongue communities and the colonial narrative of linguistic lack further entrenched the politics of monolingualism in India. The late nineteenth and early twentieth centuries witnessed the rise of regional linguistic politics across India. Despite appearances, such politics was about more than language. As regional mother tongues mediated the relationship between the individual and the state, agitation for economic, social as well as political interests were necessarily framed within language politics. In many of these movements, language was feminized and deified as a goddess in dire need of service from her devotees. Perhaps, the most striking example of such activism is the politics of Tamiltay or Mother Tamil. There are multiple imaginaries of Tamiltay in Tamil politics—Tamiltay as victimized womanhood, Tamiltay as a deprived Goddess in need of restoration to her proper place, Tamiltay as the Goddess of polity, and finally Tamiltay as Kannagi—the literary representation of quintessential, chaste Tamil womanhood. All these different imaginaries were deployed to invoke crucial elements of linguistic affect among the constituency of Tamil. The picture of wounded, victimized woman invoked a politics of protection as agitators cried, "Will she even survive?" (Ramaswamy, 1993, p. 691). The notion of the deposed Goddess called for an almost extra-rational "love, reverence and deep devotion" (Ramaswamy, 1993, p. 693). Tamil as a Goddess of polity was an argument for a distinctive Tamil national community. Finally, Tamil as a chaste woman invited Tamil speakers to participate in a programme of language standardization and purification. The "appropriative madness" that Derrida (1998, p. 24) spoke of is constituted by these impulses of protection, devotion, nationalist zeal, and a search for the ideal language.

Curiously, even as Tamil was posed as female, her devotee who *acted* in her interest was always posed as male. In the case of Hindi, on the other hand, this relationship between female language and male devotee seems to have been complicated by the introduction of the notion of a masculine language. Hindi as we know it is a somewhat modern phenomenon. Hindi linguistic politics was informed by efforts to distance it from Urdu and to claim an appropriate literary lineage from its precursors—Brajbhasha and Khariboli. Hindi was posed as the mother of Hindi speakers as well as of all Indians. Framed as a chaste Hindu woman, she was set in opposition to a promiscuous, upper-class and female Urdu. However, in the competition between the legacy of Brajbhasha and Khariboli, the idea of Hindi as woman was disrupted as leaders of the movement argued that the erotic literature of Brajbhasha was too feminine for a robust political movement. By identifying and privileging Khariboli as masculine speak, the movement posed Hindi as both a feminine mother and a robust, masculine tongue that could serve the Indian nation (Gupta, 2001, pp. 203–213).

Therefore, we see here a linguistic landscape that was populated by several regional mother tongues and Hindi serving as a contender for national language. We also see that Hindi's candidature was not without controversy. Any effort towards adopting a national language would involve a reconciliation of the linguistic claims of the regional mother tongues, Urdu, and Hindi. This search for a linguistic common ground produced some of the most-fraught engagements with the reigning Herderian model of national monolingualism in Indian policy making. In the next section, I will explore this engagement through a look at the debates about the official language of India. Even as the question of the official language is not the same as that of the national language, these debates necessarily needed to engage with the cultural and historical reasons why a certain language (read Hindi) could serve as the common linguistic denominator for India. Such arguments necessarily drew on the historical and anthropological assumptions upon which Herderian injunction of one nation-one language stands.

India and the spectre of Herder

"India stands the risk of being split up into a number of totalitarian small nationalities" (Chatterji, 1957, p. 313). This alarmist claim made in 1957 by one of the most influential literary figures of early post-colonial India signals a fundamental anxiety in India about the dangers of multilingualism for the fledgling new nation. The author, Suniti Kumar Chatterji, was responding to the conclusions of the "Report on the Official Language Commission" which had stipulated that Hindi be made the official language of India (Government of India, 1957). This elevation of Hindi would come at the expense of English which would be gradually phased out of usage in India. In his minority report within the "Report of the Official Language Commission", Suniti Kumar Chatterji argued that the new Indian state needed to balance the linguistic needs of the northern Indo-European speaking peoples with that of the southern Dravidian speaking population (Chatterji, 1957, pp. 271–314). While the languages of the North had much common with Hindi due to a shared Indo-European linguistic root, the people of the South could not easily understand Hindi as their languages were based on the Dravidian root. The Commission's conclusions were predicated on the assumption that Hindi was the language that was either spoken or understood by the largest number of Indians (Government of India, 1957, p. 36). However, at the core of this decision was a specific linguistic understanding of the emergent Indian nation. In the conclusion to the report, this image of India was laid out.

> Through the "crucible of history" as it were, over many centuries, as a result of this unceasing intercourse, a common way of life has crystallised and emerged which we call "the Indian way of life". A language is the standing record as well as contemporary expression of the culture and experience of the particular group speaking that language. The linguistic pattern in India, therefore, naturally conforms to the cultural pattern. While there is an astonishing variety of regional expressions, both linguistic and cultural, there is an unmistakable bedrock of identity underlying these multiple expressions.
> (Government of India, 1957, p. 251)

The linguistic imagination of India in this passage is founded on a curious reworking of the conventional wisdom on the relationship between language, history, and nationalism. Based on the Herderian model of linguistic nationalism, the common understanding of the relationship between language and nationalism holds that a shared language provides the foundation for nation-building as it held within it the cultural making of the national community. Therefore, language births the nation. However, in the aforementioned formulation, language does not precede the nation even as its formative importance is acknowledged. What precedes language itself is a "Indian way of life" (Government of India, 1957, p. 251) that goes on to permeate the many mother tongues spoken in India. This way of life is forged in the "crucible of history" (Government of India, 1957, p. 251). Such a formulation is very similar to Herder's use of the idea of *Volk*. And, like Herder, it seems to be used with very loose regard to an empirical definition of the concept (Hare & Link, 2019). Furthermore, this forging does not seem to have coincided with the creation and development of a shared national language that would have carried the story of the making of India within it. Language in this formulation is both elemental and superficial.

By framing the linguistic make-up of India in this manner, the report was attempting to approximate Indian realities to Herderian notions of nation formation. Therefore, we need to understand the structure of the Herderian idea before we can understand the nature of the Indian response. Forster (Forster, 2011) has illustrated that Herder proposed some foundational claims about human speech. First, that "thought is essentially dependent on and bounded by language—that is, one can only think if one has a language, and one can only think what one can express linguistically" (Forster, 2011, p. 109). Second, that "Mankind exhibits profound differences in modes of thought, concepts, and language, especially between different historical periods and cultures" (Forster, 2011, p. 110). And finally, that the differences in people's language can help us find the differences in their ways of thinking and ideas. These claims had a far-reaching impact on modern understanding of linguistics, anthropology, and historicism (Beiser, 2011; Forster, 2010, 2011).

Of interest to us is the emergence of a new Herderian historicism which would come to inform narratives of nation-building of modern India. In his discussion of Herder's impact on the development of historicism, Beiser traces Herder's efforts to produce an anthropological history of humanity which eschewed enlightenment individualism to focus on the social conception of the human past. At the crux of this socially informed historicism was the history of language. Drawing on his conviction that language held the key to our understanding of the human communities, Herderian historicism focused on tracking the history of various cultures through an anthropological focus on the particular thoughts and concepts or culture of communities. It is in this commitment to focus on the particular rather than the flattening force of European universalism that we find the construction of anti-colonial nationalism in Herderian thought (Berlin, 2009; Muthu, 2003; Noyes, 2014; Robinette, 2011). Therefore, Herder's foundational ideas about language and culture and his critique of enlightenment universalism (through a complex argument about how even as the capacity for reason is universal amongst all humans, rationality is culturally specific) enabled the modern anti-colonial nationalist arguments of the twentieth century. From this perspective, the conditions for anti-colonial nationalism belong within the ideological construct of Herderian monolingualism.

If we return to the claim made in the 1957 Report on the official languages, we can see why even as monolingualism is being bypassed, the writers cannot escape cultural historicism that enables the imagination of a united India. The Herderian idea seems like a poisoned chalice. While it allows for a convincing argument for Indian nationalism, the realities of Indian multilingualism threaten to disrupt the foundations of this argument. It is here that we can see how Herder works as a myth in linguistic and nationalist discussion in India. As discussed earlier, myths provide a means to resolve contradictions through a cohesive narrative of the community. The commitment to this myth of Hindi as a common language allows the writers of the report to hold at bay any divisive impact of regional linguistic nationalism or self-alienating impact of the continuing influence of the language of the colonizers, that is, English. The objective of the report to eventually replace English with Hindi has never really been achieved. In fact, the failure to do so has allowed the noble dream of a monolingual India survive as a nationalist myth.

Therefore, even in its failure in India, the Herderian ideal serves a purpose. Much of post-colonial scholarship on the impact of the thinker on non-western nations had focused on how the Herderian ideal is just another form of Western epistemic violence. And this violence is one that demands that the non-West lives up to an unattainable standard which would in turn leave such nations in the "waiting room of history", forever perfecting their claims to nationhood. Such a focus often blinds us to the complex impact of the ideal on Indian politics. The example of the 1957 Report on the official language illustrates that Indian policy makers were never simply victims of epistemic violence. By maintaining the status of Hindi as the aspirational, dreamed for, and mythical lingua franca, the policy makers were both rejecting the Herderian ideal while also ostensibly capitulating to it.

I would like to conclude this article with a quick case study of the most powerful versions of the dream of a common national language, Hindustani. Through a discussion of Suniti Kumar Chatterji's attempt at curating a national language for India, I will underline why such an effort was impossible.

Chatterji's Hindustani

My discussion of the linguistic landscape of nineteenth- and twentieth-century India makes it evident that any case for Hindustani as a national lingua franca had to be made against a backdrop of intense regional linguistic politics and a somewhat contentious debate about the separation between Hindi and Urdu. The Hindi/Urdu debate was founded on the alignment of both these languages with Hinduism and Islam. As religious politics came to increasingly impinge on Indian nationalist politics in the early twentieth century, the possibility of a Hindustani national language as a combination of Hindi and Urdu came to be increasingly unlikely. However, this does not mean that a secular and nationalist case for Hindustani did not have its proponents. As mentioned earlier, some of the most influential politicians of late colonial India were proponents of Hindustani. Furthermore, the case for Hindustani had supporters in southern India where most people spoke in Dravidian languages, which did not share the same root language as the northern Indian tongues. Thus, Hindustani had the potential to bring together the south and the north of India.

Suniti Kumar Chatterji, a very influential linguist of the early twentieth century, wrote one of the most sustained and detailed arguments for the making of Hindustani as the national language of India. In 1940, he gave eight lectures at the Gujarat Vernacular Society that were later collated into a book titled *Indo Aryan and Hindi: Eight lectures on the history of Aryan Speech in India and on the development of Hindi (Hindustani)*. A professor of Indian linguistics and Phonetics at the University of Calcutta, Chatterji was very closely involved with linguistic politics in late colonial India. He served as an advisor to major Indian National Congress figures such as Jawaharlal Nehru. He presided on disputes about linguistic boundaries and differentiation that arose between neighbouring regional leaders as they claimed areas to be populated by speakers of their own language. After decolonization, Chatterji became one of the most influential figures in the official linguistic and literary bodies of independent India. He served as the president of the Sahitya Academy, the premier literary institution in post-colonial India, during the 1960s and 1970s.

In *Indo-Aryan and Hindi*, Chatterji began with the following claim about his project to track the history of Aryan speech in India:

> The study of this speech-development is a human science of utmost importance, and is a very fascinating subject withal, ultimately connected as it is with our material and mental culture, our normal and natural as well as abnormal vicissitudes, and our periods of outside contact or inward isolation as a people.
>
> (Chatterji, 1942, p. 4)

Just as Herder linked language to the formation of a culture and nation, the above shows how Chatterji sought to justify his search for an ancient connection between various Indian languages to establish the credentials of modern India as a united nation.

In his project, Chatterji had to cope with two major challenges. First, he had to illustrate how historically the languages of India had been intrinsically connected with each other. This claim was challenging because Chatterji had to illustrate how the immigrant Indo-Aryan languages in Ancient India were related to the pre-existing Austric languages of India and the vastly different Dravidian languages of southern India. The problem with claiming any connection was doubly problematic due to the early twentieth-century Dravidian movement in southern India, which put forward a regional critique of caste by arguing that the influence of Indo-Aryan languages such as Sanskrit and Hindi was an instance of northern upper-caste domination of Dravidian speakers. Hence posing Indo-Aryan languages as the historical unifier of the Indian people could be potentially divisive.

Chatterji resolved this problem by arguing that the Indo-Aryan languages drew a lot of influence from the Austric and Dravidian languages. The influence of Dravidian languages was particularly important as early Indo-Aryan languages drew on Dravidian script to put the early Indian scripture like the Veda in writing. Thus, arguing that Indo-Aryan literary tradition would have been lost without the support of the Dravidian script.

The second challenge was to find a modern descendant of Indo-Aryan languages that could serve as the national language that carried the historical memory of the Indian people. But again, the challenge here was to appease the Hindi and Urdu elite while also responding to the southern Indian critique that the celebration of a northern Indian language as the national lingua franca could alienate the people of the South. Chatterji's solution was to illustrate how Hindustani was in fact a collection of different languages—Urdu, high Hindi spoken by the Hindu upper classes of northern India, everyday Hindi spoken by people all over northern India and Bazar Hindi, which was the language most widely spoken by people of various regional affiliations across northern and southern India. Chatterji suggested that it would be useful to find a Hindi that consisted of the lowest common denominator of all these languages. This was the basis of his proposal for Basic Hindi, which could serve the whole nation. The problem with Chatterji's argument about Hindustani is that by the time he arrived at Basic Hindi, his primary objective of finding a language that is connected with "our material and mental culture" (1942, p. 4) was somehow lost. In Basic Hindi we have a functional lingua franca but not a national language. It has been stripped of all memory of everyday life and historical experience. Chatterji's failure to make a case for an Indian national language is reflected in the career of Hindustani in early postcolonial India where it was unable to gain any traction.

How then did Herderian ideas of linguistic nationalism fare in post-colonial India? The establishment of regional mother tongues as official languages of the provinces on the lines of the Gandhian argument that these languages reflected Indian reality and that the use of languages other than one's own would lead to an alienation from one's own reality suggests that the influence of Herder survived. Ultimately, the resultant linguistic federation produced precisely the kind of cosmopolitanism that Herder would have called an "empty phenomena" (Berlin, 2009).

Notes

1 John Gilchrist's *A Grammar of the Hindustani Language* posed it as the language of popular speech of the country used all over India by both the literary elite and the illiterate masses. In 1800, he was appointed Professor of Hindustani at Fort William College in Calcutta, where he worked towards establishing it as a "language of command".

2 This was mentioned in a note by the Bihar Urdu Committee in 1937 in Mohandas Karamchand Gandhi, "A Welcome Move" [1937], in *The Collected Works of Mahatma Gandhi*, 95 vols, (New Delhi: Publications Divisions, Ministry of Information and Broadcasting Government of India, 1958–1982), Vol 72, p. 209.

3 Parts of this section have appeared earlier in P. Mishra (2012). "The Mortality of Hindustani". *Parallax*, *18*(3), 71–83.

References

Beiser, F. C. (2011). *The German historicist tradition.* Oxford: Oxford University Press.

Berlin, I. (2009). Return of the volksgeist. *New Perspectives Quarterly, 26*(4), 29–39.

Chatterji, S. K. (1942). *Indo-Aryan and Hindi: Eight lectures on the history of the Aryan speech in India and on the development of Hindi (Hindusthani) delivered before the research & post-graduate department of the Gujarat vernacular society in 1940.* Ahmedabad: Gujarat Vernacular Society.

Chatterji, S. K. (1957). Minority report. In *Report of the official language commission.* New Delhi: Government of India Press.

Derrida, J. (1998). *Monolingualism of the other, or, the prosthesis of origin* (P. Mensah, Trans.). Stanford: Stanford University Press.

Dodson, M. (2005). Translating science, translating empire: The power of language in colonial North India. *Comparative Studies in Society and History, 47*(4), 809–835.

Errington, J. J. (2008). *Linguistics in a colonial world: A story of language, meaning, and power.* Oxford: Blackwell.

Forster, M. N. (2010). *After Herder: Philosophy of language in the German tradition.* Oxford: Oxford University Press.

Forster, M. N. (2011). *German philosophy of language: From Schlegel to Hegel and beyond.* Oxford: Oxford University Press.

Gandhi, M. K. (1937). A welcome move. In *The collected works of Mahatma Gandhi, 95 vols* (Vol. 72, p. 209). New Delhi: Publications Divisions, Ministry of Information and Broadcasting Government of India 1958–1982.

Government of India (1957). *Report of the official language commission.* New Delhi: Government of India Press.

Gupta, C. (2001). *Sexuality, obscenity, community: Women, Muslims, and the Hindu public in colonial India* (PhD thesis), London University, Permanent Black, New Delhi.

Hare, J. L., & Link, F. (2019). The idea if volk and the origins of Volkisch research, 1800–1930. *Journal of the History of Ideas, 80*(4), 575–596.

Lelyveld, D. (1993). Colonial knowledge and the fate of Hindustani. *Comparative Studies in Society and History, 35*(4), 665–682.

Manela, E. (2007). *The Wilsonian moment: Self-determination and the international origins of anticolonial nationalism.* Oxford: Oxford University Press.

Mantena, R. S. (2005). Vernacular futures: Colonial philology and the idea of history in nineteenth century South India. *Indian Economic and Social History Review, 42,* 513–534.

Mishra, P. (2012). The mortality of Hindustani. *Parallax, 18*(3), 71–83.

Mishra, P. (2020). *Language and the making of modern India: Nationalism and the vernacular in colonial Odisha, 1803–1956.* Cambridge: Cambridge University Press.

Mitchell, L. (2005). Parallel languages, parallel cultures: Languages as a new foundation for the reorganization of knowledge and practice in Southern India. *The Indian Economic and Social History Review, 42*(4), 445–467.

Muthu, S. (2003). *Enlightenment against empire.* Princeton, NJ: Princeton University Press.

Novick, P. (1988). *That noble dream: The "objectivity question" and the American historical profession.* Cambridge: Cambridge University Press.

Noyes, J. K. (2014). Herder, post-colonial theory and the antinomy of universal reason. *The Cambridge Journal of Postcolonial Literary Inquiry, 1*(1), 107–122.

Pollock, S. (2000). Cosmopolitan and the vernacular in history. *Public Culture, 12*(3), 591–625.

Rai, A. (2005). The persistence of Hindustani. *The Annual of Urdu Studies, 20*, 135–144.

Ramaswamy, S. (1993). En-gendering language: The poetics of Tamil identity. *Comparative Studies in Society and History, 35*, 683–725.

Ramaswamy, S. (1999). Sanskrit for the nation. *Modern Asian Studies, 32*(2), 339–381.

Robinette, N. (2011). The world laid waste: Herder, language labor, empire. *New Literary History, 42*(1), 193–203.

Sawhney, S. (2009). *The modernity of Sanskrit*. Minneapolis: University of Minnesota Press.

Spivak, G. C. (2000). Translation as culture. *Parallax, 16*(1), 13–24.

Trautmann, T. R. (2004). *Aryans and British India*. New York: Yoda Press.

Trautmann, T. R. (2005). *The Aryan debate*. Oxford: Oxford University Press.

Zastoupil, L., & Moir, M. (1999). *The great Indian education debate: Documents relating to the orientalist-Anglicist controversy, 1781–1843*. London: Curzon.

7 No laughing matter

Learning to speak the "common language" in 1950s China

Janet Y. Chen

In the winter and early spring of 1956, a series of articles appeared in nationally circulating publications, with an earnest entreaty: Please do not laugh at those who are trying to learn the "common language" (*putonghua*). Beyond the headlines, permutations of the same refrain echoed in different discussions and forums. At the opening stages of a campaign aimed at "popularizing" a newly authorized lingua franca, the message was a curious one. What were people laughing at, and why? What was so comical about learning the language recently anointed as the spoken standard? At a conference a few months earlier, in October 1955, the Committee for Script Reform had prescribed the normative properties of *putonghua* as "a common language with Beijing pronunciation as its standard—the shared language of the Han nationality" (Quanguo wenzi gaige huiyi jueyi, 1955). A directive from the State Council followed, expanding the definition: "The foundation for the unification of Hanyu [the Chinese language] already exists, which is the *putonghua* that sets Beijing pronunciation as the standard, northern vernaculars as the base dialect, and exemplary modern vernacular works as the grammatical norm". Schoolteachers and students, soldiers and workers, policemen, journalists, translators, and actors—all should "gradually" learn the common language and contribute to the pursuit for uniform speech through their respective jobs (Guowuyuan guanyu tuiguang putonghua de zhishi, 1956). Simultaneously, the Communist Party's propaganda machine pumped out a constant stream of messages, reiterating that "everyone" should do their utmost to learn and to promote *putonghua*. With schoolteachers and soldiers leading the way as the "vanguard", a future of linguistic unity awaited.

Yet in concert with and in between the lines of such sanguine forecasts, persistent allusions to mockery and derision surfaced. Where did these attitudes come from? What did laughter signify about popular reactions to the ideological assumptions embedded in the project of unifying speech? This chapter answers these questions by exploring the social and political dynamics of learning to speak a new standard language in the mid-1950s. Examining the *putonghua* campaign as both political project and social history reveals a process of linguistic change that underscores fraught linkages between language and nationalism, usually presumed to exist in a straightforward relationship in the history of twentieth-century China. When the government of the People's Republic of China (PRC) cast the proposed lingua franca of New China as a "common language", distinct from the "national language" (*guoyu*) of the predecessor Nationalist regime (the Kuomintang [KMT], 1928–49), it repackaged the concept to resurrect a process of speech standardization that had been underway, in fits and starts, for half a century. In dislodging the nation-state, *putonghua* would reinforce a qualitatively different kind of political commitment by fortifying presumably shared aspirations for linguistic commonality and by embodying the "mass line" of the Chinese socialist state (Mao, 1943). The preponderance of existing scholarship, which has focused on different aspects of script reform, has tended to assume that *putonghua* became the prestige language by fiat, with little consideration of how new speech norms entered local communities or intersected with the lives of "the masses" (e.g. Bachner, 2017; Moser, 2016; Ramsey, 1987; Y. Zhou, 1997). In the 1950s, the quest for speech uniformity in China was fractured and contested. The persistence of laughter in the context of the inaugural campaign suggests that the state's ideological imperative was not fully persuasive. Indeed, the commitment of the people to the project of speech standardization could be quite tenuous, undermined by jokes, indifference, or even outright refusal. Far from being the "soul of the nation", the common language was an interloper that could not shake its association with officialdom, lingering doubts about its usefulness, or judgements about its strangeness.

What is *putonghua*?

As the language that putatively originated from the people, and deemed instrumental in forging its future unity, at the moment of its promulgation in 1955, *putonghua* was saddled with the burden of several decades of aspirations, false hopes, and conflicts. In 1913, after the demise of the imperial Qing state, the Republican government had launched an official effort to create a standardized national language befitting the new nation. Anchored by a venerated written classical language, the linguistic ecosystem comprised dozens of diverse spoken "dialects", many of them mutually unintelligible. The 1913 Conference to Unify Pronunciation sought to redress the state of linguistic fragmentation by creating a blueprint for a "national pronunciation"—a hybrid compromise combining elements of northern and southern phonology (Kaske, 2008). Both the process and the outcome were hotly contested and continued to rankle in the aftermath, in the context of sea changes wrought by the written vernacular (*baihua*) movement. When the Nationalist government assumed power in 1928, the contestation had not ceased, but the consensus among experts had migrated towards a "national language" based on Beijing dialect. In the 1930s, left-wing intellectuals further invoked the concept of a "common language", using the term *putonghua*, to critique the bureaucratic and urban privilege associated with *guanhua* (the "official language" of the imperial era) and *guoyu* (the "national language" of the KMT) (D. Wang, 2014). The definition of *putonghua* was inconsistent, however. Imbued with diverse or contradictory meanings, it could be conflated with, misunderstood as, or used interchangeably with *guoyu* (S. Hu, 1921).[1]

Entangled in the messy history of its linguistic predecessors, the *putonghua* of the Chinese socialist state also bore a Soviet imprint. Stalin's *Marxism and the Problem of Linguistics*, published in 1950, appeared in a Chinese translation the same year (Sidalin (Stalin), 1950). Thereafter—until the Sino-Soviet split—discussions of language reform (from script to speech) invariably referenced this work as the singularly authoritative source.[2] Within the Marxist-Stalinist framework of a multinational state, each nationality (*minzu*) in the PRC was sanctioned to possess cultural and linguistic autonomy. The Soviet model thus rhymes with Herder's concern with cultural particularism, while diverging in its putative embrace of multiculturalism. *Putonghua* and its written counterpart, *Hanzi* ("the writing of the Han people"), would function as a bridge for communication between the majority Han and the Tibetans, Uighurs, Mongols, as well as dozens or hundreds of other ethnic groups still to be identified and categorized (Mullaney, 2010). Government policy in the early to mid-1950s temporarily exempted "ethnic minorities" from the obligation to learn *putonghua*.[3] For the Han majority, comprising more than 90% of the population, the coherence of this ideology depended on sustaining the claim that as a single *minzu* nationality, they shared a single language—*Hanyu* ("the language of the Han people", usually rendered in English as "Chinese" or "Mandarin"). Despite the obvious incommensurability of regional speech between places such as Beijing, Canton, Shanghai, and Sichuan, all belong to the family of "Han dialects" (*Hanyu fangyan*).[4] On its surface, this configuration supports the Herderian model of one nation-one language. But to come to fruition and fulfil its role as a core component of the socialist vision of territoriality, the quest for linguistic uniformity must transcend its *minzu* origins and the confines of nationality. In this framework, the masses—united by class interest and sustained by revolutionary fervour—would embrace monolingualism, with *putonghua* superseding all other forms of speech to achieve the dream of one (multi-ethnic) China speaking in one voice. The process, as this chapter will explore, was fraught with contradictions and tensions that challenged the coherence of these assumptions.

In addition to the thorny issue of dialect, two other sets of questions hovered in the background. The first converged around the meaning of *putong* in *putonghua*—should this be interpreted as "common" in the sense of a shared lingua franca, or "common" in the sense of an ordinary, everyday form of speech? The disparate meanings caused no small amount of confusion. Parsing the differences, educators and Party cadres emphasized the "widespread", "collective", and "general usage" qualities of the common language and cautioned against treating it as commonplace or merely ordinary (X. Zhang, 1955a). The second set of questions arose from the uncertainty about the relationship of *putonghua* to the Beijing dialect and the "national language" of the deposed regime. While commentators glossed these issues in different terms, they consistently repeated the mantra that *putonghua* was not synonymous with, nor should it be conflated with, either precedent. Confusion abounded for those who had learned *guoyu* under the KMT, especially since the definition of *putonghua* anchored its phonology on the Beijing pronunciation. Repeated explanations stressed that the common language was not the equivalent of the "uncouth vernacular" of the capital; taking "Beijing pronuncia-tion" as the standard did not mean importing the entirety of *Beijinghua*; the whole nation was *not* to adopt the accent of "Old Beijing". In fact, the "coarse" elements and peculiar lexicon of the "authentic dialect" disqualified it as standard. What New China needed was a *putong* version of the Beijing dialect, stripped of its local idioms and idiosyncratic qualities (Xian, 1956; M. Yu, 1953; Y. Zhou, 1954). Despite recurrent attempts to clarify and refute, however, ambiguities endured as the mass campaign launched. The question, "What is *putonghua*?", could not be answered to general satisfaction. If *putonghua* was already "the shared language of the Han", what need was there to learn it, and why would anyone laugh?

What's so funny?

On 20 October 1955, Professor Wang Li of Peking University addressed the ple-nary session of the national conference on script reform. Two hundred and seven attendees representing 28 provinces and various government agencies had been meeting for five days, deliberating proposed changes to both the written and spo-ken language. Under the leadership of the Communist Party, China's "national language" would be reborn under three guises: simplified characters as the script, annotated with *pinyin* phonetic spelling, with the "common language" of *putong-hua* to unify the disparate spoken tongues of the nation.[5] While the conference proceedings focused primarily on script simplification, in his short address, Pro-fessor Wang introduced a different subject, directing attention to "ideological obstacles" in the work of popularizing the common language. "Many people are afraid of learning *putonghua*", Wang said, especially those whose native tongues diverge significantly from the pronunciation of the new standard.

> They think that *putonghua* is too difficult, and they are afraid of other people's mockery if they do not learn it well. . . . There is a saying: we are not afraid of heaven or earth; we are only afraid of the Cantonese speaking *guanhua*.

(Variations of this ditty implicated other dialect speakers). "This kind of taunting attitude warrants reconsideration. I suggest that we change mockery to encour-agement: we are not afraid of heaven or earth, surely not afraid of *putonghua*!" Wang concluded: "The Chinese people do not fear difficulty. We destroyed eight hundred million troops in Chiang Kai-shek's bandit gang. How could it be that we cannot conquer this linguistic fortress?" (L. Wang, 1957).

The October conference launched the campaign to attack that fortress, which proved more impregnable than expected. Subsequent publicity repeatedly alluded to "ideological obstacles" and disdainful attitudes lurking in society. An authorita-tive editorial in the *People's Daily*, published at the conclusion of the conference to affirm its resolutions, addressed the perception that the popularization of the common language sought to "destroy" local dialects. Not so, the Party newspaper declared—"dialects may and will certainly co-exist with *putonghua* for quite a long period of time". The campaign would only aim to expand the scope of the standard language, while working to "reduce gradually the boundaries of use" for dialects. To achieve this shift in balance, it was imperative to "rectify the concept of narrow localism", which manifested itself as "refusing to acknowledge *putong-hua*, unwilling to listen to *putonghua*, and even to the extent of forbidding one's children to speak *putonghua*" (Wei cujin hanzi gaige, 1955).

It is difficult to gauge the prevalence of such sentiments of suspicion and rejection. Did they represent a majority view or the disgruntlement of a small minority? Judging from the recurring discussions, they were widespread enough to cause alarm at the top, deemed "obstacles" that could derail the language reform project. As Education Minister Zhang Xiruo observed, some comrades do not understand the issues and ask, "What does speech have to do with politics?" Others may be more willing but still hesitate: "Learning *putonghua* is good and all. But it's very difficult and I'm too old to learn". Still others fret that while learning, their "southern tunes and northern tones" would be scorned as "tossing around a Beijing accent". Minister Zhang counselled patience and perseverance:

> We cannot expect to learn it all in one go, or to achieve 100% accuracy imme-diately. . . . In the process of learning, you should not be afraid of other peo-ple's mockery. Learning *putonghua* is our highest obligation, so why laugh? We say that those who ought to be disparaged and criticized are not the com-rades learning *putonghua*, but rather those who are unwilling to learn, who cling for dear life to their own dialects and won't let go.
>
> (X. Zhang, 1955b)

Among the scoffers, Yang Yiqiang discerned two sources for their disdain. One group, those "able to speak relatively fluent *putonghua*," looked down upon peo-ple for their mispronunciation, thinking: "aren't you embarrassed?" The second group, those unable to speak *putonghua*, also taunted the botched efforts of those trying to learn but asserted the "purity" of their own ineptitude: "I do not know how to speak and so I simply don't, which is the honest way to go. Not like you, posing as an expert, with your southern tunes and northern tones stinging our ears". Viewing themselves as "heroes", they proudly advertised their incompe-tence and affirmed a preference for the local dialect (Yang, 1956).

Other commentators assessed the substance of the dissenting opinions in even greater detail. Zhang Gonggui (1956), for instance, identified seven different types of negative attitudes, ranging from "I don't have a talent for learning languages" and "Strange pronunciation and odd tones, it feels unnatural", to "Why do I need to learn *putonghua*?". Among language instructors, putatively the linchpin of the process, Zhu Boshi (1955) detected four strands of "ideologi-cal obstacles":

1 "It doesn't matter"—my dialect accent is not bad, the students can understand; whether I speak *putonghua* or not doesn't matter.
2 "Feel embarrassed"—if I try to change my accent to speak *putonghua*, other people will laugh at me for putting on "bureaucratic airs".

3   "Afraid of ridicule"—If you are going to do it, you need to conform to the standard. "Neither fish nor fowl" is a disgrace and sounds bad. It would be better just to speak your native dialect.

4   "Fear difficulty"—I am old, my tongue is stiff, and it is too difficult to change.

Cumulatively, these diagnoses referred to a spectrum of popular reactions to the exhortation to learn a new spoken language. Many of the anxieties—lack of ability or confidence, ineptitude attributed to old age—clustered around acts of articulation perceived to be awkward or insurmountably difficult. Other comments registered a note of recalcitrance, variously ascribed to attachment to native dialects, indifference, or antagonism. Finally, fear of ridicule contributed to insecurity and unease about the new speech norms. Thus, in efforts to persuade the masses to speak the common language of the socialist state, agents of government authority repeatedly reprimanded those evincing "erroneous attitudes", targeting in particular the scoffers. "In the future, those unable to speak *putonghua* will be the absurd ones"—the joke will be on them (Tao, 1956; Yang, 1956). The assumption was that for the most part, "the people" were eager to learn *putonghua* but lost their fervour and grew discouraged when others mocked them. A constant refrain urged courage and fortitude, underscoring the conviction that unflagging determination could overcome deficits of natural ability or skill. From this perspective, *putonghua* was not what sounds the mouth, tongue, and throat can produce, but what a resolute heart-and-mind can accomplish. After all, as one educator noted, many are able to learn Russian or English perfectly well—so why not *putonghua*? (Tang, 1956; Zheng, 1955). To foster commitment, profuse exhortations tried to ameliorate fears and dispel "incorrect" ideas. When teachers encounter parental disapproval, they must patiently explain the relationship between the common language, socialist construction, and educational quality in order to "transform opposition into support". Complaints about difficulty and lack of time should be countered with appeals to individual resolve and willpower. Teachers themselves must adopt *putonghua* as the medium of instruction and communication—"Of course, at the outset, their pronunciation will not entirely accord with the standard and will invariably provoke other people's mockery" (Y. Wang, 1956). In their eagerness to expose "ideological obstacles" for the purpose of overcoming them, commentators and news reports also revealed a range of attitudes militating against the idea of a standard spoken language, casting doubt on the vision of a nation unified in speech.

Examined more closely, the entreaty "please do not laugh" could be disaggregated into several permutations. The most frequently repeated rendering points to how attempting to speak the putative prestige language could subject the speaker to ridicule—for making mistakes, sounding "foolish", or according to a nebulous saying, *buhaoting* or *nanting* ("sounding bad").[6] Such disparagement could actually buttress the status of the prestige language. For instance, teasing a classmate for not speaking *putonghua* "well", worries about "becoming the butt of jokes" because of inaccurate pronunciation, or school leaders "looking down on those who have trouble learning"—these views implicitly reinforced a perceived standard (Jiaoshimen yingdang chengwei tuiguang putonghua de jiji fenzi, 1955; S. Zhou, 1956). As one primary school instructor explained, students unaccustomed to the sounds of the "standard pronunciation" often start laughing when they hear it.

> A student, reading aloud in a strange voice and odd manner, sometimes sets the entire class off roaring in hilarity. This affects classroom order. The teacher must pay attention and prevent it, as well as cultivate the students' habit of speaking the standard pronunciation.
>
> (S. Chen, 1956)

On the other hand, in other contexts, "sounding bad" could signal a denial of *putonghua*'s claim to higher status—"useless" for communication, aesthetically distasteful ("stinging to the ears"), or emotionally alienating. In a bold inversion of authority, students laughed at teachers for bumbling through lessons and for speaking *putonghua* in a comical or incomprehensible manner (Peterson, 1997, pp. 111–112). In a related but slightly different rendering, a particular mode of mockery singled out those trying to speak *putonghua* (whether fluently or poorly) for putting on airs, affecting a higher status, or imitating government cadres. In this variation, *putonghua* marked the speaker as an outsider. In one middle school in Yunnan, for instance, a class of 83 students resolved to learn *putonghua* (Quanti dou xuehui shuo putonghua, 1956). They succeeded in doing so, after patiently helping reluctant classmates overcome their doubts. Yet students from other classes refused to learn and heaped scorn, laughing at them for "showing off" and jeering at their "pretentious foreign flavor" (Quanti dou xuehui shuo putonghua, 1956). In another example, Jiang (1956) urged people "not to sneer" in an extended anecdote featured in a provincial education journal. In this story, Teacher Wang had completed a one-month *putonghua* training course. Upon his return, he attended a teachers' meeting, where he saw Teacher Xing and greeted him warmly. "So strange! Teacher Xing did not reply. Instead he opened his eyes wide, as if searching for something, and looked Teacher Wang over, from head to toe". After a moment's silence, Xing said slowly: "I haven't seen you for some days, how come your accent has changed? It seems you are no longer a local!" Everyone burst out laughing. Someone said: "Not a local but also not a foreigner!" They all started talking at once and stared at Teacher Wang, who felt "somewhat embarrassed". In this narrative, a newly acquired "accent" subjected a teacher to jokes and scorn from his colleagues. Instead of rising in status in the community, he became an outsider—not as alien as a foreigner and not quite an outcast, but no longer "one of us". Rather than embracing *putonghua* as a "solemn political responsibility", his colleagues rejected the linguistic obligation ascribed to their position as schoolteachers. They certainly refused its ideological significance. While the moral of the story praised Teacher Wang and admonished those who poked fun at him, the social dynamics captured in the anecdote undermined the message.

From mockery to refusal

In addition to laughter, whether contemptuous or good-natured, challenges to *putonghua* emerged in other ways. One observer described four types that were "a drag on *putonghua*"—"the unequivocally opposed", "the vacillators", "the conceited and apathetic", and the "wait and see-ers" (S. Zhou, 1956, p. 7). Verging on intransigence, "Some people say: 'This [*putonghua*] can never work, because language is a matter of the people's freedom, there is no way you can force people to speak a prescribed language'" (Rao, 1956). According to Zhu Boshi, such sentiments had roots in the pre-Liberation period. As a schoolteacher who had worked in diverse locales (Fujian, Jiangxi, Wuhan), Zhu had struggled with the incommensurability of regional dialects. When he required students speak *putonghua* in the classroom in years past, "they talked back, saying either 'it is difficult to change our accent' or 'each person has the freedom to speak as he chooses, uniformity should not be imposed' or 'if you demand that everyone speak *putonghua*, dialects will perish'".[7] Quoting an aphorism from the *Classic of Poetry*, Zhu lamented that his appeals fell on deaf ears: "The speaker talked with great earnestness, but the audience paid little attention". Yet in the post-Liberation period, despite the acute and obvious need for a common spoken language, similar "ideological obstacles" remained. "We must recognize that learning *putonghua* is not a simply a matter of individual hobby or interest, but related to the national economy, the people's livelihood, and the socialist construction of the fatherland" (Zhu, 1955).

Such utilitarian arguments, prominently featured in the propaganda campaign, positioned the common language as an instrument to accelerate the project of socialist construction. Beyond the national imperative, a common language would also redress the long-standing linguistic divides that had troubled communities and hampered communication.

> We need to clearly understand the situation. For the people of the same province to go looking for a "translator" in order to converse, or to make stupid mistakes because of a linguistic impasse—this is a laughable, backward situation.
>
> (Tao, 1956)

Contrary to popular belief, the common language did not aim to "destroy dialects". As a matter of "historical development", local vernaculars will "naturally be eliminated and weeded out", but this process would take a long time to unfold.

> In this regard, there is no coercion, no possibility of adopting violent methods. If someone wishes to speak in dialect with his fellow villagers, no one can interfere. The problem is that . . . we cannot hold native place association meetings every day.
>
> (Q. Hu, 1955)

As linguist Xu Shirong put it, the practical benefits were obvious. With improvements in transportation creating opportunities for unprecedented mobility, "who knows how many people will be leaving their hometowns to travel to other places, for study or work". Native dialects were inadequate for this new world; in the wrong contexts they may cause inconvenience, "sometimes trouble and vexation" (Xu, 1956). One familiar trope in these discussions described misunderstandings (serious or humorous) arising from the incommensurability of dialects. Due to mispronunciation, an innocuous phrase such *sanshiyi ge ren* (三十一个人, "thirty-one people") could be misconstrued as *shasi yi ge ren* (杀死一个人, "killed one person"); an attempt to *mai xiezi* (买鞋子 "buy shoes") could be garbled as *mai haizi* (买孩子 "buy a child") (Z. Zhang, 1956, p. 12; Xu, 1956).

In the winter of 1955 and into the spring of 1956, the campaign thus proceeded with "bursts of fervor" ("gongs and drums") interspersed with allusions to lurking problems and obstacles. Professor Wang Li tried to address some of the latent issues, by posing three questions: Is learning *putonghua* "putting on official airs"? Is learning *putonghua* "forgetting your origins"? Is learning *putonghua* difficult? On all three counts—decidedly not, Wang declared (L. Wang, 1956). In the first instance, *putonghua* should not be conflated with the Beijing dialect or its imperial predecessor, "*guanhua*" (the "official language" denoting bureaucratic privilege). As the professor explained:

> In feudal society, officials did speak this way and used this kind of language to intimidate the people. But we cannot conclude that this language belongs to officials just because of this. We ought to say: the speech of any place belongs to the people.

As evidence, Wang avowed that under the leadership of the Communist Party, the "bureaucratic masters" had been destroyed and "the people" had become the new masters. "The Beijinghua that is also called '*guanhua*' still exists—therefore we can see that [the *putonghua* we are referring to] is not the language of officials, but the language of the people". Moreover, how can the language of Beijing, the nation's capital, be considered "putting on bureaucratic airs"?

In the second instance, there are "those who say that abandoning the language of one's ancestors means 'forgetting one's origins'". Not true, the professor soothed. To learn *putonghua* is to acquire an additional language, not to displace dialects.

> It's not the case that from now on you will be prohibited from speaking the vernacular of your hometown. . . . A thousand years ago our Hanyu was not as splintered as today. Several thousand years prior to that, there was only one kind of Hanyu . . . the language of our distant ancestors was unified.

In other words, far from forsaking one's heritage, learning *putonghua* constituted a return to one's origins. Finally, addressing the third issue of difficulty, Wang assured readers that "Anything that is important and worth doing has its share of difficulties". Contrary to popular perception, learning *putonghua* is "actually not that difficult for southerners", certainly far easier than a foreign language. When several members of the Central Committee for Popularizing Putonghua raised this point at a meeting, the professor said. "These are not empty words of comfort, but based on theory and verified with facts" (L. Wang, 1956). Wang Li's contortions to clarify the "actual" situation, mollify discontent, and refute misunderstandings disclosed attitudes that contradicted the ideological dictates of the government campaign. The insistence that *putonghua* was *not* difficult to learn; *not* the language of bureaucrats; would *not* destroy dialects—he was protesting a little too much.

The assurances Wang Li offered were also undermined by the campaign's adamant messaging, which portrayed the new lingua franca as a tidal wave soon to inundate the entire country. In the State Council's February 1956 directive, a 12-point action plan ordered swift, nationwide implementation. The first order of business stipulated: "Starting from the autumn of 1956, excepting ethnic minority regions, the language and literature classes of all primary and middle schools in the nation shall be conducted using *putonghua*" (Guowuyuan guanyu tuiguang putonghua de zhishi, 1956). Although reality soon revealed this mandate to be far off the mark (a target not achieved even after 30 years, much less six months), the spring of 1956 did turn out to be the "high tide". By the autumn, waning publicity indicated the attenuation of the campaign. As an editorial in *Teachers' News* described, the movement had launched in 1955 as "a gentle breeze caressing the grass" and evolved into "gathering clouds and surging storms". The State Council's directive in February 1956 precipitated thunder and lightning, resulting in much progress. Thereafter, however, some teachers started asking: "Is the *putonghua* campaign a gust of wind that has passed?" Although She Hua, the editorialist, insisted that "*putonghua* instruction is not a gust of wind", his discussion of numerous and diverse sources of obstacles suggested otherwise. According to She, those responsible for propaganda grumbled: "We have already publicized it [*putonghua*]; to do it again is just the same old stuff". Attitudes combining provincialism, "close enough" (*chabuduo*), and "it has nothing do with me" undermined the campaign. He concluded:

> We should not treat it as a gust of passing wind. Instead we should amplify the force of the *putonghua* campaign. . . . The unification of Hanyu cannot be realized within three or five years. We need to continue the work of popularizing *putonghua* with determination and over a long period of time.
>
> (She, 1956)

With such indicators of uncertainty and doubt percolating, in September the language reform committee in Beijing dispatched an inspection team to the south, to assess the behind-the-scenes situation, particularly in middle and primary schools (Shanghai Municipal Archive B105-5-1689, pp. 42–49).[8] After spending some eight weeks touring Zhejiang, Jiangxi, and Shanghai, the inspectors reported progress and some achievements, but also documented an array of disturbing views:

- Some warned their children: "We would rather sell the family home, but we will never sell out the vernacular of our hometown". Speaking *putonghua* was akin to "forgetting their origins" and considered a betrayal of one's ancestors.

- When children learned *putonghua* at school and spoke it at home, some parents slapped them.
- Some considered learning *putonghua* to be a form of "putting on official airs" or talking like a bureaucrat. They denigrated it as "speaking nonsense".
- Some teachers think *putonghua* belongs to the purview of language instructors and "have nothing to do with the other subject teachers".

Reviewing a litany of negative feedback, the inspection team concluded that despite a promising start, insufficient commitment and lack of "vigorous support from the leadership" signalled to the people that the previous political significance imputed to speech standardization had elapsed (Shanghai Municipal Archive B105–5–1689, p. 47).

Other observers echoed these assessments. In its annual report, the Shanghai education bureau summarized the work of 1956 with a similar praise-and-blame formula. On one hand, the report enumerated specific achievements: a team of four staff members dedicated to the speech campaign in schools; an array of classes, lectures, broadcasting programmes, and publications; a cohort of cadres trained to lead the future effort. Most importantly, "schoolteachers and some of the masses have gained a specific understanding of the significance of *putonghua*. With their misgivings gradually assuaged, the number of people learning and speaking *putonghua* increases daily". The report lauded these achievements as "a solid foundation for the future work of popularizing *putonghua* in Shanghai" (Shanghai Municipal Archive B1–2–1901/2, pp. 37–40). The discussion of "lessons learned" that followed, however, belied the depiction of success. Cadres in charge failed to recognize linguistic change as "a long term and routine task", different from ordinary political campaigns. Overzealous and impatient for results, they "demanded too much all at once". The failure to grasp the guiding principle of "promote key points, gradually popularize" in turn generated other problems. After a surge of publicity at the end of 1955 and in the early months of 1956, "propaganda work in society virtually ceased". As the initial fervour dissipated, "teachers and students no longer paid much attention to speaking *putonghua*". Teacher qualifications—one of the keys to success—remained abysmal.[9] Observations in seven schools indicated that only 10 percent of teachers were able to speak "relatively standard" *putonghua*; the rest spoke "various kinds of dialect *putonghua*". At the most egregious end of the spectrum, some instructors relied on the blackboard to communicate in writing; "otherwise the students cannot understand". More generally, students replicated the teachers' pronunciation mistakes. The report also repeated observations about rampant "erroneous ideology": lack of urgency and attention; abdication of responsibility ("it has nothing to do with me"); fear of incompetence; and lack of confidence among older teachers ("my dialect accent is too strong, impossible to learn"). As a result, the language teachers who embraced the *putonghua* mission described their experience as "doing battle as orphan soldiers. Without support from school administrators, the results are negligible" (Shanghai Municipal Archive B1–2–1901/2, pp. 39–40, 65).

Such candid assessments, conveyed in confidential reports, also filtered into public disclosures. For instance, in a letter published in Shanghai's *putonghua* bulletin, one middle school teacher lamented that the "upsurge" and fanfare of the previous year had become a "cold front". He felt stranded as a "lone soldier in combat", without reinforcements from below or support from above (J. Yu, 1957). At the same time, narratives of individual commitment testified to the compelling promise of unified speech. When a middle school teacher from Nantong (Jiangsu province) sent a query about the neutral tone (*qingsheng*) to the editors of the journal, *Language Reform*, his letter enclosed a line-by-line inventory of its inconsistent usage in practice manuals. The irregularities confounded new learners: "For the same character, some Beijingers think that it should be pronounced with the neutral tone, others think not. Each has his/her own pronunciation and habit. This poses extreme difficulties for those of us in dialect regions studying *putonghua*". Despite the complaining tone, the teacher's study of the finer points of pronunciation evinced diligent attention and a seriousness of purpose (G. Wang, 1957). Beyond the classroom, the well-known stage actor Hou Baolin attested to the critical importance of standardizing speech for dramatic performance. He enjoined his colleagues to moderate the linguistic peculiarities of their respective genres (whether Cantonese opera or Henan ballads) and shift their pronunciation towards the standard. Hou singled out Beijing crosstalk (*xiangsheng*), his own speciality, as a local tradition imbued with "thick dialect flavor". Despite the correlation between *putonghua* and Beijinghua, the ubiquitous use of local idioms rendered crosstalk routines incomprehensible to outsiders. Vowing to be "a courageous and staunch propagandist for *putonghua*", Hou urged his fellow performers to redouble their efforts to conform to new speech norms (Hou, 1956).

More generally, progress reports from the provinces divulged mixed results from the first phase of the campaign, with testimonies of success interspersed with explicit acknowledgements of extensive problems. Some jurisdictions reported significant time and resources devoted to instruction of the new speech norms. Other provinces had barely started. Half of the primary school teachers in Anhui, for example, reportedly received *putonghua* training in the summer of 1956 (some 30,000). Fujian, in contrast, lagged far behind—only 366 middle school teachers had attended summer classes. In these accounts, the tenuous commitment of cadres and futile efforts to dislodge "ideological obstacles" lurking within teachers materialized as recurring themes. In Heilongjiang, an inspection of seven districts revealed a patchy linguistic terrain: some schools were putting forth tremendous effort, but others blithely disregarded the responsibility to implement *putonghua* instruction. Some language instructors viewed using the common language as the medium of instruction to be a "waste of time", since dialect speech dominated the school environment. Meanwhile, subject teachers mutter that *putonghua* "has nothing to do with them", and some even laugh at those who speak it. Overall, the prevailing opinion in Heilongjiang presumed that "the high tide of popularizing *putonghua* has passed", resulting in "passive and apathetic attitudes" (Quanguo tuiguang putonghua gongzuo qingkuang jianbao, 1956).

Conclusion

In retrospect, Chen Runzhai could date the diminishing fervour for the common language to the middle of 1956. Writing in the *People's Daily* one year later, Chen explained that of the many reasons that could account for the palpable chill, erroneous understandings of the nature and history of the nation's complex linguistic ecology constituted the primary cause. Based on faulty assumptions, "some people viewed the task of popularizing *putonghua* as very simple. They thought that we only need to circulate some slogans; without much work everyone will learn it". But given the wide spectrum of differences between dialects and Beijing phonology, "we cannot expect every place to proceed in lockstep, and we should not be so impatient as to expect to accomplish the goal in one leap" or to insist on "a single standard". A differentiated approach, taking into account "the linguistic circumstances of each dialect region", would be more productive. Moreover, proficiency requirements should be set according to age, occupation, and residence location (rural/urban). While teachers and students needed to be held to higher expectations, the "ordinary masses" required an approach based on "actual conditions", governed by "the principle of volition". "We cannot do it by force or command, and we cannot forbid them from speaking dialect. Otherwise, it will provoke the dissatisfaction of the masses", to the detriment of the broader goals of language reform (R. Chen, 1957).

In August 1957, the Ministry of Education appraised the state of the *putonghua* campaign and evaluated the accomplishments of the past 18 months. Nationwide, education officials counted more than 600,000 schoolteachers who had received some form of "Beijing pronunciation training" (about one-third of the language teachers in the country). More than two million listeners had tuned in for lessons on the radio. Some 4.5 million volumes and 1,380,000 phonograph records of instructional materials had been distributed. Nonetheless, "the chief difficulty is that in society, there is insufficient understanding of the importance and meaning of *putonghua*. Therefore there is significant resistance in implementation". Across the country, progress was uneven, "from hot to cold". Publicity had halted completely in some jurisdictions, "to the extent that some people have begun to wonder whether the campaign will continue". Given the circumstances, and in light of the forecasted "heavy workload" of the ongoing Anti-Rightist campaign, the Ministry of Education decided *not* to issue another directive on *putonghua*. Instead, the memo expressed hope that each province and city would "persevere in continuing the work of popularizing *putonghua*"—building upon the foundational achievements of the past months, rather than "giving up and forfeiting halfway" (Guanyu jixu tuiguang putonghua de tongzhi, 1957, pp. 25–26). Local jurisdictions should incorporate promotion of the common language into their "routine work", rather than oscillating "from hot to cold" (Jixu nuli tuiguang putonghua, 1957).

The campaign did continue, but at a fraction of its former decibel level. Since there were no real consequences for not learning *putonghua*, it paled in comparison to other political goals and receded in importance. As the Anti-Rightist Campaign intensified in the fall of 1957, the persecution of those who had opposed or voiced reservations about script simplification dominated the politics of language reform (Seybolt & Chiang, 1979, pp. 3–5). Among the victims caught in the dragnet was Wang Li.[10] In the Great Leap Forward that followed, the winds of exaggeration extended to *putonghua*, with claims that perfect speech unity could be achieved within weeks or months. But like much of the Great Leap, this was fantasy, conjured up for political purposes. In 1966, Chen Boda, one of the leaders of the Cultural Revolution, gave speeches to Red Guard groups around the country. The transcripts indicate that he apologized to the young revolutionaries for "not speaking *putonghua* very well", saying: "let me get an interpreter". No one laughed.

Notes

1 S. Hu (1921) famously coined a definition that equated *guoyu* with *putonghua*: "What we call *guoyu* refers to a common language [putonghua] that is largely the same, with only minor differences, in the region extending from the Great Wall to the Yangtze River, from the three eastern to the three southwestern provinces".

2 Soviet advisers also played instrumental roles in different aspects of Chinese language reform in the mid-1950s, particularly 1954–57 (Li, 2017; M. Zhou, 2003).

3 From 1949–57, during what Zhou Minglang (2003) has characterized as a "pluralistic stage", government policy emphasized the rhetoric of equal language rights. A more coercive "monopolistic phase" began in 1958 (pp. 43–60).

4 Mair (1991) proposed using the term "topolect" in place of dialect, as a more neutral and accurate rendering of Chinese linguistic categories.

5 Of the trio, a draft of the simplification scheme was issued in January 1955 and subsequently revised. *Pinyin* phonetic spelling received more attention the following year (February 1956) with the promulgation of a "draft" scheme.

6 For an illuminating discussion of the affective differences embedded in the judgement *bu haoting*, see Blum (2003).

7 In describing the situation prior to 1949, Zhu's anachronistic reference to *putonghua* avoided the KMT nomenclature of *guoyu*.

8 Sources from the Shanghai Municipal Archive draw from the records of the local education bureau and the municipal government. They are cited by the archive's catalogue and page number system.

9 Eddy U (2004) found that in the 1950s Shanghai's secondary schools were staffed with large numbers of politically suspect or academically unqualified teachers. Party and state agencies transferred their "rejects" to schools, where they received haphazard training to become instructors.

10 Wang Li's views on linguistics and higher education first landed him in political trouble in 1957–58. A dutiful self-criticism won him a reprieve until the Cultural Revolution (Seybolt & Chiang, 1979, pp. 260–287; Zhang & Wang, 1992).

References

Bachner, A. (2017). *Beyond sinology: Chinese writing and the scripts of culture*. New York: Columbia University Press.

Blum, S. (2003). Good to hear: Using the trope of standard to find one's way in a sea of linguistic diversity. In M. Zhou (Ed.), *Language policy in the people's republic of China* (pp. 123–141). Boston, MA: Kluwer.

Chen, R. (1957, April 6). Genju shiji qingkuang caiqu butong fangshi tuiguang putonghua [Select different methods based on the actual situation to popularize the common language]. *Renmin ribao*, p. 7.

Chen, S. (1956, June 15). Jiao xuesheng jianghao putonghua [Teach students to speak the common language well]. *Jiaoshibao*, p. 3.

Guanyu jixu tuiguang putonghua de tongzhi [Notification regarding continuing to popularize the common language] (1957, August 21). *Shanghai municipal archive B105-7-18*, pp. 25–26.

Guowuyuan guanyu tuiguang putonghua de zhishi [State Council directive regarding the popularization of the common language] (1956, February 12). *Renmin ribao*, p. 3.

Hou, B. (1956). Women you juexin zuo putonghua de xuanchuanyuan [We have the determination to be the propagandists of the common language]. *Zhongguo yuwen*, 7, 38.

Hu, Q. (1955 [1999]). Zai quanguo wenzi gaige huiyi shang de fayan [Speech at the national conference on script reform]. In *Hu Qiaomu tan yuyan wenzi* (pp. 94–139). Beijing: Renmin chubanshe.

Hu, S. (1921). Guoyu yundong de lishi [The history of the national language movement]. *Jiaoyu zazhi*, 13(11), 8–9.

Jiang, X. (1956). Yindang guli shuo putonghua [We should give encouragement to speak the common language]. *Jiangsu jiaoyu*, 5, 28.

Jiaoshimen yingdang chengwei tuiguang putonghua de jiji fenzi [Teachers should become the activists for popularizing the common language] (1955, November 25). *Guangming ribao*, p. 1.

Jixu nuli tuiguang putonghua [Continue to work hard to popularize the common language] (1957, December 25). *Renmin ribao*, p. 7.

Kaske, E. (2008). *The politics of language in Chinese education, 1895–1919*. Boston: Brill.

Li, Y. (2017). *China's soviet dream: Propaganda, culture, and popular imagination*. London: Routledge.

Mair, V. (1991). What is a Chinese "dialect/topolect"? Reflections on some key Sino-English linguistic terms. *Sino-Platonic Papers*, 29, 1–31.

Mao, Z. (1943 [1967]). Some questions concerning methods of leadership. In *Selected Works of Mao Tse-tung* (Vol. 3, pp. 117–122). Beijing: Foreign Languages Press.

Moser, D. (2016). *A billion voices: China's search for a common language*. Melbourne: Penguin Books.

Mullaney, T. (2010). *Coming to terms with the nation: Ethnic classification in modern China*. Berkeley, CA: University of California Press.

Peterson, G. (1997). *The power of words: Literacy and revolution in south China, 1949–1995*. Vancouver: UBC Press.

Quanguo tuiguang putonghua gongzuo qingkuang jianbao [*Bulletin on the national situation of popularizing the common language*] (1956, October 24, vol. 5 and December 15, vol. 6).

Quanguo wenzi gaige huiyi jueyi [Decisions of the national conference on script reform] (1955). In Quanguo wenzi gaige huiyi mishuchu (Ed.), *Quanguo wenzi gaige huiyi wenjian huibian* (pp. 216–217). Beijing: Wenzi gaige chubanshe.

Quanti dou xuehui shuo putonghua [All will learn to speak the common language] (1956, January 28). *Zhongguo qingnianbao*, p. 1.

Ramsey, S. R. (1987). *The languages of China*. Princeton, NJ: Princeton University Press.

Rao, X. (1956, January 4). Zai woguo fangyan fuza qingkuang xia tuiguang putonghua xingde tong ma? [In our nation's complicated dialect situation, is it possible to popularize the common language?]. *Guangming ribao*, p. 3.

Seybolt, P., & Chiang, G. (1979). Introduction. In P. Seybolt & G. Chiang (Eds.), *Language reform in China: Documents and commentary* (pp. 1–27). New York: M. E. Sharpe.

She, H. (1956, October 9). Putonghua jiaoxue bushi yizhenfeng [Teaching and learning the common language is not a gust of wind]. *Jiaoshi bao*, p. 3.

Sidalin (Joseph Stalin) (1950). *Makesi zhuyi yu yuyanxue wenti* [*Marxism and the problem of linguistics*]. Beijing: Jiefangshe.

Tang, T. (1956). Dadan xuexi putonghua [Courageously learn the common language]. In Wenzi gaige chubanshe (Ed.), *Putonghua lunji* (pp. 120–121). Beijing: Wenzi gaige chubanshe.

Tao, H. (1956, January 12). Jianglai buhui shuo putonghua cai kexiao li [In the future those unable to speak the common language will be the absurd ones]! *Zhongguo qingnian bao*, p. 3.

U, E. (Eddy U). (2004). The hiring of rejects: Teacher recruitment and crises of socialism in the early PRC years. *Modern China*, *30*(1), 46–80.

Wang, D. (2014). Guanhua, guoyu, putonghua: Zhongguo jindai biaozhunyu de "zhengming" yu zhengzhi [Official language, national language, common language: The politics and "rectification of names" for the standard language in modern China]. *Xueshu yuekan*, *46*, 155–170.

Wang, G. (1957). Qingsheng nanyu zhuomou [The neutral tone is difficult to grasp]. *Pinyin*, *3*, 47–48.

Wang, L. (1956). Tantan xuexi putonghua [Let's talk about learning the common language]. *Shishi shouce*, *6*, 15–17.

Wang, L. (1957). Wang Li daibiao de fayan [Representative Wang Li's speech]. In *Diyi ci quanguo wenzi gaige huiyi wenjian huibian* (pp. 142–143). Beijing: Wenzi gaige chubanshe.

Wang, Y. (1956). Xiaoxue jiaoshi bixu liji xuexi bing tuixing yi Beijing yuyin wei biaozhunyin de putonghua [Primary school teachers must immediately learn and popularize the common language based on Beijing pronunciation as the standard]. *Jiaoyu banyuekan*, *1*, 14.

Wei cujin hanzi gaige, tuiguang putonghua, shixian Hanyu guifanhua er nuli [Promote reform of Chinese writing, popularize the common language, realize the standardization of the Chinese language] (1955, October 26). *Renmin ribao*, p. 1.

Xian, D. (1956, January 4). Beijing tuhua bing bushi putonghua [Beijing's uncouth vernacular is not the common language]. *Guangming ribao*, p. 3.

Xu, S. (1956). Weisheme yao tuiguang putonghua [Why we need to popularize the common language]. In Zhongguo wenzi gaige weiyuanhui (Ed.), *Dajia doulai xuexi he tuiguang putonghua* [Let us all learn and popularize the common language] (pp. 25–27). Beijing: Tongsu duwu chubanshe.

Yang, Y. (1956, March 14). Chaoxiao bieren xueshuo putonghua de taidu shi cuowu de [The attitude of mocking other people learning to speak the common language is erroneous]. *Guangming ribao*, p. 3.

Yu, J. (1957). Gujun zuozhan [Lone soldier in combat]. *Tuiguang putonghua jianbao*, *9*, 2.

Yu, M. (1953). Tan minzu biaozhunyu wenti [On the question of nationality and standard language]. *Zhongguo yuwen*, *4*, 13–14.

Zhang, G. (1956, February 15). Yinggai jiechu xue putonghua de jizhong sixiang zhang'ai [We need to remove several types of ideological obstacles in learning the common language]. *Guangming ribao*, p. 3.

Zhang, G., & Wang, J. (1992). *Wang Li zhuan* [*The biography of Wang Li*]. Beijing: Guangxi jiaoyu chubanshe.

Zhang, X. (1955a, November 18). Dali tuiguang yi Beijing yuyin wei biaozhunyin de putonghua [Resolutely promote the standard common language based on Beijing pronunciation]. *Renmin ribao*, p. 3.

Zhang, X. (1955b). Dajia doulai tuiguang he xuexi putonghua [Let us all popularize and learn the common language]. *Shishi shouce, 24*, 24–26.

Zhang, Z. (1956). *Weisheme yao tuigaung putonghua [Why we need to popularize the common language]*. Beijing: Guangdong renmin chubanshe.

Zheng, Y. (1955). Tan putonghua de xuexi [On learning the common language]. *Yuwen xuexi, 11*, 12–13.

Zhou, M. (2003). *Multilingualism in China: The politics of writing reforms for minority languages, 1949–2002*. Berlin: Mouton de Gruyter.

Zhou, S. (1956). Tuiguang putonghua zhong de sixiang wenti [Ideological problems in popularizing the common language]. *Yuwen zhishi, 1*, 7.

Zhou, Y. (1954). Pinyin wenzi yu biaozhunyin [Phonetic script and standard pronunciation]. *Zhongguo yuwen, 6*, 23–24.

Zhou, Y. (1997). *Zhongguo yuwen de shidai yanjin [The evolution of the Chinese language]*. Beijing: Qinghua daxue chubanshe.

Zhu, B. (1955). Yuwen jiaoshi yao dali xuanchuan, tuiguang, bing xuehao putonghua [Language teachers must do their utmost to propagandize, promote, and learn putonghua]. *Yuwen xuexi, 12*, 4–6.

8 Nationalism, multilingualism, and language planning in post-colonial Africa

Nkonko Kamwangamalu

In 1884, seven European countries, Belgium, Britain, France, Germany, Italy, Portugal, and Spain, held a conference in Berlin, Germany, with only one item on the agenda: the geopolitical partition of Africa. This partition, which came to be known as the *scramble for Africa*, set in motion an issue that post-colonial generations of African policy makers and linguists have been addressing over the years and which is the focus of this paper, namely, the determination of a language to serve as the medium of instruction in the continent's educational systems (Bamgbose, 2000; Djité, 2008). The challenge for the African continent has been whether to replace former colonial languages with indigenous languages in state institutions such as education and, in doing so, cut off students from the international scholarly community or to retain former colonial languages as the sole mediums of instruction and, in this process, perpetuate linguistic neocolonialism and imperialism and the nation-state ideology inherited from former colonial powers (Phillipson, 1992). It seems that in post-colonial Africa, the pendulum has, despite Africa's linguistic diversity, continued to swing in the direction of the inherited ideology of the nation-state and the related ideology of socioeconomic development (Djité, 2008; Kamwangamalu, 2016; Koffi, 2012). The ideology of the nation-state, championed by the eighteenth-century German philosopher Johann Gottfried Herder, is based on the notion of homogeneity: a *Volk* (nation), a culture, a language, a polity must be homogeneous—diversity is unnatural and destructive of the bonds of sentiment that hold a people together (Pagden, 1994). In Herder's vision, a viable polity can only be founded on a national language resistant to the penetration of foreign tongues (Nicolas, 2011; Noyes, 2014). Accordingly, it is noted that linguistic homogeneity is a *sine qua non* for a polity to qualify as a nation, for social and political cohesion demand one language, one metadiscursive order, one voice (Pagden, 1994).

Drawing on the ideology of the nation-state, European colonial powers in Africa embraced monolingualism in a European language as the norm, treated Africa's multilingualism as a problem, and considered African languages as inadequate for advanced learning and socioeconomic development (Bamgbose, 2000). The related ideology, the ideology of socioeconomic development, is the belief, by the metropole and African elites who came into power when colonialism ended, that development in all its forms (economic, political, social) is possible only through the medium of a European language (Kamwangamalu, 2018; Newton, 1972; Weinstein, 1990). This paper explores why in post-colonial Africa, the inherited monolingual model favouring European languages as the sole medium of instruction in school persists. It does so in light of theoretical developments in language economics (Grin, Sfreddo, & Vaillancourt, 2010) and critical theory (Bourdieu, 1991; Tollefson, 2006, 2013), especially Bourdieu's notions of *habitus* and *capital*. I argue that these theoretical frameworks not only shed light on why inherited colonial language policies persist, but also offer a lens through which this issue of the medium of instruction can be resolved for the benefit of former colonial languages as well as of Africa's indigenous languages. But, first, I provide the background to language planning and practice in education in Africa, with the focus on language and nationalism and the related two ideologies—the ideology of the nation-state and the ideology of socioeconomic development—that have informed language policy decision-making in the continent since the colonial era to the present. Next, I briefly describe the theoretical frameworks just mentioned—language economics and critical theory—for they offer the theoretical underpinnings against which the issue of the medium of instruction in African education can be understood better. Drawing on these frameworks, and following Haarmann (1990) and Kamwangamalu (2016), I propose, in the next and last section, *prestige planning* for African languages so that they become, like former colonial languages, a viable medium of instruction in the continent's educational systems.

Essentially, prestige planning is concerned with raising the prestige of any given language so that members of the target speech community develop a positive attitude towards it. I argue that negative attitudes towards African languages as the medium of instruction in school might change if an education through the medium of these languages were associated with positive economic outcomes, such as access to employment. Finally, I offer a case study showing how the proposed framework of prestige planning can be implemented in Africa, for the issue of implementation was raised at the workshop out of which this paper has evolved. Successful case studies of prestige planning in various parts of the world are also presented in support of the proposed prestige planning framework for Africa's indigenous languages.

Nationalism and language policies and practices in colonial and post-colonial Africa

Determining the relationship between language and nationalism has been a thorny issue in Africa since the continent liberated itself from colonial rule in the late 1950s. Nationalism, says Paulston (2003), is a complex and dynamic phenomenon; that is why some scholars, such as Shafer (1972), say it is impossible to fit nationalism into a short definition. Accordingly, Paulston (2003) remarks that nationalism is best understood in terms of its salient features, which she lists as including "group cohesion, the goal of political self-determination, stubborn or terminal loyalty, territory, and a perceived threat of opposing forces" (p. 403).

Taken together, these features represent what Hans Kohn (1944, cited in Paulston, 2003, p. 403) calls "open nationalism" in contrast with "closed nationalism". The former is territorially based, hence "geographic nationalism"; as opposed to the latter, which is ethnically based, hence "ethnic nationalism".

According to Kohn (1944), language figures prominently in ethnic nationalism, but it is not necessarily the prime symbol of the nation in geographic nationalism. It is worth noting, however, that in colonial and post-colonial Africa, language has been central in both geographic and ethnic nationalism. Colonial authorities, for example, imposed their languages in all higher domains (including education) to secure control over the territories they colonized, but they simultaneously used ethnic languages to sow divisions and rivalries among ethnic groups to prevent them from cohering and creating a united front against colonialism. The most recent example is the then apartheid South Africa, where the apartheid government imposed Afrikaans as one of the two official languages of the state (besides English); at the same time, however, the apartheid government used ethnic languages such as Zulu, Xhosa, and Sotho to create rival, language-based territories, which came to be known as ethnic homelands (Kamwangamalu, 2009, 2018). There was, for example, a Zulu ethnic homeland for Zulu speakers, a Venda ethnic homeland for Venda speakers, a Xhosa homeland for Xhosa speakers, etc.

Geographic nationalism involving a former colonial language has been at the heart of the nation-state ideology in both colonial and post-colonial Africa. Soon after the European powers partitioned Africa, they were confronted with the question of what to do with the languages spoken by the people they had colonized. In response, the European powers all invariably used the ideology of the nation-state, which was popular in nineteenth-century Europe, to impose monolingualism in their respective languages in the conquered territories. For colonial authorities, monolingualism was necessary because by definition, the ideology of the nation-state requires unitary symbols, among them one nation, one language, one culture, to list just a few.

If for the colonial authorities the question was what to do with the languages of the colonized people, for the elites who took power when colonialism ended the question was what to do with the languages that the colonial authorities left behind. Inspired by the ideology of the nation-state, post-colonial African leaders opted for the continual use of former colonial languages as the sole official languages in their respective independent nations. The literature justifies retention of inherited colonial language policies as follows:

- to avoid ethno-linguistic conflicts in Africa's multilingual polities, since choosing one African language as the medium of instruction would anger those whose languages were not selected (Newton, 1972);
- to promote national unity because a former colonial language is ethnically neutral for it does not belong to or privilege any specific indigenous ethnic group, and, therefore, presumably (dis)advantages everyone equally, both socioeconomically and politically (Weinstein, 1990); and

- to use the language of wider communication for literacy and national socio-economic development because African languages apparently lack higher literacy forms and linguistic complexity that European languages have (Revel, 1988; Spencer, 1985).

Taken together, the three arguments have all the marks of the ideology of the nation-state, as already defined, as well as of the related ideology, the ideology of socioeconomic development. The two ideologies portray linguistic diversity or multilingualism as a threat to nation-building and "a social deficiency that causes social and economic backwardness" (Wiley, 2006, p. 143), whereas unilingualism, especially in a former colonial language, is seen as the key to socioeconomic development. Language policies framed within the "multilingualism as a problem" paradigm are usually aimed at eliminating the source of the problem, that is, "eradicate multilingualism and replace it with monolingualism" (Strauss, 1996, p. 6). African leaders have attempted to eradicate multilingualism by theoretically or constitutionally according national or official status to selected indigenous languages, as was the case for Chichewa, the national language in Malawi, or for the nine official African languages in South Africa. At the same time, however, the leaders have covertly ensured that those languages do not enjoy significant use in higher domains such as education, the parliament, government and administration, or in the operation of the economy.

The ideology of the nation-state and the ideology of socioeconomic development continue to impact language policy decision-making in Africa, as evident from language practices in education in the continent. Here, African languages are used as the medium of instruction only in the first three years of elementary school, after which former colonial languages take over as instructional mediums for the remainder of the educational system, including primary, secondary, and tertiary education (Djité, 2008; Koffi, 2012). In this regard, in a comment on English-medium education in Uganda, Kwesiga (1994) remarks sarcastically that African mothers who have knowledge of this much-sought-after language start teaching their children English before they are born.

As Fishman (1996) remarks on the relationship between colonial powers and their former colonies, it seems that "although the lowering of one flag and the raising of another may indicate the end of colonial status, these acts do not necessarily indicate the end of imperialist privilege in neo-colonial disguise" (p. 5). In other words, "while the engine of colonialism long ago ran out of steam [in Africa], the momentum of its languages remains formidable, and it is against their tyranny that smaller languages fight to survive" (Master, 1998, p. 717). The prominence of former colonial languages in the higher domains has contributed to negative attitudes among the populace towards the use of indigenous languages as the medium of instruction in school. In the next section, I draw on theoretical developments in language economics and critical theory to explain the persistence of inherited colonial language policies and, with them, the dominance of former colonial languages in education in post-colonial Africa.

Persistence of colonial language policies in education— insights from language economics and critical theory

The majority of African countries became independent nations in the early 1960s. The move from colonialism to independence was a massive social change, the aftermath of which can be explained in terms of Cooper's (1989) functionalist theory of social change. The theory contends that all parts of a system are inter-related, such that changes in any part of the system ripple throughout the system, causing changes in other parts. Therefore, it was expected that in Africa, the change from colonialism to political independence would trigger changes not only in politics but also in other institutions of the state, including education (Alexander, 1999). The literature shows, however, that not much has changed with respect to the status of African languages in education and such related formal domains as the government and administration, the economy, the media, and so on (Alexander, 2009; Bamgbose, 2000; Kamwangamalu, 2013a, 2013b; Mchombo, 2014).

The official language in developed nations, observe Laitin and Ramachandran (2016), is typically one which is spoken and used widely by a majority of the population. However, in developing countries in Africa (and elsewhere), the official language is often one that is neither indigenous nor spoken by citizens outside of an elite minority. Also, even when widely spoken African languages are recognized as official languages, they are not allowed extended use in formal domains such as education, for example, where their use is restricted to only the first three years of elementary school, as noted earlier (Djité, 2008; Koffi, 2012). Along these lines, Djité (2008) remarks that the language policies of African countries generally prioritize communication with the outside world, chiefly the former metropoles, and thus favour a small elite class that has access to and use these languages to serve their own interests. Vigouroux and Mufwene (2020) concur, noting that language policies of most African states have actually marginalized from local politics and lucrative economic activities the vast majority of citizens who do not command them.

The literature on language policy and planning in post-colonial Africa has, over the years, attempted to explain why inherited colonial language policies, which favour former colonial languages over African languages as instructional mediums, have persisted in the continent (Newton, 1972; Revel, 1988; Weinstein, 1990). The focus of such literature has mostly been on Africa's linguistic diversity, which it portrays as a problem. In particular, the argument portraying multilingualism as a problem is often perceived to be twofold.

First, there are too many languages simultaneously with limited resources, such that governments cannot afford to provide children with an education in their respective languages. The cost-related arguments to explain monolingualism underlying the "language as a problem paradigm" (Ruiz, 1988), notes Strauss (1996), appear to be fundamentally reductionist and to have all the characteristics of the nation-state ideology (p. 4), as previously described. Actually, there is evidence that post-colonial nations in Africa and elsewhere incur more costs in retaining former colonial languages than promoting indigenous languages as the medium of instruction in school. For example, as cited in Djité (2008, p. 67), Vaillancourt and Grin (2000) remarked, very much to the point, that it costs more to train teachers to use a language in which they are not proficient—a former colonial language—than to train teachers to teach through the language(s) they know and speak well—an African vernacular. Laitin and Ramachandran (2016) explain the costs in terms of the distance from and the exposure to the official language. They highlight the importance of both the distance from and exposure to the official language in determining learning outcomes and consequently, the growth and development of nation-states. More specifically, Laitin and Ramachandran theorize that the official language, by acting as a gatekeeper for access to education, jobs, and elite political networks, imposes costs of participation due to its linguistic distance from popular speech and due as well to the low exposure people have to that official language in everyday life. In other words, the official language's greater linguistic distance from everyday speech, together with people's lower exposure to it in daily life, result in increased learning costs and consequently reduces the level of human capital in society. Using data from 11 African countries where English serves as the medium of instruction, the authors show that exposure to English at home is a significant factor in explaining student performance. This is probably why in sub-Saharan Anglophone Africa, highly educated parents, for example, tend to encourage their children to speak English at home, a domain traditionally reserved for indigenous languages (de Klerk, 2000).

The second argument portraying multilingualism as a problem is that the promotion of any indigenous language for official use often elicits opposition from the elites of those languages not chosen. It seems, as Lo Bianco (1996) remarked, that issues relating to multilingualism "are understood and framed in relation to obstacles they present to institutions or more generally to social cohesion" (p. 7). Also, there is evidence that even when social cohesion is not at stake, policy makers generally resist language policies calling for the use of indigenous languages in formal domains such as the educational system, the government and administration, and so on. A case in point is the objection by legislators in Nigeria to the proposal that Yoruba, one of Nigeria's national languages, be used as the language of debate in the House of Assembly (Bamgbose, 2001). Bamgbose points out that the legislators rejected the proposal despite the fact that about 90% of them speak Yoruba as mother tongue. The legislators themselves explain that they rejected Yoruba because "[the use of Yoruba in the House of Assembly] *is capable of demeaning and reducing the intellectual capacity of legislators* [emphasis added]" (Bamgbose, 2001, p. 190). As I have noted elsewhere (Kamwangamalu, 2016), the contempt for Yoruba and the indigenous languages amongst the legislators is illustrated by their assigning of official roles to those languages—a procedure intended to suggest an equal status with former colonial languages, while simultaneously not allowing the languages to be used, and the majority of their speakers to participate, in the conduct of the business of the state. In the next section, I argue that theoretical developments in critical theory and language economics offer better insights into why inherited colonial language policies and practices persist in higher domains, including education, in post-colonial Africa.

Critical theory and language economics

Tollefson (1991, 2006) describes critical language policy as an approach to language planning that investigates the processes by which systems of inequality are created and sustained through language. The goal of critical linguistics is (i) to describe and explain hegemonic practices, which Gramsci (1988) defines as institutional practices that ensure that power remains in the hands of the few, (ii) to understand how dominant social groups use language for establishing and maintaining social hierarchies, and (iii) to investigate ways to alter those hierarchies (Tollefson, 1991). Along these lines, Bourdieu (1991) says that all human actions take place within social fields, that is, areas of struggle for institutional resources and forms of privilege and power. He notes that the individuals who participate in this struggle, Bourdieu calls them "agents", have a set of dispositions or *habitus*, which incline them to act and react in certain ways in a given linguistic market (p. 32). In Bourdieu's work, the concept of *linguistic market* refers to the fact that language use indexes of social, political, and economic inequality and that different variants of a language do not enjoy the same degree of prestige in a given place at a given time. The choices that individuals make about which language to use in a given market is informed by the economic value with which a language is associated since some languages are valued more highly than others.

Bourdieu's approach to language practices is in agreement with developments in language economics, a field of study whose focus is on the interplay between linguistic and economic variables. Briefly, language economics is concerned with the relevance of language as a commodity in the acquisition of which individual actors may have good reason to invest and considers language learning as a social investment that yields benefits for the investors (Grin, 2001, p. 66). It follows that it is extremely important to understand the interplay between linguistic and economic variables, especially in the African context, for this understanding sheds light on why there is so much demand for foreign language skills in Africa's labour market, but virtually no comparable demand for African languages. Thus, it is not surprising that African parents, for example, prefer an education through the medium of a former colonial language over an education through the medium of their own native languages. This is because an education through the medium of a former colonial language enhances individuals' socioeconomic status and prestige, while an education through the medium of an indigenous language does not. I, accordingly, argue that, for African parents to accept an education through the medium of an indigenous language for their children, education must, like an education through the medium of a former colonial language, be associated with positive economic outcomes. As Vaillancourt (1996) remarks, "individuals invest in language skills for their children or themselves according to the benefits and costs associated with these investments" (p. 81). Drawing on Haarmann (1990) and Kamwangamalu (2016), this paper proposes prestige planning for African languages to make these languages an economically viable medium of instruction in Africa's educational systems.

The ideas presented in the foregoing discussion are useful in two significant ways. One, they offer the lens through which we can understand why African parents favour former colonial languages over African languages as the medium of instruction in the educational systems. Two, with this understanding, we can explore ways in which former colonial languages and African languages can coexist productively in education for the benefit of all rather than a select few, the elite.

Prestige planning for Africa's indigenous languages

The African continent does not have a history of successful prestige planning for its indigenous languages. There are, however, the cases of Somali in Somalia, Amharic in Ethiopia, kiSwahili in Tanzania, Ile Ife in Nigeria, and Afrikaans in South Africa that African scholars often reference as success stories (Alidou, 2006; Bamgbose, 2007; Batibo, 2001). These cases are successful insofar as they demonstrate that children learn better when they are taught through the medium of a familiar language, which may or may not necessarily be their mother tongue or primary language, rather than through the medium of a foreign language. From the perspective of the prestige planning framework I am proposing, the success of these case studies, except of Afrikaans in South Africa, is a limited one, for the economic returns derived from an education through the medium of either of the languages (Amharic, kiSwahili, Somali) are comparatively lower than those derived from an education through the medium of a former colonial language, be it English, French, Portuguese, or Spanish.

Prestige planning for African languages has, in general, consisted only in giving official recognition to selected indigenous languages to symbolically bring them to equality with former colonial languages. The latest example is post-apartheid South Africa, where the government has adopted 11 languages including English and Afrikaans, and nine other African languages as official languages of the state. Scholars are in agreement, however, that no official South African indigenous language (e.g. Zulu, Sotho, Xhosa) has the same socioeconomic status as English or Afrikaans, which were previously the only two official languages of the then apartheid state (Kamwangamalu, 2003, 2001). Success in language planning, says Ager (2005), is about "succeeding in influencing language behavior" (p. 1039). In the African context, this entails changing the negative attitudes that the populations have had, since the colonial era to the present, towards indigenous languages as the medium of instruction in school. It is worth emphasizing that these ingrained negative attitudes might change if an education through the medium of indigenous languages were associated with positive economic outcomes, such as access to employment. I propose prestige planning undergirded by language economics and critical theory, as already described, to promote use of African languages in education. The central assumption of this proposal is concerned with promoting African languages in the educational system as first and foremost an economic or marketing problem in the sense that, unlike former colonial languages, knowledge of African languages does not provide adequate compensation in the formal labour market. For a legislation designed to elevate the status of indigenous languages in education to succeed, it must meet at least two intertwined conditions.

First, the legislation must simultaneously create a market or demand for these languages in Africa's linguistic marketplace. This entails associating an education through the medium of these languages with economic returns and raising awareness of their value in the formal labour market. Put differently, individuals who are interested in learning or being schooled through the medium of an African language must know what that education will do for them in terms of upward social mobility. Would it, for instance, be as rewarding as an education through the medium of a former colonial language? What benefits, as Grin (2005) asks, would individuals actually reap, particularly in the labour market, because of their academic skills in an indigenous language? I argue that the response to these questions lies in the relationship between language and economic returns. This explains why, as Grin (1999) observes, "people learn certain languages and why, if they have the choice of using more than one, they prefer to use one or the other" (p. 16). As economists would say, individuals respond to incentives and seek to acquire those language skills whose expected financial benefits exceed their expected costs (Bloom & Grenier, 1996, pp. 46–47).

The second condition that a legislation promoting use of indigenous languages in education must meet is this: certified skills or knowledge, that is, school-acquired knowledge of African languages must become one of the criteria for access to employment in the public and private sector, much as is the case for skills in any former colonial language. In the proposed prestige planning framework, indigenous languages are seen as potential cash cows and as a commodity to which the market assigns a value. To view language as a commodity is, as Pennycook (2008) notes, "to view language in instrumental, pragmatic and commercial terms, which is precisely the dominant discourse on language in many contemporary contexts" (p. xii). Thus, at the core of the proposed prestige planning framework is "linguistic instrumentalism", which Wee (2003) describes as, "a view of language that justifies its existence in a community in terms of its usefulness in achieving specific utilitarian goals, such as access to economic development or social mobility" (p. 211).

Prestige planning for African languages—a critique

As one would expect, the framework of prestige planning being proposed in this study has its critics. The main critique, made at the workshop out of which this paper has evolved, concerns the implementation of the proposed framework. One workshop participant, for example, referred to the framework as "wishful thinking". Accordingly, the status quo must prevail. In other words, the continual use of former colonial languages in African education must remain the norm. Such a perspective must be challenged, for no single former colonial power, let alone any European country for that matter, uses a language for instruction or any official purposes that is not spoken by the majority of its population. The Germans, the British, the Portuguese, and the French are schooled through the medium of their respective national languages: German, English, Portuguese, French. Likewise, other European countries, such as Poland, Czech Republic, Netherlands, Austria, to list a few, use their respective languages—Polish, Czech, Dutch, German—in all formal domains, including education. Also, European languages have been used in African education and other formal domains for nearly two hundred years; yet, illiteracy rates in the continent remain high. As Laitin and Ramachandran (2016) and Djité (2008) point out, more than 80–90% of the population in most African countries do not speak the official language, and this is especially true for the older generations. Along these lines, the United Nations Educational, Scientific and Cultural Organization (UNESCO, 2014) remarks that Africa has the highest illiteracy rates in the world. It notes that of the 11 countries with the lowest recorded literacy in the world, ten are in Africa. In 1990, for example, there were 138 million illiterate persons in sub-Saharan Africa (UNESCO, 2003). However, recent statistics from the UNESCO Institute for Statistics (2013) show that more than one in three adults in the continent cannot read, 182 million adults are unable to read and write, and 48 million youths (ages 15–24) are illiterate.

Bearing these statistics in mind, Djité (2008) asks, how much longer can Africans wait to become proficient in the official languages of their respective nations? What price must Africans pay to learn the languages of their former colonial masters, languages whose social distribution remains limited and is largely restricted to a minority elite group? Drawing on previous works (e.g. Kamwangamalu, 2009, 2010, 2016), the section that follows offers a case study showing how the proposed prestige planning for Africa's indigenous languages can be implemented in specific settings, with the focus on the Southern African monolingual Kingdom of Swaziland, recently renamed *eSwatini* to avoid persistent confusion with a European country with a similarly sounding name, Switzerland.

The implementation of prestige planning for African languages

Anticipating the concern over the feasibility of the proposed framework of prestige planning for Africa's indigenous languages, Kamwangamalu (2016) offers a set of case studies detailing how the proposed framework of prestige planning can be implemented not only in monolingual nations such as Lesotho and Swaziland in Southern Africa but also in multilingual nations such as Kenya and Tanzania in the east of the continent. For the purpose of the present study, and due to space limitations, I will present only one randomly selected case study: the landlocked Kingdom of Swaziland. Swaziland, a former British colony, became an independent nation in 1968. As already mentioned, the country was recently renamed eSwatini, meaning the land of the Swazis, to distinguish it from Switzerland, a country with which it has often been confused. Swaziland has a population of about two million people speaking only one indigenous language, siSwati, which has the status as a co-official language with English. It must be noted that though the two languages, siSwati and English, have the status as co-official languages, only English is conjoined with employment opportunities: English is seen as a personal asset, as a stepping stone to getting a better job, and as a social status marker (Schmied, 1991, p. 170); it has greater prestige than siSwati both locally and internationally; it is the language of the government and administration and of international communication; it is the language by which an individual's actual or potential socioeconomic standing in the community is measured. It is not surprising, then, that in terms of upward social mobility, the people of Swaziland value English more than their own native language, siSwati (Chisanga & Kamwangamalu, 1997).

The question arises of how the proposed prestige planning framework can be implemented for siSwati so that it, too, can be perceived as an instrument for upward social mobility. What is needed is a legislation that creates a market or demand for siSwati, that is, a legislation that genuinely supports the demand in the labour market for skills in the language. Creating a demand for siSwati (or for any African language for that matter) simply means requiring the language for access to employment in at least the local labour market. As Dominguez (1998) puts it, creating such a market means communicating the benefits that the product, siSwati, carries and persuading the market to buy the produce. The legislation thus created would not only give official recognition to siSwati but also require speakers to have skills in and use of the language in domains such as employment and in the national economy activity in particular. Its central goal is to create an environment where an indigenous African language, siSwati, would be viewed by both its speakers and potential users as a viable complementary medium of instruction in the schools and a commodity in which they would have an interest to invest. This legislation is intended to impact consumer language behaviour. Therefore, it must have a clear agenda aimed at the behaviour to be changed, and it must be communicated to the population through the medium of the target language they understand. Also, a legislation aimed at prestige planning for an indigenous language such as siSwati would have a planned response to the questions raised in Cooper (1989): (i) who plans (ii) what (iii) for whom, (iv) when, (v) where, (vi) how, and (vii) why. Cooper provides a detailed response to these questions, as Koffi (2012, pp. 214–224) does in his discussion of literacy planning in rural sub-Saharan Africa. Therefore, the paragraphs that follow focus on how the proposed prestige planning framework can be implemented for the siSwati language in the context of the monolingual Kingdom of Swaziland. More specifically, in response to the "how" question, the legislation would include the following details:

1   It would explain why it (the legislation) is needed in the first place (e.g. not everyone has access to English-medium education. Therefore, not everyone has access to employment opportunities in the public and private sector. There is a wider gap between those who have access to English, that is, the elite and those who do not, that is, the majority of the population, and promoting siSwati in education and for access to employment would potentially reduce the gap etc.).

2   It would highlight the benefits, for example, access to education, employment, that speakers and potential users of siSwati would accrue by accepting

the language as a complementary medium of instruction in the schools along-side English.

3   It would vest the target language, siSwati, with some of the power and perqui-sites currently associated with English to entice parents to find in the indig-enous language an alternative to English-medium education. For instance, the legislation would require firms and public institutions to provide services in siSwati, as happened for French in Quebec or Gaelic in Scotland (e.g. Walsh, 2006), and it would make academic competence in siSwati one of the requirements (in addition to academic qualifications) for access to employ-ment in both the public and the private sector, much as is currently the case for English.

4   It would make siSwati an integral part of the curriculum both at primary and secondary as well as tertiary education levels. siSwati would, for instance, become the medium of instruction for some subjects (e.g. his-tory, the language subject, home economics, etc.) throughout the education system. Since siSwati is not yet well developed enough to be used for all school subjects, English would be used as an instructional medium for such subjects. In the meantime, siSwati would have to be updated with a scien-tific lexicon as needed to accommodate the twenty-first-century needs, and resources, both human and material, would have to be committed to achieving those needs.

5   It would call on all stakeholders, including firms, governmental institutions, faith-based organizations, schools, language activists, the mass media, com-munity leaders, non-governmental organizations, and so on, to be involved in the dissemination of the legislation (Kamwangamalu, 2016, pp. 176–179).

The literature provides sufficient evidence that language planning and policy activities succeed if they lead to desirable economic outcomes. Vaillancourt (1996), as well as others, has demonstrated that legislators in the province of Que-bec, Canada elevated the socioeconomic status of French by, all else being equal, adopting legislation requiring business firms to provide goods and services in the French language. Similarly, Tollefson (2002) reports on the success of the Mac-edonian language in Macedonia. In particular, he remarks that when the Republic of Macedonia was created within Yugoslavia, the Macedonian language served as the medium of government operations and education. The use of Macedonian in these higher domains guaranteed access to jobs in the administration and schools, and communication industries also enjoyed more clients for their books, newspa-pers, and music.

Fishman (2006) makes a similar comment regarding prestige planning for the Basque language in Spain, pointing to the success of what he calls "Basqueciza-tion activities", that is, activities intended to promote the Basque language in that country. He explains that Basquecization activities were successful because par-ticipation in these activities yielded certification at various levels of competence, entitling their bearers to qualify for promotions, raises, job tenure, and other per-quisites of success in the workplace.

Like Fishman, Giri (2010) explains why speakers of Sino-Tibetan languages in Nepal are attracted to Nepali as the medium of instruction rather than to their own indigenous languages. She says that in Nepal, Nepali and English are status symbols and, increasingly, serve as tools in the hands of the ruling elites who use these languages to create linguistic hegemony within the polity. As a result, speakers of Sino-Tibetan languages choose Nepali as their second language because their own indigenous languages do not have the same value as Nepali in the linguistic marketplace.

Conclusion

In Africa, language-in-education policies and practices continue to be informed by inherited colonial language ideologies, especially the ideology of the nation-state, as espoused by the German philosopher, Johann Gottfried Herder, and the ideology of socioeconomic development, according to which development, in all its forms, is possible only through the medium of a European language, as discussed earlier. Indeed, as Bauman and Briggs (2003) note, Herder believes strongly that a nation must be associated with one language. Linguistic diversity, in Herder's view, is unnatural and destructive of the bonds of sentiment that hold a people together. According to Bauman and Briggs, Herder believes that "it is the possession of its own distinctive language that constitutes the touchstone of a people or *Volk*, the *sine qua non* of its national identity and spirit: 'Only through language can a people exist'" (p. 169). However, despite his championing of linguistic homogeneity, Herder arguably never envisioned one continent colonizing and imposing its languages on another, as happened with Europe's colonization and imposition of its languages in the African continent. On the contrary, Herder was very critical of colonial powers, describing them, in 1797, as presumptuous, intrusive, manipulative monsters who have "destroyed the germs of other people's cultures" (Noyes, 2014, p. 110). Also, it must be noted that in some of his own writings, Herder embraces linguistic diversity. In this regard, Bauman and Briggs (2003) note that:

> Herder's entire understanding of the social organization of language is founded on a recognition of linguistic diversification at every level of integration from the individual to the international. Because of individual differences of experience and learning, no two individuals speak exactly the same language.
>
> (p. 169)

It is against the background of Herder's view of linguistic diversity and of his criticism of colonial powers that this paper has sought to propose an alternative to inherited colonial language ideologies, including the ideology of the nation-state and the ideology of socioeconomic development, both of which have informed Africa's language-in-education policies since colonialism ended 60 years ago to the present. One must ask whether it is pedagogically justified to continue investing only in Western education, or what Coulmas (1992) rightly describes as a "monolingual, elitist system" (p. 149), even if that education, practised for nearly two hundred years, has failed to spread literacy among the populations in the continent (Kamwangamalu, 2009, 2010; Kwesiga, 1994; Mchombo, 2014; UNESCO, 2013, 2014). By not contesting this state of affairs, the populations that are the target of language planning unwittingly endorse the status quo and collude in their own subjugation by the elites; they collaborate, as Bourdieu (1991) puts it, "in the destruction of their instrument of expression" (p. 7)—the indigenous languages. To change the status quo, and drawing on critical theory and language economics, I have proposed prestige planning for African languages if these languages are to become, like inherited colonial languages, an instrument for upward social mobility. For prestige planning to succeed in Africa, the selected African languages must bear economic returns for their users, for the attribution of real value has been the key ingredient for the success of prestige planning elsewhere. Prestige planning envisages associating selected indigenous languages with an economic value in the labour market and requiring academic skills in these languages as one of the criteria for access to employment. In other words, as Alexander (1999, 2009) notes aptly, unless African languages are given a market value, that is, unless their instrumentality for the process of production, exchange, and distribution is enhanced, no amount of policy change at the school level can guarantee their use in high-status functions and, thus, the eventual escape from the dominance and hegemony of inherited colonial languages.

References

Ager, D. (2005). Prestige and image planning. In E. Hinkel (Ed.), *Handbook of research in second language teaching and learning* (pp. 1035–1054). Mahwah, NJ: Lawrence Erlbaum Associates.

Alexander, N. (1999). An African renaissance without African languages? *Social Dynamics, 25*(1), 1–12.

Alexander, N. (2009). Evolving African approaches to the management of linguistic diversity: The ACALAN project. *Language Matters, 40*(2), 3–18.

Alidou, H. (2006). *Use of African languages and literacy: Conditions, factors and processes (Benin, Burkina Faso, Cameroon, Tanzania and Zambia).* Association for the Development of Education in Africa (ADEA). Retrieved June 28, 2015, from www.adeanet.org/adea/biennial-2006/Alpha/vo/PDF/A3_3_hassana_en.pdf

Bamgbose, A. (2000). *Language and exclusion: The consequences of language policies in Africa.* Munster: LIT Verlag.

Bamgbose, A. (2001, August). *Language policy in Nigeria: Challenges, opportunities and constraints* [Keynote address]. Nigerian Millennium Sociolinguistics Conference, University of Lagos, Nigeria.

Bamgbose, A. (2007). Multilingualism and exclusion: Policy, practice and prospects. In P. Cuvalier, T. du Plessis, M. Meeus, & L. Tech (Eds.), *Multilingualism and exclusion* (pp. 1–21). Pretoria: Van Shaik Publishers.

Batibo, H. (2001). *Language decline and death in Africa: Causes, consequences and challenges.* Clevedon: Multilingual Matters.

Bauman, R., & Briggs, C. L. (2003). *Voices of modernity: Language ideologies and the politics of inequality*. Cambridge: Cambridge University Press.

Bloom, D. E., & Grenier, G. (1996). Language, employment, and earnings in the United States: Spanish-English differentials from 1970 to 1990. *International Journal of the Sociology of Language, 121,* 43–68.

Bourdieu, P. (1991). *Language and symbolic power* (J. B. Thompson Ed., G. Raymond & M. Adamson, Trans.). Cambridge: Polity Press.

Chisanga, T., & Kamwangamalu, N. M. (1997). Owning the other tongue: The English language in Southern Africa. *Journal of Multilingual and Multicultural Development, 18*(2), 89–99.

Cooper, R. L. (1989). *Language planning and social change*. Cambridge: Cambridge University Press.

Coulmas, F. (1992). *Language and the economy*. Oxford: Blackwell.

de Klerk, V. (2000). Language shift in Grahamstown: A case study of selected Xhosa speakers. *International Journal of the Sociology of Language, 146,* 87–100.

Djité, P. G. (2008). *The sociolinguistics of development in Africa*. Bristol: Multilingual Matters.

Dominguez, F. (1998). Toward a language-marketing model. *International Journal of the Sociology of Language, 134,* 1–13.

Fishman, J. A. (1996). Introduction: Some empirical and theoretical issues. In J. A. Fishman, A. Conrad, & A. Rubal-Lopez (Eds.), *Post-imperial English: Status change in former British and American colonies, 1940–1990* (pp. 3–12). Berlin: Mouton de Gruyter.

Fishman, J. A. (2006). Language policy and language shift. In T. Ricento (Ed.), *An introduction to language policy: Theory and method* (pp. 311–328). Oxford: Blackwell.

Giri, R. A. (2010). Cultural anarchism: The consequences of privileging languages in Nepal. *Journal of Multilingual and Multicultural Development, 31*(1), 87–100.

Gramsci, A. (1988). *A Gramsci reader: Selected writings* (D. Forgacs, Ed.). London: Lawrence & Wishart.

Grin, F. (1999). Economics. In J. A. Fishman (Ed.), *Handbook of language and ethnic identity* (pp. 9–24). Oxford: Oxford University Press.

Grin, F. (2001). English as economic value: Facts and fallacies. *World Englishes, 20*(1), 65–78.

Grin, F. (2005). The economics of language policy implementation: Identifying and measuring costs. In N. Alexander (Ed.), *Mother tongue-based bilingual education in Southern Africa: The dynamics of implementation* (pp. 11–25). Proceedings of a symposium held at the University of Cape Town, October 16–19, 2003. Cape Town: Volkswagen Foundation & PRAESA.

Grin, F., Sfreddo, C., & Vaillancourt, F. (2010). *The economics of the multilingual workplace*. London: Routledge.

Haarmann, H. (1990). Language planning in the light of a general theory of language: A methodological framework. *International Journal of the Sociology of Language, 86,* 103–126.

Kamwangamalu, N. M. (2001). A linguistic renaissance for an African renaissance: Language policy and planning for African mass development. In E. Maloka & E. Le Roux (Eds.), *Africa in the new millennium* (pp. 131–143). Pretoria: Africa Institute of South Africa.

Kamwangamalu, N. M. (2003). When 2+9=1: English and the politics of language planning in a multilingual society: South Africa. In C. Mair (Ed.), *The politics of English as a world language* (pp. 235–246). New York: Rodopi.

Kamwangamalu, N. M. (2009). Reflections on the language policy balance sheet in Africa. *Language Matters, 40*(2), 133–144.

Kamwangamalu, N. M. (2010). Vernacularization, globalization, and language economics in non-English-speaking countries in Africa. *Language Problems and Language Planning, 34*(1), 1–23.

Kamwangamalu, N. M. (2013a). English in language policy and ideologies in Africa: Challenges and prospects for vernacularization. In R. Bayley, R. Cameron, & C. Lucas (Eds.), *The Oxford handbook of sociolinguistics* (pp. 545–562). Oxford: Oxford University Press.

Kamwangamalu, N. M. (2013b). Effects of policy on English-medium instruction in Africa. *World Englishes, 32*(3), 325–337.

Kamwangamalu, N. M. (2016). *Language policy and economics—the language question in Africa*. London: Palgrave Macmillan.

Kamwangamalu, N. M. (2018). The issue of the medium of instruction in Africa as "an inheritance situation". *Current Issues in Language Planning, 19*(2), 133–135.

Koffi, E. (2012). *Paradigm shift in language planning and policy—Game theoretic solutions*. Berlin: Mouton de Gruyter.

Kohn, H. (1944). *The idea of nationalism: A study of its origins and background*. New York: Palgrave Macmillan.

Kwesiga, J. B. (1994). Literacy and the language question: Brief experiences from Uganda. *Language and Education: An International Journal, 8*(1–2), 57–63.

Laitin, D., & Ramachandran, R. (2016). Language policy and human development. *American Political Science Review, 110*(3), 457–480.

Lo Bianco, J. (1996). *Language as an economic resource: Language planning report 5.1*. Paper presented at a workshop in Pretoria, July 14, 1995. Pretoria: Government of South Africa, Department of Arts, Culture, Science and Technology.

Master, P. (1998). Positive and negative aspects of the dominance of English. *TESOL Quarterly, 32*(4), 716–727.

Mchombo, S. (2014). Language, learning, and education for all in Africa. In Z. Babac-Wilhite (Ed.), *Giving space to African voice* (pp. 21–47). Boston, MA: Sense Publications.

Newton, E. S. (1972). Linguistic pluralism: Third world impediment to universal literacy. *The Journal of Negro Education, 41*(3), 248–254.

Nicolas, R. (2011). The world laid waste: Herder, language labor, empire. *New Literary History, 42*(1), 193–203.

Noyes, J. K. (2014). Herder, postcolonial theory and the antinomy of universal reason. *The Cambridge Journal of Postcolonial Literary Inquiry, 1*, 107–122.

Pagden, A. (1994). Colonialism and the origins of nationalism in Diderot and Herder. In G. Prakash (Ed.), *After colonialism: Imperial histories and postcolonial displacements* (pp. 129–152). Princeton, NJ: Princeton University Press.

Paulston, C. B. (2003). Linguistic minorities and language policies. In C. B. Paulston & G. R. Tucker (Eds.), *Sociolinguistics: The essential readings* (pp. 394–407). Oxford: Blackwell.

Pennycook, A. (2008). Praise for language as commodity: Global structures, local marketplaces. In P. K. W. Kwan & R. Rubdy (Eds.), *Language as commodity: Global structures, local marketplaces* (p. xii). London: Continuum.

Phillipson, R. (1992). *Linguistic imperialism*. Oxford: Oxford University Press.

Revel, J. F. (1988). *La connaissance inutile [Useless knowledge]*. Paris: Grasset.

Ruiz, R. (1988). Orientations in language planning. In S. L. McKay & S. L. C. Wong (Eds.), *Language diversity: Problem or resource?* (pp. 3–25). New York: Newbury House.

Schmied, J. (1991). *English in Africa: An introduction.* London: Longman.

Shafer, B. C. (1972). *Faces of nationalism.* New York: Harcourt Brace Jovanovich.

Spencer, J. (1985). Language and development in Africa: The unequal equation. In N. Wolfson & J. Manes (Eds.), *Language of inequality* (pp. 387–397). Berlin: Mouton de Gruyter.

Strauss, G. (1996). The economics of language: Diversity and development in an information economy. *The Economics of Language: Language Report, 5*(2), 2–27.

Tollefson, J. W. (1991). *Planning language, planning inequality.* London: Longman.

Tollefson, J. W. (2002). The language debates: Preparing for war in Yugoslavia, 1980–1991. *International Journal of the Sociology of Language, 154,* 65–82.

Tollefson, J. W. (2006). Critical theory in language policy. In T. Ricento (Ed.), *An introduction to language policy: Theory and method* (pp. 42–59). Oxford: Blackwell.

Tollefson, J. W. (2013). Language policy in a time of crisis and transformation. In J. W. Tollefson (Ed.), *Language policies in education—critical issues* (2nd ed., pp. 11–34). London: Routledge.

United Nations Educational, Scientific and Cultural Organization (2003). *Education in a multilingual world: UNESCO education position paper.* Retrieved May 25, 2018, from http://unesdoc.unesco.org/images/0012/001297/129728e.pdf

United Nations Educational, Scientific and Cultural Organization (2014). *Adult and youth literacy.* Retrieved from https://unesdoc.unesco.org/ark:/48223/pf0000229504

United Nations Educational, Scientific and Cultural Organization Institute for Statistics (2013). *Adult and youth literacy: National, regional and global trends, 1985–2015.* Retrieved from http://uis.unesco.org/sites/default/files/documents/adult-and-youth-literacy-national-regional-and-global-trends-1985-2015-en_0.pdf

Vaillancourt, F. (1996). Language and socioeconomic status in Quebec: Measurements, findings, determinants, and policy costs. *International Journal of the Sociology of Language, 126,* 69–92.

Vaillancourt, F., & Grin, F. (2000). *The choice of a language of instruction: The economic aspects. Distance learning course on language instruction in basic education.* Washington, DC: World Bank Institute.

Vigouroux, C., & Mufwene, S. (Eds.). (2020). *Bridging linguistics and economics.* Cambridge: Cambridge University Press.

Walsh, J. (2006). Language and socio-economic development: Towards a theoretical framework. *Language Problems & Language Planning, 30*(2), 127–148.

Wee, L. (2003). Linguistic instrumentalism in Singapore. *Journal of Multilingual and Multicultural Development, 24,* 211–224.

Weinstein, B. (Ed.). (1990). *Language policy and political development.* Norwood, NJ: Ablex.

Wiley, T. G. (2006). The lessons of historical investigations: Implications for the study of language policy and planning. In T. Ricento (Ed.), *An introduction to language policy: Theory and method* (pp. 135–152). Oxford: Blackwell.

9   Language and national consciousness in the post-colonial Caribbean

Andrew M. Daily

In the late 1950s, unemployed sugar worker Évariste Suffrin began to preach on street corners around Lamentin and Fort-de-France in the French Overseas Department of Martinique. He distributed self-made tracts and prayers and invited passers-by to visit the temple he had built on a fallow strip of cane field near his Lamentin home. Suffrin's doctrine, which he called the dogma of Cham (*le dogme de Cham*), excerpted and rearranged his eclectic readings in history, religion, and contemporary events and borrowed from doctrines that ranged from Catholicism to Afrocentrism to popular social science writing in order to construct an original symbolic and ritual system. Chamism, Suffrin claimed, was the true science of "universal and eternal renovation", a doctrine that would not only redeem French Antilleans and the Black race, but all humanity in a "better tomorrow" (Glissant, 1973a, p. 88).

That we know about Suffrin and Chamism, that Suffrin entered the archives at all, is thanks to the Martinican novelist and philosopher Édouard Glissant, who visited Suffrin's temple in the late 1960s and collected his writings, filmed and recorded his rituals, and met with him for long conversations about his doctrine. While most Antilleans dismissed Suffrin as a crank and a charlatan, in Suffrin's *dogme* Glissant discerned an original interpretation of the Antillean situation and a unique cultural vision that resisted French colonialism. But his dogma also teetered on the edge of madness and offered a case study in how colonial traumas created challenges to constructing a national consciousness. For Glissant, the "Suffrin case" illustrated the difficulties Antilleans would face in articulating a disalienated and decolonized self and underlined how colonialism, language, and subjectivity were deeply intertwined.

Scholars have produced a sophisticated literature that analyses the entanglements of language and colonial power. From the initial moment of encounter, language proved another territory to be conquered and contested. Mastery of indigenous languages and literatures facilitated the expansion of commercial trade networks and later the colonial state. Colonial linguists studied and standardized indigenous languages according to the strictures of colonial science, while cadastral surveys renamed and reorganized colonized space. Sacred languages were secularized and trade tongues formalized. Administrators constrained the practice of some indigenous languages while encouraging the expansion of others and built school systems that disseminated colonial languages as the medium for education and knowledge. Throughout the colonial encounter, language proved a key site for constructing colonial power and for contestation and resistance.[1]

As anti-colonial movements gained followers and strength in the first decades of the twentieth century, language emerged as another front in the struggle against the colonial state. Mastery of language had facilitated the establishment and expansion of colonial power, so inevitably control of language, too, emerged as part of the struggle between colonizer and colonized. Anti-colonial approaches to language focused on three main areas of intervention: the divide between elite and popular language; the choice of a post-colonial national language; and language and its place in national culture. Anti-colonial elites, educated in colonial schools and therefore in the colonizer's language, recognized that anti-colonial writing and organizing, often conducted in French, English, Dutch, and so on, created a gulf between elites and the colonized masses, who by and large spoke only indigenous languages. To build mass-based anti-colonial movements required going to the people and addressing them in their language(s). This multiplicity of languages presented a second problem: how to determine a national language post-independence. Here nationalists were divided. Some advocated a single official post-colonial language; others were comfortable with recognizing the linguistic multiplicity of their new nations; and still others advocated retaining the colonizer's language as a national lingua franca to unite polyglot and multiethnic polities. But what language could serve as the language of post-colonial national culture? If language was the carrier and disseminator of national culture—and therefore national identity—which language expressed the nation and contained and preserved the people?[2]

The Kenyan writer Ngũgĩ wa Thiong'o (1986) presented an influential account of language and decolonization in the lectures collected in his book, *Decolonising the Mind*. For Ngũgĩ, language possessed a "dual character: it is both a mean of communication and a carrier of culture" (p. 13). On the one hand, language is "the language of real life" (p. 13), a reflection of the social relations between individuals and the means by which they communicate with each other. It is, simply, the language of the people and their community. On the other hand, he argued, language was synonymous with culture. It was the "set of spiritual eyeglasses" (p. 14), the "collective memory bank of a people's experience in history" (p. 15) that transmitted the "moral, ethical and aesthetic values" (p. 14) that defined a people as a people. In other words, language was not simply a means of communication or transmission, but carried, encrusted within its structures, rhythms, sayings, and idioms, a people's essential culture.

> Language carries culture, and culture carries, particularly through orature and literature, the entire body of values by which we come to perceive ourselves and our place in the world. . . . Language is thus inseparable from ourselves as a community of human beings with a specific form and character, a specific history, a specific relationship to the world.
>
> (p. 16)

Language possessed an almost mystic character as a medium and archive that preserved, despite colonial depredations, the history and culture of a people. To decolonize fully, therefore, Africans had to abandon the colonizer's language. In Ngũgĩ's account, a people, their culture, and their nation were intimately bound up in language.

Herder, language, and anti-colonialism

Ngũgĩ's (1986) linguistic theory echoed, or perhaps reflected, the enduring influence of romantic nationalism and in particular the influence of the Herderian model of national language and nation. Johann Gottfried Herder's work, written in response to both the hegemony of French culture and the scientism of Enlightenment theories of language, constitutes an influential and still bitterly debated corpus of ideas about the links between language and peoples. Often dismissed as the intellectual progenitor of *völkisch* German nationalism (and, as such, part of the special path [*sonderweg*] that led to Nazism), recent scholarship has underlined his thought's humanistic, cosmopolitan, and anti-imperialist elements.[3] Despite varying interpretations of his legacy, at its core Herder proposed a causal bond between language and nation. For Herder, national language (*nationalsprache*) served as "the 'preserve' or 'receptacle' for the 'entire collection of a people's thoughts'" (Benes, 2008, pp. 44–45). In his *Treatise on the Origins of Language* (1772), *Ideas on the Philosophy of the History of Mankind* (1784–91), and other writings, Herder understood language as the repository of national identity, as the means by which national character, culture, genius, and civilization [*bildung*] were preserved and transmitted from generation to generation. Each people possessed a language proper to them, shaped organically through its interactions with its landscape and reflecting its history. To lose contact or fluency with this language threatened to dissolve a people as a people (Herder, 2002, pp. 139–164; Herder, 2004, pp. 104–120). Imperialism and colonialism, Herder argued, constituted severe threats to this natural harmony. "What, generally, is a foisted, foreign culture, a formation [*bildung*] that does not develop out of [a people's] own dispositions and needs? It oppresses and deforms, or else it plunges straight into the abyss" (Herder, 2002, p. 382). To restore themselves and their culture, peoples had to discard imposed or exterior languages and recover their own speech.

Herder's philosophy of language and culture formed a powerful framework for both thinking about the linguistic relationship between the colonizer and the colonized and for constructing post-colonial national cultures. Recent scholarship reads Herder as an important philosophical source for anti-colonial thought and a forerunner of post-colonial cosmopolitanism. Barnard (2004) defends Herder from those who simply reduced him to a *völkisch* nationalist and writes at length about Herder's affinities with Heine, Rousseau, and others, framing his thinking as a precursor to debates about cultural globalization. Significantly, Barnard starts his book with a discussion of Herder's writing about Jewish history and culture. Barnard argues that Herder saw Jews as "a nation par excellence" (p. 19) and derived many of his principles of the organic nation from his studies of Hebrew poetry and the "Mosaic constitution" (p. 21). Barnard notes how Herder linked land, law, and people, writing:

> Moses bound the hearts of his people to their native soil and made them look throughout their dispersal upon Palestine as their true homeland. "The Land belonged to the Law, and the Law belonged to the Land of Jehovah". Hence, however dispersed and distant from its shores, the eyes and hopes of the Jewish people did not cease being focused on their ancient land, a nostalgic focus that helped them retain their identity.
>
> (pp. 20–21)

Here in gestate form is Herder's mature theory of a people and its organic *bildung*. Far from a proto-Nazi, Barnard instead suggests affinities between Herder's writing about the Jewish condition in eighteenth-century Germany and the later writings of Theodor Herzl (pp. 25–26).

Noyes (2015) casts Herder as an early critic of colonialism and imperialism. Engaging directly with Herder's work on colonialism and empire, he traces not only Herder's specific criticisms of Europe's rapacious imperialism, but identifies Herder's philosophical contribution to critiques of empire, what Noyes calls his "antinomy of universal reason" (pp. 301–302). Herder, Noyes asserts, argued that

> [r]eason exists only in the plural, and the plurality of reason ensures that life will be cognized in countless different ways. The diversity of reason follows the diversity of languages, sociolects, idiolects, cultural communities, and individuals. Herder speaks of "the human paths" to reason in the plural.
>
> (Noyes, 2015, p. 301)

In Noyes's reading, Herder rejected European claims to possess universal reason and premised his philosophy of language and nation on the contention that all peoples possessed reason but expressed universal human reason in forms determined by their linguistic and cultural contexts. For Noyes, Herder's epistemology thus foreshadows debates in post-colonial and post-structuralist theory.

Barnard (2004) and Noyes (2015) convincingly argue that Herder should be rescued from the nationalist box into which many condemned him. And they further demonstrate that Herder's thought speaks to contemporary debates about nation, language, reason, and cosmopolitanism. Nonetheless they both pass over certain troubling implications of Herder's thinking, his thinking about diasporic Jewry in particular and diasporic peoples in general, implications that bear on Herder's potential contribution to post-colonial theory. They fail to interrogate the implications of Herder's linking a nation's *bildung* to its geography, or in other words, the privileged role that Herder accorded place in the emergence and development of a nation's particular language and culture. Herder's writings about language, nation, reason, and empire presume that peoples are sedentary and topographically fixed, and as such he had little to say about peoples set in motion. For Herder, exile and diaspora cannot create new cultures and languages but only destroy and contaminate their organic unity.

Creolizing the national concept

Put simply, the Herderian model of culture and nation presents distinct problems for diasporic peoples. Arguments that Herder eschewed cultural chauvinism and opposed European empire are compelling, but it remains equally true that his cultural monadism left little room for diasporic linguistic and cultural forms. Herder, for example, argued that while Hebrew poetry and culture had once been great, Jewish culture became *unsittlich* (demoralized or degenerated) when Jews were displaced from their geographical homeland (cited in Grossman, 1994, p. 64). If a nation's *bildung* is closely related to its geographical homeland, how do peoples defined by displacement, exile, hybridization, and cultural mixing construct a nation? Which cultural practices do they embrace and which do they discard? What language(s) do they speak? How do they define their relationship to the myriad cultures that combined in their making? Do they choose one culture and discard the others? Caribbean cultural and political nationalisms grappled, and not always easily, with these conundrums. Deciding which language and culture on which to construct a post-colonial national culture divided nationalists throughout the colonial period and remained a vexing question in decolonization's wake. Most intellectuals and nationalist movements settled on a sort of Herderian faith in creolization itself and attempted to build post-colonial nationalisms on a creole base with mixed and often uneasy results.[4] The Herderian model and the romantic nationalisms it inspired fit poorly in Caribbean cultural and political space.

How to found a Caribbean identity preoccupied Édouard Glissant in the 1960s and 1970s. In his activism with the Front Antillo-Guyanais pour l'autonomie (FAGA), his intellectual and pedagogical work at the Institut Martiniquais d'Etudes (IME), and in his novels, plays, and essays, Glissant diagnosed the Caribbean paradox: Caribbean peoples required a cultural nationalism to break metropolitan political and cultural hegemony, but due to their particular histories they lacked a clear cultural base upon which to construct a cultural identity and attendant political subjectivity. The problem, Glissant (1989) argued, was that Caribbeans lacked a "cultural hinterland" (*arrière-pays culturel*) (p. 63), which he defined as the "ancestral community of language, religion, government, traditional values—in brief, a worldview—[that] allowed these peoples, each in its own way to offer continuous, open resistance" (pp. 62–63). In a hinterland, colonized peoples preserved their pre-colonial world and could draw on it to resist colonialism and, in the moment of decolonization, build a decolonial future.[5] However, unlike Algerians or Indians or Senegalese, Caribbean and New World peoples did not possess or have access to a distinct cultural hinterland. The pre-colonial Arawak languages of the Caribbean were largely extinct, and in any case, the dominant population—the Black descendants of enslaved peoples—had no historical relationship to Arawak. Nor did they have a clear relationship to African languages. Enslaved peoples came from many regions and cultures of Africa, and while most enslaved people in the French Caribbean originated in the Senegambia region, African languages were also practically extinct. Finally, Antilleans could also claim East Asian, Indian, Levantine, and European cultural ancestry. What language should Antilleans draw from to articulate or develop a national and cultural identity? Caribbeans were creolized peoples, formed from populations and cultures that included Africa, Europe, America, and Asia. And the realities of the Middle Passage and subsequent labour migrations cut most Caribbeans off from their pre-colonial cultures. Such a state of affairs, Glissant suggested, left them particularly subject to metropolitan cultural hegemony and made constructing a post-colonial culture and subjectivity a difficult task.[6]

Historically, intellectuals had offered two solutions to the Antillean situation. The first, articulated by Aimé Césaire, Léon Gontran Damas, and other négritude writers, was to continue to write in French, but to rediscover their négritude through an archaeology of the African elements present in their cultures. French remained the medium, but in form and subject, they rejected Frenchness for new modes of expression informed by Africanness and Blackness. A second approach, consistent with the Herderian model of the nation as well as Ngũgĩ's proposal for post-colonial African literatures, argued that Antillean writers should abandon French for Creole. In this interpretation, Creole was the "mother tongue" for Antilleans, as well as the only "indigenous" language they possessed, one that reflected their polyglot and multicultural origins.[7] While the two positions differed over the status of Creole, both believed that access to a Caribbean hinterland was a relatively linear process of cultural and linguistic recovery.

Glissant's critique of the Creolist position was straightforward and rooted in the realities of the language itself. To begin, Creole was itself a colonial language, produced in the colonial encounter. Further, it was an oral language and to codify it as a written language risked destroying what made it Creole. Third, adopting Creole would not smooth the communication between Caribbean peoples. While French-based Creoles were spoken across the Caribbean, differences in local dialect made French Creole more a family of languages than a common tongue. Moreover, the Anglophone and Hispanophone Caribbean spoke entirely separate Creoles. Glissant (1971c) further argued that adopting Creole risked the exoticization and "folklorization" (p. 59) of Antillean cultural expression, in which living cultures are ossified as part of state-sanctioned cultural heritage projects. And finally, privileging Creole risked isolating Antilleans from the wider Americas and the world. Creole language, he argued, did not in the final analysis provide the cultural hinterland required to resist colonization.[8]

His critique of the négritude position was rooted in research that Glissant and his colleagues carried out at the IME, a research institute and secondary school that Glissant established in 1967 to develop "a non-parodic Martinican culture" (1971d, p. 136) and to "enlarge consciousness about the Caribbean milieu" (1971d, p. 137). He hoped the IME would combat Antilleans' ignorance of their own history and culture, as well as combat the cultural annihilation wrought by French assimilationist ideology. To this end, Glissant recruited researchers and activists from across the Caribbean to research Caribbean culture and to teach their research to young Antilleans. The Institute's historical and ethnographic work demonstrated that it was much more difficult to recover pre-colonial culture than the négritude writers had suggested. Césaire, Damas, and the others who wrote for the 1940s journal *Tropiques* also had turned to ethnographic techniques to recover the non-French elements of their culture. Their thesis was that despite European colonization and cultural and linguistic creolization, Black Antillean culture at its essential core remained African. The task was a hermeneutic one, to articulate a method to reread Antillean folktales, songs, dance, and mores for their African elements. Césaire and Ménil's (1942) analysis of the Creole folktale "Conte de Yé" was typical of négritude's hermeneutics. Césaire and Ménil situated the tale as expressive of African culture, linking the tale of Yé to African tales and characters and to African beliefs like the *zombi*.[9] Négritude's approach to cultural nationalism was consistent with Herder's theses about culture and nation. The forms and beliefs of African culture, despite enslavement and colonization, survived in Antilleans' popular cultural forms. To renew Antillean culture required breaking with France and excavating the Africanist cultural past.[10]

Roland Suvélor (1971), a researcher at the IME, used the "Conte de Yé" to articulate a competing interpretation of Antillean culture, an articulation that troubled the négritude intellectuals' transparent analogy between folklore and national consciousness. His study contested the romanticization of creole folklore and language by both metropolitans and Martinicans, and instead centred on how the slave trade, slavery, racism, and colonialism reshaped the stories Antilleans told and the mentalities those stories expressed (pp. 22–24). Suvélor grounded his study of the "Conte de Yé" in academic discussions of folklore and in Glissant's theses on Antillean psychosocial structures.[11] He argued that two qualities defined Martinican folklore when compared to other folkloric traditions: First, it was formed from the violent experience of deportation and enslavement such that Martinican folklore, like Guadeloupean, Guianese, and other New World cultures, hybridized African and European elements; and second, the formal and subjective qualities of Martinican stories reflected what he called "acculturation" and "deculturation" (p. 28), a dialectical process constantly in transformation. The encounter between Africans and the European slave system initiated the acculturation/deculturation dialectic: while the enslaved adopted many of the values and beliefs of the master, African forms survived. Grounding his analysis in a strict separation between form and content, Suvélor proposed that folktales took up "European" material and reworked and reframed it in African idioms. While the form of African folkways survived the slave ship, its meaningful content was filled with European ideas and values (pp. 25–29).

Turning to the "Conte de Yé", Suvélor applied his method and distinguished between the tale's formal qualities and its content to underline the tale's cultural ambiguities. In the tale, a version of which he published in *Acoma* #3, Yé suffers from hunger and begs God for relief by climbing Morne-Lacroix to "knock against the sky to appeal to and summon God" (Suvélor, 1971, p. 30). God's response to Yé's appeal was to provide him with a "formula" (Suvélor, 1971, p. 30) to sate his hunger. In Suvélor's reading, the tale expressed the collision between African forms and Christian content. In *Tropiques*, Césaire and Ménil (1942) read the tale as an example of the preservation of African collective sensibilities (pp. 7–11). Suvélor (1971, 1972) in contrast argued that while it retained African motifs, it expressed an essentially European and Christian morality. God's intervention on Yé's behalf expressed its African formal qualities: instead of communicating with God through prayer or good works, Yé travelled to the deity's realm—in this case, Morne-Lacroix—and summoned God by knocking on the sky. Further, God's cure for Yé's hunger was to give him a formula—a spell or medicine in African belief systems—rather than granting Yé a miracle or a work of grace. Despite these formal qualities, the god of the tale was explicitly the Christian God and clearly differentiated from the Devil, a distinction that would have been meaningless in an authentically African account of the tale. Suvélor argued that the tale's moral lesson was essentially Christian, which is to say, a European one. He concluded that the tale was ambiguous, for while it preserved African poetics in its formal structure, its content and ultimate moral reflected the master's Christian faith (Suvélor, 1971, pp. 30–31; Suvélor, 1972, pp. 54–58). Suvélor's analysis showed the inextricable entanglements of Antillean culture and nation. Antillean culture was at root fundamentally Creole and distinguishing or isolating the various elements that combined to make it was a fool's errand. Whereas the négritude writers hoped to recover an African cultural hinterland through ethnographic research, Suvélor suggested that Antilleans' cultural hinterland had to be discovered in their concrete history of creolization. Monadic notions of culture and nation derived from Herder were inapplicable to the lived experience of the Caribbean.

Articulating how Antilleans, lacking access to a distinct cultural hinterland, could resist French cultural hegemony occupied Édouard Glissant's contributions to the Institute's work. In a series of essays, he theorized Antillean psychosocial structures and how they were expressed in the social and cultural life of the French Caribbean (Glissant, 1971a, 1971b, 1971c, 1973c). Glissant suggested in these essays that Antilleans recognized and disavowed their social and cultural structures as colonial impositions, but only did so unconsciously. Because their disavowal was latent and not self-conscious, their rejection of colonial forms was not experienced as resistance but as "disequilibrium". "Tensions here are, above all, the mark of this refusal of imposed historical structures, and a negative unconscious, traumatic, and confused search for a secure relationship to lived "space-time"" (Groupe des Recherches, 1971, p. 33). In Glissant's analysis, disequilibrium affected all aspects of Antillean life from familial structure to class conflict to language. Because Antilleans continued to live under an imposed culture (French culture) and lacked access to a cultural hinterland, they unconsciously rejected the imposed culture, but because their refusal was unconscious rather than conscious, instead of producing liberated cultural forms, it led to disequilibrium.

Linguistic disequilibrium, which Institute researchers called "verbal delirium", emerged as a central focus of the Institute's research. Glissant and his colleagues, Marlène Hospice and Hector Elisabeth, set out to analyse how French colonialism and hegemony warped and transformed Antillean speech and linguistic codes.

In their studies, the IME researchers cast a wide view over Antillean society. Hospice (1973) examined elite delirious language in publications put out by the pro-assimilation Socialist Party, Elisabeth (1973) focused on quotidian social interactions in Fort-de-France, and Glissant (1973a) studied Suffrin's dogma. All three studies were empirical and grounded in research into Antillean language use. Elisabeth, for example, conducted fieldwork in popular locales and presented case studies from a bus station, a political rally, a bar, and a bus. Hospice, consonant with her literary training, analysed political tracts and pamphlets and concentrated in particular on a 1972 pamphlet circulated by the Socialist Party that addressed debates about autonomy. Glissant attended and recorded Suffrin's rituals, interviewed Suffrin, and collected his pamphlets and other writings.

In Glissant's introduction to their work (Glissant, 1973b), he outlined an analytic matrix to sort and understand the modalities and occurrences of verbal delirium observed in their case studies. First, the social and class position of subjects shaped their speech, such that delirium had "elite" and "popular" forms. Next, they inventoried delirium's "modalities" and sorted it by content into nine categories: accumulative process; formula; evidence; expository sequence; the vision of the other; the vision of the self; the vision of the vision of the self by the other; humanism; and the conception of history.[12] A final defining feature of verbal delirium, which reflected the Group's psychoanalytic approach, is that it serves an unconscious ideological purpose: to reconcile alienated subjects to the colonial situation. Whereas madness completely refused the situation's traumatic force through "the total refusal of the situation" (p. 65), delirium " 'let off' this pressure" (p. 65). "Habitual delirium", Glissant wrote, "is almost uniformly lived as de-appropriation" (p. 65).[13] Verbal delirium, they argued, constituted a counter-therapy that foreclosed any reckoning with the evacuation of Antillean being through an attempt to master the situation through pseudo-mastery. Because Antilleans unconsciously sensed the disjunction between Antillean reality and its representation, verbal delirium served to repress this unease and renew their investment in French identity.

On first reading, the Institute's diagnosis of the Antillean colonial-linguistic situation seems to call for an approach similar to what Herder and Ngũgĩ proposed. If Antillean language was alienated to the point of delirium, to reclaim not just their selves but their integrity as subjects required them to appropriate and master a language. If the use of colonial language produced alienation verging on the edge of sanity, the obvious answer was to appropriate a non-colonial language. But as Glissant (1971c) had outlined, there was no non-colonial language available to appropriate. While Antilleans had invented and enriched Creole, it remained a colonial language, a product of their displacement from Africa, and their enslavement in the Caribbean. Creole was not equivalent to the pre-colonial languages of Africa or Asia, or the national languages of Europe, because it emerged not from the community's work upon itself, but from the violence and disappropriation of the colonial encounter. The cultural hinterland that other colonized peoples could access through language was unavailable. Nonetheless, the researchers did not believe that Antilleans were condemned to perpetual colonized delirium and non-mastery. While they could not access a non-colonial language, they could invent non-colonized idioms.

In his study of Suffrin and his *dogme de Cham* [dogma of Cham], Glissant (1973a) synthesized the Institute's work and outlined his theory of creolized idiom as resistance to colonialism. His reading of the dogma analysed its delirious structure, but also engaged with Suffrin's discourse in order to theorize possible lines of escape from the impasses of the Antillean colonial situation. Applying the matrix outlined in the Group's theoretical essay, Glissant considered Suffrin's symbolism, rhetoric, and use of language. He noted Suffrin's literalist use of symbols: "In his temple he has an actual garbage can and a basket respectively labeled: 'dustbin of history' and 'historic birthing bed'" (p. 85).[14] He also noted how Suffrin's rhetoric accumulated formulaic scholastic terminology and alliterative repetition.[15] Certain words were expressed in repeated formulas ("triggers", as Glissant put it (p. 86)), often rooted in theatricalized alliteration and assonance: "polygamy" and "polyandry", "evolution" and "involution", "exclusion" and "excommunication" (p. 86). Suffrin also switched between French and Creole: His tracts were written and his discussions delivered in French, but his commentary and discussion were almost always in Creole (pp. 84–92). In its content, the dogma was equally contradictory. On a "manifest" level, it was a "national claim" that sought to grasp Martinique's lived history. On a "latent" level, however, it reproduced the religious permissions and prohibitions of Catholic doctrine and narrated an imagined history that replaced the critical recovery of lived experience. And Suffrin's solution to Martinique's colonial situation was to write to "the great of this world" (p. 89) and convince them that only his dogma could preserve the "well-being of civilization and of humanity" (p. 88). The dogma, despite its criticisms of racism and colonialism, remained wed to a belief in Europe and the civilizing mission.

And yet at the same time, the dogma of Cham, in Glissant's analysis, represented a genuine attempt to create an idiomatic means of expression to represent the lived realities of Antillean life. Steeped in a mystic-religious and delirious ritual and language, it nonetheless possessed a "creative energy that revealed itself not only at the level of language but in the manipulation of the concrete" (p. 89). Suffrin's dogma apprehended and critiqued the poverty and racism that defined Antillean life and created forms and poetics that strove towards disalienation and mastery. In his idiosyncratic use of French, English, and Creole, and in his borrowing and recontextualizing of cultural and intellectual elements from a range of sources and cultures, Suffrin created a new idiom to understand Antilleans and their place in the world.[16] In other words, Suffrin *creolized* European cultures to speak about and to the Antillean experience. Rather than imitating European models or subjects, Suffrin created an elaborate system of meaning from the heterodox cultures and artifacts that defined Caribbean life. While his discourse ultimately collapsed into a "tragic and spectacular effort to re-appropriate historical suffering" (p. 89), it did so in much the same way Marx described religion as "the expression of real suffering and a protest against real suffering . . . the heart of a heartless world, and the soul of soulless conditions" (Marx, 1994, p. 57). The dogma of Cham was a "real cultural claim" (Glissant, 1973a, p. 88), an original effort to express Antillean being in the language of the Antilles (pp. 89–90).

For Glissant (1973a), the value of Suffrin's discourse was that it set aside worrying about a proper Antillean *langue* and instead worked to enunciate a uniquely Antillean *parole*.[17] Because Creole was a colonial language and because exoticization and folklorization risked turning Antillean cultural expression into fetishism, Institute researchers believed that promoting Creole as a *langue* of resistance was ultimately counterproductive.[18] Creolizing French, however, and inventing a creolized French *parole* and idiom, seemed more promising. The problem with Creole literature was that while the Creolist poets switched their language from French to Creole, they did not similarly transform their literary forms, idioms, subjects, or styles. A poet such as Gilbert Gratiant, for example, wrote in Creole, but his form, subjects, imagery, in short, his entire poetics, remained essentially European. Better in that case, Glissant argued, to write in the colonizer's tongue and produce new aesthetic forms and idioms that creolized French and expressed a Caribbean and American being and poetic sensibility than to Europeanize Creole. In essays collected in *L'Intention poétique* (1969), Glissant (1997 [1969]) had lauded writers such as Saint-John Perse, William Faulkner, and Alejo Carpentier—all of whom wrote in colonial languages— precisely because their work invented an American discourse that idiomatically and formally creolized French, English, and Spanish. In the poetry and espe- cially in the experimental novel, *Malemort*, published in 1975, that he wrote while directing the IME, Glissant worked to invent a similar poetics for the French Antilles. And his work for the IME led ultimately to his major theoretical statement published in 1981, *Le Discours Antillais* [*Caribbean Discourse*], in which he theorized a creolizing approach to culture and subjectivity and articu- lated the danger if such a cultural and social effort was not consciously articu- lated and disseminated.[19]

In their critique of the primacy accorded *langue* in conceptions of national- ism, both romantic and anti-colonial, the researchers at the Institute zeroed in on a blind spot in Herder and in the German philosophical tradition he influenced. Put simply, the German philosophical tradition that stretched from Herder to Hei- degger theorized people and nation *a priori* as tied to and bound by place and allowed little room for the migrant and the mobile (Casey, 1998). As Emmanuel Levinas (1998) put it in a critique of Heidegger:

> It is absolutely not a philosophy of the émigré! I would even say that it is not a philosophy of the emigrant . . . he or she who emigrates is fully human: The migration of man does not destroy, does not demolish the meaning of being.
>
> (p. 117)

Heidegger's (1971) famous illustration of the "fourfold" (p. 148) in his essay, "Building, Dwelling, Thinking", notably describes the bridge's "gathering" (p. 151) as taming and controlling the stream's waters, subordinating liquidness and flow to the building accomplished by the bridge. In this tradition, consistent with Herderian philosophy, the migrant or the diasporic cannot be conceived as anything other than out of place and lacking in worldliness.

This lack becomes clear when we return to Herder's writing on European Jewry. On the one hand, Herder lauded the historical Jewish nation for its contributions to world history and culture, but on the other hand, as Grossman (1994) has pointed out, his writing about diasporic Jewry was often critical and dismissive. Grossman concedes Herder's anti-imperialism, but also highlights how the idea of an organic national community on which it was founded excluded Jews in particular and diasporic peoples in general. While Herder thought that Hebrew poetry and language had once been great, when Jews were removed from their lands, they "lost contact with the sources of their poetry" (p. 68). "Hellenization" (p. 68) and exile caused them to become "morally degenerated because it has allowed its language and culture to become 'überfremdet'" (p. 68). Überfremdet can be translated as "foreignized" or "extremely foreign". Grossman (1994) concludes that for Herder, diasporic peoples were

> "[f]oreign peoples", uprooted and existing outside their native geography, inorganically mixing languages and cultures. *Bildung*, culture (art, literature) and climate-geography all operate together to generate the *Sitten* of a people. Lacking any one of these, a people becomes *unsittlich*, that is, immoral or degenerate.
>
> (p. 74)

Herder was critical of imperialism and critical of Atlantic slavery, but his theories of language and community inevitably cast diasporic peoples as degenerated shadows of their former organic communities. In fact, in his critical defence of Herder as a theorist of anti-imperialism, Noyes (2015) suggests that part of Herder's objection to slavery was precisely that it was an extreme example of "the domination of one people by another more powerful one" (p. 76).

Herder's concepts of nation and culture remained wed to that most Enlightenment of intellectual manoeuvres: the transformation of a European particular into a universal category. He read the properties of the nascent European nation-state back into the historical record and discovered in the past the origins not of a universal mode of being, but of a particularly European politico-cultural institution and imagination. In other words, Herder elevated a European particular—an organic linguistic nation-state rooted in a particular geography—to a universal and imposed it on the diverse particulars of the world—the multiplicity of the different ways of organizing nation, language, culture, and community. To translate this move into Glissant's critical language, Herder attempted to impose the One—the false universal—on the Many—the lived diversality of the world. Glissant's move, much like Levinas's (1998) critique of Heidegger, is to remind us of the contingency of the universal and to show the repressed diversality that always rests behind it. For diasporic peoples, the search for the root is as fruitless as the effort to assimilate, as both deny that diasporic Being that exists in perpetual tension between the particular and the universal (Glissant, 1997, pp. 214–222).

Conclusion

Despite the implicit critique of Herder's rooted concept of nationality, it should be asked whether the creolized sense of nation that Glissant advocates escapes the horizon of Herderian thought. Is not the concept of cultural hinterland a reflection of the Herderian concern with the geographical roots of culture and language? Can we think of the nation outside of the terms set out in the Herderian paradigm? While the diasporic critique of monadic culture and settled nationality pushes past the Herderian frame, it too remains, in many ways, captive to the same concentration on culture, language, history, and was first outlined in the late eighteenth century.

Recent scholarship has attempted to rescue Herder from his association with *völkisch* nationalism and present his work as a valuable resource for scholars researching the intellectual architecture of anti-imperialist nationalism. Herder's thought nonetheless remains structured in Eurocentric terms, bound to a vision of nation and culture that reflects a fundamentally European understanding of the world and which is imperfectly suited to understanding diasporic peoples and, more pressingly, to critiquing contemporary nationalist retrenchments. While Herder's philosophy has anti-imperialist and even anti-racist implications, it is not difficult to see how his understanding of national culture can be picked up and appropriated by new constellations of racist and cultural chauvinist thought. Anti-immigrant, anti-Muslim, and colourblind racist advocates in contemporary Europe could all find in Herder's oeuvre intellectual resources to support their campaigns against immigration, refugee asylum, and multiculturalism. His Eurocentric categories, which privilege sedentary national cultures, and his general dismissal of diasporic peoples, all outline the lineaments of what we might call a cosmopolitan racism.[20]

Across the humanities, scholars have called for a decolonization and critical reengagement with not just the canon but the methods and epistemologies that structure the humanistic fields. Researchers in Caribbean and Africana studies have advanced a similar call to creolize the canon, to read and reread the foundational works of Western intellectual history both against the grain and in critical dialogue with Afro-diasporic intellectual production (Gordon, 2014; Monahan, 2017). Reading the Western intellectual sources of nationalism and their dissemination throughout the colonial and post-colonial world requires further research. In Suffrin, Glissant saw that work being done, albeit in an unsystematic and fragmented manner; the need, as Glissant put it, was to transform his critiques into a "concrete task" (Glissant, 1973a, pp. 89–90). To subject Eurocentric categories to creolization is not just an intellectual exercise, but a matter of pressing political import.

Notes

1 See, for example, Fabian (1991), Franklin (2011), Comaroff and Comaroff (1997), Heller and McElhinny (2017).
2 There is a rich literature across multiple fields ranging from education to state building to literary production. Texts relevant to my discussion include: Bray and Koo (2004),

Blommaert (2006), May (2006), Blommaert (2014), Laitin (1992), Apter (2005), Schnepel (2004), and Salhi (2002).

3 Classic statements of this interpretation include: Berlin (1976). More recent approaches include: Sternhell (2009). For an overview of recent scholarship on Herder, see Zammito, Menges, and Menze (2010).

4 For a critique of some of creolism's blind spots as a post-colonial national identity, see Jackson (2012).

5 Glissant drew on Che Guevara's foco theory of guerrilla war. In Guevara, a "hinterland" represented a place of retreat and refreshment where a guerrilla foco could gather its forces, educate, rest, and plan its attack on the centres of power. See Glissant (1989, pp. 62–63).

6 Haitian vodou and other Afro-Creole religions and their continuing role in popular resistance to colonialism offer an interesting counterexample to Glissant's theory. Elsewhere, Glissant acknowledged vodou as a resource for resistance. Generally speaking, Glissant agreed with the widespread French Antillean position that Haiti and its Revolution represented the "missed opportunity" that Guadeloupeans, Guianese, and Martinicans had let pass them by. See Glissant (1989, pp. 87–92).

7 The definitive statement of this approach is: Bernabé, Chamoiseau, and Confiant (1993). However, arguments in favour of Creole were already widespread by the late 1950s and early 1960s. A number of Glissant's contemporaries, including Gilbert Gratiant, Daniel Boukman, and Sonny Rupaire, chose to write in Creole. See Schnepel (2004, pp. 57–84).

8 For Glissant's full discussion of Creole: Glissant (1989, pp. 120–133, 159–170, 182–191).

9 An English translation of this text can be found in Richardson and Fijalkowski (1996, pp. 101–104).

10 See Christina Kullberg's discussion of *Tropiques* and its ethnographic project in: Kullberg (2013, pp. 27–40).

11 First, he argued that folklore expressed mankind's relationship to the world; its origins were in the "shock" early humans experienced face to face with existence. Folklore and stories were early attempts to account for and master natural phenomena. Nature, he continued, posed several problems, most pressingly the precariousness of survival. Early forms of cultural expression thus turned to nature's forces—tempests, winds, rain, drought, night, the seasons, and so on—to tame them and make them graspable for human thought. Humans created the "religious imagination, magical thought, stories, myths, dances, chants" and other collective cultural forms to propitiate and control nature's force. The product of the collective, Suvélor insisted that these forms of organizing and controlling the human experience in the world could not be individually differentiated. In a conceptualization drawn from Lévi-Strauss, it was only when human society attained a certain level of civilizational security that collective cultural forms were transformed into modes of expression—"theatre, poetry, science, religion, philosophy"—that accommodated individual mastery. While the old materials did not completely disappear, they were remade when they reappeared under the new forms (Suvélor 1971, pp. 23–24).

12 Their typology was complex and detailed. In this note I list the forms followed by examples they provided. *Accumulation* is marked by an "assonant" and "rhythmic" accrual of unnecessary totemic words: "Racism varies by individual, according to their physical, educational, moral, spiritual, technical, and scientific development"; *Formula* is the uncritical repetition of clichés: "Racism—a thing shared across the world . . ."; *Evidence* designates not empirical evidence, but common sense: "France knows the colored people from having rubbed shoulders, administered them, ruled them . . ."; *Expository sequence* describes the proliferation of a discourse and its multiplication of tangents (no example was provided for this modality); *Vision of the other* is, in this case,

the view of France: "The nation of Chateaubriand, of Hugo, of Lamartine . . ."; *Vision of the self* is a picture of the self that is both self-deprecatory and "hyper-valorized": "Antilleanism: Prefiguration of the world of tomorrow"; *Vision of the vision of the self by the other* is an imagined description of how the other sees the self, comparable to Fanon's concept of "comparison": "For the whites, the Antillean is a negro like all other negroes . . ."; *Humanism* is the automatic recourse to a "vague universalism" (no specific example provided); and *conception of history* is the refusal of history (and historicity) in favour of a clichéd pseudo-history: "What good to return to the affairs of slavery"?

In addition, these modalities are sorted into four overarching "forms" of delirium: communication, dramatization, representation, and persuasion. The first two forms are popular, the latter two elite. "Delirium of communication" is an aggressive turn in language, defined by an inventive yet violent "invective". "Dramatization" imitates elite discourse in an attempt to overcome alienation in search of "personality and history". "Representation" is "complete alienation" expressed through "parodic culture". "Persuasion" is ideological, the defense of what exists, a "rationalization of unease". While their analysis was rigidly structural and schematic, they emphasized that delirium's modes and forms combined in unique ways in empirical manifestations of delirium (Glissant 1973b, pp. 56–62).

13 "De-appropriation" is the French word used to translate the Heideggerean coinage *"enteignis"*, which Heidegger theorizes is a necessary de-appropriation that accompanies (and even makes possible) the appropriation of Being described as *ereignis*. See Dastur (2013, p. 61).

14 Other examples included: He baptized his followers in a "bath of redemption"; the colours "blue white red symbolize the black race"; and "beneath the alter, in a cardboard cradle, a black doll and white doll are exhibited side by side".

15 Suffrin called the Church "the Essene religious authority", referred to the Black race as "heteromorphic human matter", and called himself an "oniromancien" (a portmanteau of oneiric, magicien, and romancier (novelist)).

16 Similar arguments have been proposed for other areas of Caribbean culture. See, for example, Hebdige (1987).

17 In French, the terms *langue* and *parole* describe the distinction between language as a set of rules and language as living speech. *Langue* denotes the grammatical and syntactical rules that govern a language, while *parole* denotes how language is creatively and productively used.

18 Ultimately, Creole could not be a *langue* because the "rules" of Creole were not fixed. That would change in the 1960s and 1970s as linguists and anthropologists began to study and formalize Antillean Creoles. See Schnepel (2004, pp. 93–98).

19 On the links between Glissant's work with the Institute and the genesis of *Le Discours Antillais*, please see my forthcoming book, *After Négritude: Anticolonial Activism in Postwar France and the Caribbean*.

20 On "colorblind racism", see Bonilla-Silva (2017). For the European and French contexts, see Fernando (2015), Keaton, Sharpley-Whiting, and Stovall (2012), and Wekker (2016).

References

Apter, E. (2005). *The translation zone: A new comparative literature*. Princeton, NJ: Princeton University Press.

Barnard, F. (2004). *Herder on nationality, humanity, and history*. Kingston: McGill University Press.

Benes, T. (2008). *In Babel's shadow: Language, philology, and the nation in nineteenth-century Germany*. Detroit, MI: Wayne State University Press.

Berlin, I. (1976). *Vico and Herder: Two studies in the history of ideas*. London: Viking Press.

Bernabé, J., Chamoiseau, P., & Confiant, R. (1993). *Éloge de la créolité [In praise of creoleness]*. Paris: Gallimard.

Blommaert, J. (2006). Language policy and national identity. In T. Ricento (Ed.), *An introduction to language policy: Theory and method* (pp. 238–254). Oxford: Blackwell.

Blommaert, J. (2014). *State language and ideology in Tanzania* (2nd ed.). Edinburgh: Edinburgh University Press.

Bonilla-Silva, E. (2017). *Racism without racists: Color-blind racism and the persistence of racial inequality in America* (5th ed.). New York: Rowman & Littlefield.

Bray, M., & Koo, R. (2004). Postcolonial patterns and paradoxes: Language and education in Hong Kong and Macao. *Comparative Education, 40*(2), 215–239. https://doi.org/10.1080/0305006042000231365

Casey, E. S. (1998). *The fate of place: A philosophical history*. Berkeley, CA: University of California Press.

Césaire, A., & Ménil, R. (1942). Introduction au folklore martiniquais [Introduction to Martinican folklore]. *Tropiques: Revue Culturelle, 4*, 7–11.

Comaroff, J. L., & Comaroff, J. (1997). *Of revelation and revolution, volume 2: The dialectics of modernity on a South African frontier*. Chicago, IL: University of Chicago Press.

Dastur, F. (2013). The later Heidegger: The question of the other beginning of thinking. In F. Raffoul & E. Nelson (Eds.), *The Bloomsbury companion to Heidegger* (pp. 55–66). London: Bloomsbury Academic.

Elisabeth, H. (1973). Du délire verbal en milieu populaire [Of verbal delirium in a popular context]. *Acoma, 4–5*, 69–83.

Fabian, J. (1991). *Language and colonial power: The appropriation of Swahili in the former Belgian Congo 1880–1938*. Berkeley, CA: University of California Press.

Fernando, M. (2015). *The republic unsettled: Muslim French and the contradictions of secularism*. Durham, NC: Duke University Press.

Franklin, M. J. (2011). *Orientalist Jones: Sir William Jones, poet, lawyer, and linguist, 1746–1794*. Oxford: Oxford University Press.

Glissant, É. (1971a). Structures de groupes et tensions de groupes en Martinique [Group structures and group tensions in Martinique]. *Acoma, 1*, 35–43.

Glissant, É. (1971b). Introduction à une étude des fondements socio-historiques du deséquilibre mental [Introduction to a study of the socio-historical foundations of mental disequilbrium]. *Acoma, 1*, 78–93.

Glissant, É. (1971c). Théatre, conscience du peuple [Theatre, conscience of the people]. *Acoma, 2*, 41–59.

Glissant, É. (1971d). L'Institut Martiniquais d'Etudes [The Martinican institute of studies]. *Acoma, 1*, 136–137.

Glissant, É. (1973a). Le cas Suffrin [The Suffrin case]. *Acoma, 4–5*, 84–92.

Glissant, É. (1973b). Sur le délire verbal [On verbal delirium]. *Acoma, 4–5*, 56–62.

Glissant, É. (1973c). Action culturelle et pratique politiques: Propositions de base [Cultural action and practical politics: Basic proposals]. *Acoma, 4–5*, 16–20.

Glissant, É. (1989 [1981]). *Caribbean discourse: Selected essays* (J. M. Dash, Trans.). Charlottesville: University of Virginia Press.

Glissant, É. (1997 [1969]). *L'Intention poétique [Poetic intention]*. Paris: Gallimard.

Gordon, J. A. (Ed.). (2014). *Creolizing Rousseau*. New York: Rowman & Littlefield.

Grossman, J. (1994). Herder and the language of diaspora Jewry. *Monatshefte, 86*(1), 59–79. Retrieved April 1, 2020, from www.jstor.org/stable/30153274

Hebdige, D. (1987). *Cut n'mix: Culture, identity and Caribbean music.* London: Routledge.
Heidegger, M. (1971). Building, dwelling, thinking. In M. Heidegger (Ed.), *Poetry, language, thought* (pp. 141–159). New York: Harper and Row.
Heller, M., & McElhinny, B. (2017). *Language, capitalism, colonialism: Toward a critical history.* Toronto: University of Toronto Press.
Herder, J. G. (2002). *Philosophical writings* (M. N. Forster, Ed. & Trans.). Cambridge: Cambridge University Press.
Herder, J. G. (2004). *Another philosophy of history and selected political writings.* Cambridge: Hackett Publishing Company.
Hospice, M. (1973). Sur le mécanismes du persuasion [On the mechanisms of persuasion]. *Acoma, 4–5*, 93–103.
Jackson, S. L. (2012). *Creole indigeneity: Between myth and nation in the Caribbean.* Minneapolis, MN: University of Minnesota Press.
Keaton, T. D., Sharpley-Whiting, T. D., & Stovall, T. (Eds.). (2012). *Black France/France noire: The history and politics of blackness.* Durham, NC: Duke University Press.
Kullberg, C. (2013). *The poetics of ethnography in Martinican narratives: Exploring the self and the environment.* Charlottesville, VA: University of Virginia Press.
Laitin, D. D. (1992). *Language repertoires and state construction in Africa.* Cambridge: Cambridge University Press.
Levinas, E. (1998). *Entre nous: On thinking-of-the-other* (M. B. Smith & B. Harshav, Trans.). New York: Columbia University Press.
Marx, K. (1994). A contribution to the critique of Hegel's philosophy of right: Introduction. In J. O'Malley (Ed.), *Marx: Early political writings* (pp. 57–70). Cambridge: Cambridge University Press.
May, S. (2006). Language policy and minority rights. In T. Ricento (Ed.), *An introduction to language policy: Theory and method* (pp. 255–272). Oxford: Blackwell.
Monahan, M. J. (Ed.). (2017). *Creolizing Hegel.* New York: Rowman & Littlefield.
Ngũgĩ, T. W. (1986). *Decolonizing the mind: The politics of language in African literature.* Portsmouth: Heinemann.
Noyes, J. K. (2015). *Herder: Aesthetics against imperialism.* Toronto: University of Toronto Press.
Richardson, M., & Fijalkowski, K. (Trans.). (1996). *Refusal of the shadow: Surrealism and the Caribbean.* New York: Verso Press.
Salhi, K. (2002). Critical imperatives of the French language in the francophone world: Colonial legacy—postcolonial policy. *Current Issues in Language Planning, 3*(3), 317–345. https://doi.org/10.1080/14664200208668044
Schnepel, E. M. (2004). *In search of a national identity: Creole and politics in Guadeloupe.* Hamburg: Helmut Buske Verlag.
Sternhell, Z. (2009). *The anti-enlightenment tradition.* New Haven, CT: Yale University Press.
Suvélor, R. (1971). Folklore, exotisme, connaissance [Folklore, exoticism, knowledge]. *Acoma, 2*, 22–24.
Suvélor, R. (1972). Yé et les maledictions de la faim [Yé and the curses of hunger]. *Acoma, 3*, 54–58.
Wekker, G. (2016). *White innocence: Paradoxes of colonialism and race.* Durham, NC: Duke University Press.
Zammito, J. H., Menges, K., & Menze, E. A. (2010). Johann Gottfried Herder revisited: The revolution in scholarship in the last quarter century. *Journal of the History of Ideas, 71*(4), 661–684. https://doi.org/10.1353/jhi.2010.0006

10 The myth of multilingualism in Singapore[1]

Ying-Ying Tan

The Herderian mantra

The Herderian philosophy on language and thought is primarily a Whorfian one. Fishman (1982) in fact labels Whorf as a "neo-Herderian champion" (p. 5). The Whorfian idea is a well-rehearsed one, namely, that language determines thought, and therefore language is a manifestation of values and ideas. In the context of the nation, nations are thus differentiated because the languages spoken by the national groups make these communities conceptualize the world in ways that are different from speakers of other languages. Yet it is the extension and application of this seemingly innocuous idea that has resulted in the reading of Herder as an "ethnic nationalist" (Wright, 2004, p. 32). According to Wright (2004), ethnic nationalists are "essentialists . . . who believe that nations are a natural phenomenon whose linguistic and cultural cohesion derive from a common past and whose destiny is to be a single political unit" (p. 33). The strongest critics of Herder see the Herderian philosophy as a doctrine for pushing nationalist unification agendas based on the ideology of a common language being a primordial and necessary condition for building a nation. Bauman and Briggs (2003), in their exposition on Herder's philosophy, explain this idea as follows:

> The desired goal of unification rests upon discursive unity, provided by the authority of tradition and a unified adherence to the national spirit. And here too, linguistic homogeneity is a necessary condition: "One people, one fatherland, one language".
>
> (p. 193)

In this view, the nation needs to have a single national language, which therefore leads to a general perception that Herder heralds the ideal of a monoglot nation (e.g. Blommaert, 2009; Canagarajah, 2012).

While Herder's influence is relatively moderate in sociolinguistic literature, his ideology of the monoglot nation has not been received well. Most of his critics oppose this ideology because of their commitment to diversity, multilingualism, and the fight for language rights (e.g. Blommaert, 2005; Canagarajah, 2012). Much also has been said in the other chapters in this volume about Herder's flawed assumptions of bounded territories and monolingualism. Meanwhile, others such as Fishman (1982) and Piller (2016) have taken on positions defending Herder. It is not the purpose of this piece here to expand on those critiques. What I aim to do here, rather, is to take Herder out of Europe and look at the applicability of the Herderian philosophy to post-colonial states in Asia, where linguistic homogeneity is not a given, and nation-building requires also the creation of a national consciousness. In language policy terms, this means "taking on the European model of linguistic nationalism" (Tupas, 2018, p. 154) which, according to Tupas, while not referring to Herder, assumes "a stable and straightforward link between one language and one nation" (Giordano, 2014, p. 247, as cited in Tupas, 2018, p. 154).

This paper looks specifically at Singapore and the application of the Herderian philosophy. Singapore is exceptional in that unlike all other Southeast Asian nations that have promoted linguistic nationalism at various points over the last century, it is believed to be the only Southeast Asian state that has a carefully crafted set of language policies that resist linguistic homogeneity (Tupas, 2018, p. 154). Being a young nation that has gone through nation-building in recent history, and given Singapore's reputation as a successful multilingual state, does Singapore then show herself to be a counterexample to the Herderian mantra? The aim of this paper is to look at how Herder can be used to understand the building of the nation in Singapore, and in particular, explore the relationship between language(s) and the nation. What then does the case of Singapore imply for the Herderian mantra and in the process, what does the Herderian mantra reveal about the nature of multilingualism in Singapore? In answering these questions, this paper also explores and traces the development of multilingualism in Singapore. This paper argues how multilingual Singapore is a myth created to balance the development of the Herderian ideal and the realities of how languages come to represent the nation.

Building the Singaporean nation through language

In 1965, when Singapore became independent, this newly minted nation found herself working through a multilingual ecology while climbing out of the shadows of colonialism. One would therefore expect the story of language and nation-building in Singapore to be a familiar one, that is, one that involves using language to "symbolize resistance against colonial rule" (Tupas, 2018, p. 154). Elsewhere in Southeast Asia, one can see the consequence of this kind of linguistic nationalism, for example, in the "Myanmarization" of Myanmar (Aye & Sercombe, 2014), the "Lao-ianization" of Laos (Cincotta-Segi, 2014), and the "Thai-ization" of Thailand (Kosonen & Person, 2014). It is the same post-colonial tale of how these new nations go in search of a common national language as they grapple with their new identities and how this negotiation is to be carried out between the local vernaculars and the foreign colonial language. Contrary to the Herderian model, however, Singapore's language policies at first glance were not intentionally monolingual. The state policies in fact seemingly promoted multilingualism, with no clear directives to build or move towards a language that would form the "soul" of the nation.

To date, no one has seriously questioned Singapore's multilingualism. This is not unexpected as its language policies are clearly geared towards giving recognition and status to multiple languages. While one could see a hint of the Herderian idea in the political psyche of Singapore's governing body from as early as 1955, ten years before Singapore became independent, there was no deliberate state effort to seek out that *one* common language. In the 1955 *All-Party Report*, which can be said to be one of the first documents on language policies in Singapore, it was clear that having multiple common languages was an acceptable condition.

> Without one or more common languages officially encouraged in Singapore and fostered in the schools, the ideal of unifying the various races into one people cannot be realised, and the links of common understanding, outlook and identity of interest, cannot be speedily forged.

While the above does not specifically speak of the spirit or soul of the nation, it is clear that "links of common understanding, outlook, and identity of interest" are necessary for the building of a new nation, as it puts people of diverse backgrounds and ethnicities into a united frame of thinking. And the way to do so is through language, though in this case, the Singapore governing body in 1955 was not pushing for monolingualism. They instead saw the possibility of uniting the people by "one or more" common languages. This is a clear departure from the ideal of the monoglot nation.

Having multiple tongues turned out in fact to be the bedrock of Singapore's language policies when she became independent in 1965. In the Independence Act of 1965, Malay, Mandarin, Tamil, and English were made the four official languages of Singapore. This was deemed a good solution to the management of ethnolinguistic diversity in Singapore then. The governing body of the newly independent Singapore needed to very quickly create cohesiveness amongst its ethnically and linguistically diverse populace who were educated in different languages and who mostly spoke the region's vernacular, Bazaar Malay, as the lingua franca. While Singaporeans can be broadly classified into three major ethnic groups— Chinese, Malays, and Indians—they spoke many more languages. According to the census data of 1957, a total of 33 languages of different language families were reportedly spoken in Singapore (Bokhorst-Heng, 1998, p. 288). They comprised Indic languages such as Hindi, Urdu, Punjabi, and Sindhi; Dravidian languages such as Tamil, Telugu, Malayalam, and Kannada; and Austronesian languages such as Malay, Boyanese, Bugis, and Javanese. And just within the Chinese community, which made up 75.4% of the population then, more than 13 Chinese languages were spoken, including Southern Min languages such as Hokkien, Teochew, Hainanese, and Foo Chow; Gan languages such as Hakka; and Yue languages such as Cantonese. English was used only by 1.8% of the population then (Bokhorst-Heng, 1998, p. 288).

Allowing for multiple common tongues is however not the same as having unmanaged multilingualism. The state of multilingualism as it was presented then in 1965 was not a desirable one. The sentiment that linguistic diversity was a problem is best reflected in Lee Kuan Yew's (2000), then the prime minister, description of the Singaporean army: that it was "saddled with a hideous collection of dialects and languages [and that Singapore] faced the prospect of going into battle without understanding each other" (p. 146). A multilingual nation was clearly regarded as a bane, yet there was no available common tongue for the diverse population. The solution was to present language policies making use of what I would consider to be "hierarchical multilingualism" (Mohanty, 2010) and "controlled multilingualism" (Gazzola, 2006). The term *hierarchical multilingualism* was used by Mohanty (2010) to describe the different statuses of the dominant Indian languages as opposed to the regional and tribal languages. *Controlled multilingualism*, on the other hand, is a methodological tool used by the European Union (EU) to perform translation and interpretation of EU parliamentary proceedings of over 25 languages by using a smaller, controlled set of languages. I find these two terms particularly useful in the Singaporean context. Singapore's language policy set itself out to create "hierarchical multilingualism" by elevating some languages to the official status, and even within the official languages, to structure further hierarchies by promoting English over the other languages. There was also "controlled multilingualism" as only a small number of languages were used to group numerous disparate communities, and having these languages serve as conduits for what would otherwise be unrelated and diverse groups. All these strategies are aimed to reduce diversity.

Even though English, Mandarin, Malay, and Tamil are the four official languages in Singapore, there is an obvious hierarchy between these languages. English was, from the onset, planned to become the most dominant language, even though English was spoken only by a very small percentage of the population in the years leading to Singapore's independence. The institutionalization of English as an official language was most strongly argued for on the basis of pragmatism. The economic opportunities that English could bring were at the forefront of the government's concerns, and Lee Kuan Yew (2011) could not have put it more directly when he said "Singapore would be economically isolated from the wider world if Chinese was chosen . . . Had we not chosen English, we would have been left behind". English was presented as the only option for the nation's survival. It was clear that English had more linguistic capital as compared to the other languages, official or otherwise.

English was also touted to be the language of neutrality. English was a natural choice precisely because it was used only by a very small percentage of the population then, and it was not the dominant language that belonged to any local speech community. English was perceived to be in a good position to serve as the language of interethnic communication without privileging or discriminating any group over the other. English was therefore seen as a good medium to ensure equality amongst the ethnically and culturally diverse population. And since English was believed to be a neutral language, it was also well positioned to be the common language for all Singaporeans. Homogeneity was seen as an optimal condition for nation-building. The Herderian philosophy begins to rear its head here; the only difference is that while Herder talked about using an established language of the masses, Singapore was using a foreign, colonial language.

As to be expected, one could not ask the population to take to English immediately, let alone use it competently. English was the language of the members of the privileged class, who either had ties to the British colonial government, or who were wealthy enough to send their children to English schools. For the rest of the population, English remained very much a foreign tongue. Threatened by the imposition of English, barely eight weeks after separation from the Malaysian Federation in 1965, Chinese-language activists publicly asked the government to guarantee the status of the Chinese language as one of the official languages of Singapore (Lee, 2000, p. 147). The ruling government needed to assure the Singaporean population, especially the prominent and powerful Chinese intellectuals, that English was not going to be institutionalized as an official language at the expense of languages that were more local and "Asian".

In the spirit of "controlled multilingualism", Malay, Mandarin, and Tamil were assigned as official languages and given the status of "mother tongue". There is an inextricable link between these languages to the ethnic classifications of the Singaporean population. These three languages are to serve as the control languages for the three ethnic communities which would otherwise have a dozen or more languages within each group. As mentioned earlier, Singapore's population is broadly classified as Chinese, Malay, and Indian. Ethnic classification is based primarily on one's father's ethnic assignment. Based on the rules of ethnic assignment, the Chinese is the most dominant group in Singapore, with 76.8% of the population belonging to this group, followed by the Malays at 13.9%, and the Indians at 7.9% (Singapore Department of Statistics, 2011), and this distribution has remained relatively unchanged since the nation's independence. Each ethnic group is correlated to one "mother tongue". In fact, the assigned "mother tongue" can be said to be the "superordinate language" (Gupta, 1998, p. 117) of each official ethnic group as the official languages of Mandarin, Malay, and Tamil are assigned to each group correspondingly. Therefore, if one is ethnically classified as "Chinese", then one's mother tongue is deemed to be Mandarin; that of a "Malay", Malay; and that of an "Indian", Tamil. This assignment of a "mother tongue" however was not based on the actual linguistic repertoire of any given individual (see Y. Y. Tan, 2014 on the "mother tongue" in Singapore). In other words, even if one does not speak or use Mandarin, as long as one has been classified as "Chinese", one's "mother tongue" would still be Mandarin. This has in fact been the case for many in the Chinese community, for even as late as 1980, only 10% of them were reported to use Mandarin at home, with over 80% of them using other non-Mandarin Chinese languages (Khoo, 1981).

The importance of the "mother tongue" is further reinforced by the state's language acquisition policies, with every school-going child having to mandatorily acquire his or her "mother tongue" in school. This was one of the ways in which the state could maintain a semblance of equality in the treatment of the various language communities. Lee Kuan Yew (2000), "not wanting to start a controversy over language" (p. 146), introduced the teaching of the three "mother tongues" into English schools in 1965. At the same time, English was introduced as a mandatory second language in the Chinese, Malay, and Indian schools. These Chinese-, Malay-, and Indian-medium schools which provided education in Chinese, Malay, and Indian languages were gradually closed over the period from 1970 to 1984. In 1987, English was officially implemented as the medium of instruction in all schools, and the "mother tongues", since then, were taught as the other compulsory language. The "mother tongue" that a child would have to learn in school then depends entirely on the ethnic classification of the child: Mandarin for the Chinese child, Malay for the Malay child, and Tamil for the Indian child. The average post-1965 bilingual Singaporean is therefore a product of a state-engineered bilingual education programme, which Pakir (1991) describes as "English-knowing bilingualism".

It is apparent that the state's multilingual policy was a controlled one, with attempts to reduce linguistic diversity to a small number of official languages and a favouritism towards English as the dominant language. One might even go so far as to say that the language policies are more monolingualism- than multilingualism-oriented, despite its formulation. This is echoed in Phillipson and Skutnabb-Kangas (1996).

> A language policy is basically monolingual when it linguistically allocates resources primarily to one language and correspondingly idolizes and glorifies this dominant language while demonizing, stigmatizing, and rendering invisible other languages. The ideological underpinning involves a rationalization of the relationship between dominant and dominated, always to the advantage of the dominant, making the learning of the dominant language at the cost of other languages seem not only instrumentally functional but beneficial to and for the dominated.
>
> (p. 437)

The rationalization for the state's choice of the four official languages is based precisely on the idea of instrumentalism. The Asian "mother tongues" are given the customary functions of being the carriers of Asian values (see P. K. W. Tan, 2014; Wee, 2002). And as an interesting aside, it is not a coincidence that the Asian "mother tongues" are accorded the job of transmitting Asian values. This is a Whorfian/Herderian idea at its most basic form. For Herder, there is a strong link between the language and the soul of the human. The soul, specifically, encompasses the feelings, sensations, and ways of life.

> For our mother-tongue was simultaneously the first world that we saw, the first sensations that we felt, the first efficacy and joy that we tasted! The side ideas of place and time, of love and hate, of joy and activity, and whatever

the fiery, turbulent soul of youth thought to itself in the process, all gets made eternal along with it. Now *language really becomes tribal core* [Stamm]!

(Herder, 2002, p. 143)

The "mother tongues" in Singapore, in a Herderian fashion, are the carriers of Asian cultures. However, in the scheme of the larger, national agenda, the transmission of Asian values takes a backseat. After all, English is the language that provides the currency and mileage. Given the way the language policies of Singapore have privileged English, the functions of English for the workings of the Singaporean society have worked out exactly according to plan. English in Singapore today serves the function of being the official language, language of administration, and the medium of education. English is also the lingua franca, serving as the link language of communication for Singaporeans of different ethnic groups. Despite this, the state policy remains cautious about according English the status of the common language, or even as the "mother tongue" for Singaporeans. It is almost as if the state is consciously resisting the Herderian ideology and maintaining the façade of multilingualism in policy terms, even though the intent, as I have explicated in this section, is clearly Herderian.

One can see how multilingualism in Singapore is a myth. According to Barthes (1972), "myth is a system of communication; it is a message" (p. 107). Multilingualism in Singapore is a construction, meant for both internal and international image-making. A policy and image of multilingualism has to be created and communicated as a part of nation-building, as it is deemed an important tool to harmonize ethnic differences and linguistic diversity. And Monica Heller (as cited in Coulmas, 2018) describes this aptly: "Multilingualism is an idea produced by the nation-state construct of unified languages, cultures, populations, and territories" (p. 55).

Linguistic reality-check

Another aspect of myth, according to Barthes (1972), is that "myth hides nothing; its function is to distort, not make disappear" (p. 120). In this section, I will show how multilingualism in Singapore is a myth because the nature of multilingualism has been seemingly distorted.

With the way English has dominated language policies in Singapore, it comes as no surprise that the census data over the last 30 years has shown a steady increase of English speakers in the home, with an alarming decline in the use of other languages. The use of English is so widespread that, according to the Singapore Census of Population in 2010, 32.3% of the population claimed English as their dominant home language, an increase from 23% in 2000, 18.8% in 1990, and 11.6% in 1980 (Khoo, 1981). This suggests an increasing trend of English replacing the other languages in the home domain—a point also made by a few others (e.g. Pakir, 2000; Wee, 2002, 2013). Home language is in fact only one of many other reflections of actual language use. Linguistic landscape studies on public signs in Singapore have also pointed to an overwhelmingly English monolingual scene (P. K. W. Tan, 2014; Tang, 2016). Elsewhere, with empirical data collected from over four hundred participants, using constructs of *language inheritance, language expertise, language function,* and *language identification,* I have shown that English has in fact penetrated the psyche of the everyday Singaporean to the point that it can be considered to be the real linguistic mother tongue for Singaporeans (Y. Y. Tan, 2014). The penetration of English even goes into the construction of ethnicity. Wong and Tan (2017) show how the Singaporean Chinese community uses English as a tool to imagine and construct their Chinese ethnicity, tearing down the essentialistic link between Chinese language, culture, identity, and ethnicity. All that said, English dominance does not necessarily equate to English monolingualism. How multilingual is Singapore, and Singaporeans, truly?

In what follows, I present some numbers from a sociolinguistic survey I conducted in Singapore in 2018. A total of 2841 Singaporeans participated in the survey, of whom 1193 were Chinese, 877 were Malay, and 771 were Indian. I cast the net wide without special restrictions, and participants were recruited as long as they were Singaporean, aged above 18, and were literate in English. The survey had about 50 questions, concerning the participants' language background, linguistic competence, language use, attitudes, and knowledge of language policies. I will not present the results of the entire survey in this chapter, given that not all of them will be relevant, but will instead show some pertinent figures derived from the survey, so as to present the realities of multilingualism in Singapore. I will do so by looking at *linguistic capacity* and *linguistic practice.* These are the two most common and widely accepted ways of looking at multilingualism (see Coulmas, 2018 for a more extensive exposition).

Linguistic capacity

Multilingualism can be defined by one's linguistic capacity. Multilingualism is the ability of individuals and communities to communicate in more than one language (Haberland & Yagmur, as cited in Coulmas, 2018, pp. 52–53). If we take this view of multilingualism and apply it to Singapore, the Singaporean society as a whole is highly multilingual. Of the 2841 Singaporeans who participated in the survey, only 0.8% of the participants indicated that they are monolingual, and, specifically, in English. Almost all the participants (99.2% of them) indicated that they know at least two languages. This is not at all unexpected, given that Singapore's bilingual education system makes it mandatory for Singaporean children to go through ten years of compulsory education in English and their designated official "mother tongue". However, Singaporeans are not simply bilingual, but multilingual, as more than half of those surveyed (56.1%) indicated that they know more than two languages. As can be seen in Figure 10.1, 28.9% of the participants are multilingual in English, Mandarin, and one or more non-Mandarin Chinese languages. This number could have been higher if not for the Mandarinization programme put in place to homogenize the Chinese population (see Wong & Tan, 2017). One can also see a growing interest among Singaporeans in acquiring new

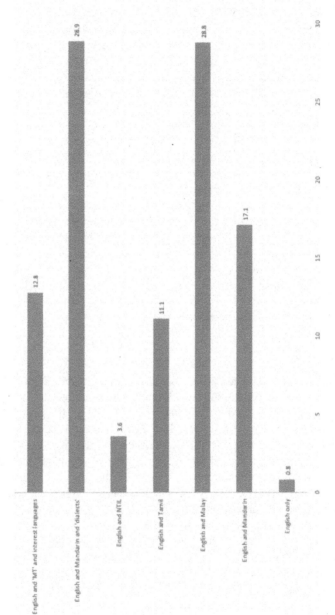

Figure 10.1 Linguistic capacity of Singaporeans (in %)

languages, with 12.8% of the population indicating linguistic capacity in languages such as French, Korean, Japanese, Thai, Vietnamese, Spanish, and many others (I refer to as "interest languages").[2]

Linguistic capacity also takes into account linguistic proficiency. Participants were asked to report on the written and spoken proficiency of the languages they are capable of. Figures 10.2 and 10.3 show their responses.

As can be seen from Figures 10.2 and 10.3, English has the highest reported written and spoken proficiency across speakers of all three ethnic groups, averaging over six out of the highest score of seven. The reported proficiencies of the three other official languages, Mandarin, Malay, and Tamil, are relatively lower, with Mandarin and Tamil scoring below five, and Malay just a little over five. Besides these four official languages, as can be expected, the other languages like the non-Mandarin Chinese languages (labelled as "dialects" for ease of reference), the non-Tamil Indian languages (labelled as "NTIL"), and foreign languages as such as Thai, French, and Vietnamese (labelled as "Interest") have scores below the median.

Nonetheless, the picture of multilingualism here, as presented in terms of linguistic capacity, is a very encouraging one. Singaporeans on the whole show themselves to be capable of multiple languages and rather competently too. However, linguistic capacity is only one of several ways to view multilingualism. It is one thing to claim competence, but the competence may not be shown in the ways that multilingualism is practised in reality.

Linguistic practice

As opposed to linguistic capacity, multilingualism can also be defined as the co-use of and regular interaction amongst community members in more than one language (Li Wei, as cited in Coulmas, 2018). Looking at multilingualism in terms of use and practice, the picture looks significantly different.

Participants were asked a series of questions that looked at their use of languages in their everyday lives and daily interactions. Figure 10.4 presents the responses of the participants in their use of languages in four ways, namely: speaking to self, recounting a short story, writing a diary, and posting on social media. As can be seen, English dominates in these four areas, and the Indian community, in particular, uses English over 80% of the time in all of them. The other three official languages, Mandarin, Malay, and Tamil, are used by the respective ethnic communities, but the use of these languages does not exceed 30%.

Participants were also asked a series of questions that looked at their use of languages in their daily interactions with others. Figure 10.5 presents the responses of the participants in their use of languages with their parents, their siblings, their friends, and with their classmates or colleagues at school or work. Once again, English can be seen to dominate. English is clearly the preferred language of communication outside the home, and on average, we can see English being used 75% of the time. With parents, the situation is slightly more balanced. The Chinese and Malay communities use English and Mandarin and Malay respectively with their

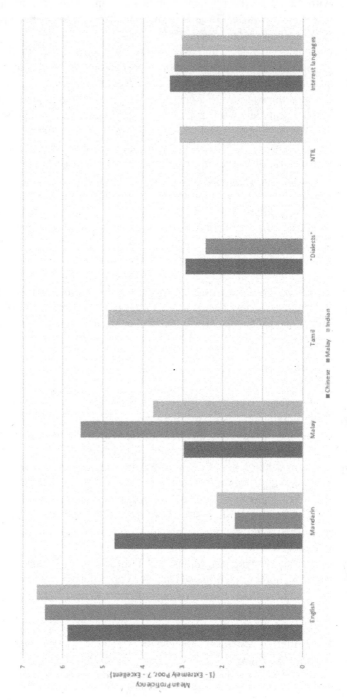

Figure 10.2 Mean written proficiency of languages by Singaporeans of three ethnic groups

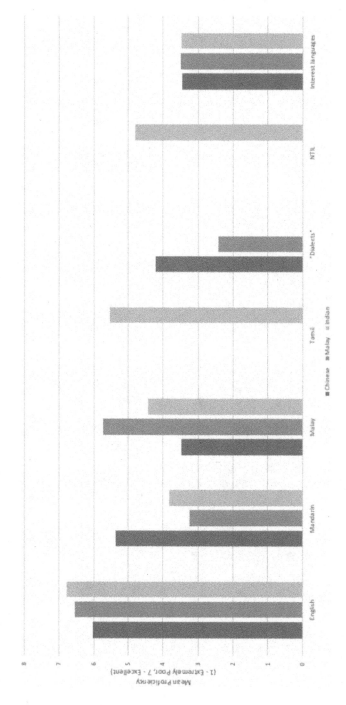

Figure 10.3 Mean spoken proficiency of languages by Singaporeans of three ethnic groups

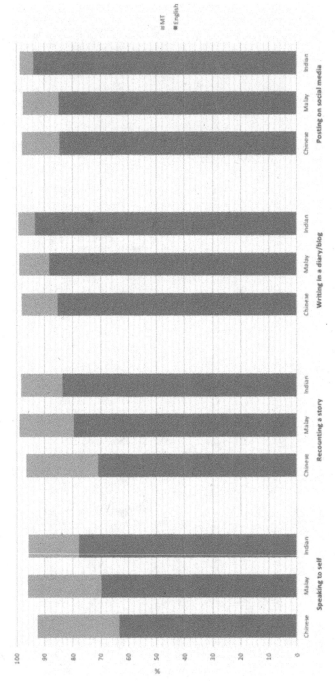

Figure 10.4 Use of language in everyday lives by Singaporeans of three ethnic groups

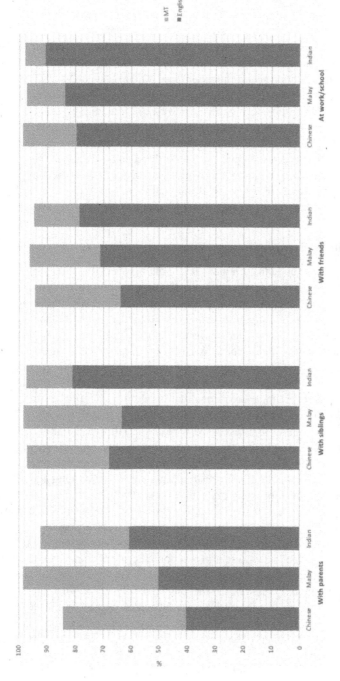

Figure 10.5 Use of language in daily interaction with others by Singaporeans of three ethnic groups

parents about 50% of the time. Of course, part of this may be due to the fact that at least half of the participants' parents would have been born before Singapore became independent and would not have had been affected by the language and education policies implemented in 1965. These parents would not have had a compulsory English education, and the linguistic mediums available to the participants to communicate with their non-English speaking parents would invariably have had to be either one of the other three official languages, or any of the other non-Mandarin or non-Tamil languages that were already spoken in the home.

In terms of linguistic practice, here we can see a slightly different picture of multilingualism. While we can still see the presence of other languages being used and practised every day, it is clear that English is dominating the scene. It is not quite yet English monolingualism we see here, but one can see the potential of Singapore becoming an increasingly monoglot nation if we give some time for the languages to run their course. Multilingualism in Singapore is a myth precisely because multilingualism seemingly exists, but its true nature is distorted.

Monolingualism of a foreign tongue

Certainly, monolingualism is not ideal. This is especially when, all things being equal, having more languages is better than having only one. As illustrated in the earlier section, Singapore still appears to be multilingual, albeit it being a predominantly English one. Singapore cannot be said to be in a bad place linguistically, even if it were to become an English monoglot. It would simply be yet another Anglophone nation in the world. What is unfortunate though, and what marks the difference between Singapore and other English-speaking nations in the world, is that English in Singapore remains very much someone else's language, and the English spoken in Singapore is one that is felt to be inferior as compared to the Englishes spoken elsewhere. There is, in other words, a deep sense of "linguistic insecurity" (a notion first discussed by Robert Hall in 1950 and later coined by Labov in 2006), despite the fact that English is used in almost every aspect of the Singaporean life. The insecurity is most acutely felt when the community complains about the standard of English in Singapore. Not too long ago, Sumiko Tan (2011), a prominent journalist and editor at the *Straits Times* (Singapore), observed that Singapore was "an inarticulate nation". She bemoaned the standard of English in Singapore as "low compared to other English-speaking countries" and lamented that Singaporeans speaking English was "almost painful to hear". The majority of the readers who sent in reaction letters to S. Tan's column agreed with her. Most of them echoed the sentiment that Singaporeans had a "sub-standard" or even "atrocious" command of the language. A letter sent in to the *Straits Times* (Singapore) forum page called on the education department to teach standard British English so as to help Singaporeans avoid a decline into "an adulterated form of British English" (The Straits Times, 2011). Foo and Tan (2019) blame this on the state. They claim that the state has forcefully denied Singaporeans of their linguistic ownership of English through the narrative of linguistic insecurity; the message that the population has poor English language standards, and this means that they must necessarily defer to the linguistic norms of the "superior" native speakers, making any local linguistic innovation substandard. The state needs to bear some responsibility indeed. After all, the state launched the Speak Good English Movement (SGEM) in 2000 to "promote good English". In a speech before this language campaign was launched, Singapore's then Prime Minister Goh Chok Tong (1999) proclaimed to Singaporeans that "to become an engineer, a technician, an accountant or a nurse, you must have standard English" and that they "should speak a form of English that is understood by the British, Americans, Australians, and people around the world". Since then, the SGEM has been a yearly event, the theme and focus of each campaign revolving around ideas such as speaking "Standard English" intelligible to all (2000–06), effective communication (2007 and 2009), making a choice to use Standard English (2008), using "proper" English (2010 and 2014), being ambassadors of "good" English (2011).

Singaporeans now find themselves in a conundrum, and this condition is most aptly and succinctly described by Derrida (1998): "Yes, I only have one language, yet it is not mine" (p. 2). Even if English were to be Singapore's common and only language, it is not (yet) to be a Singaporean language. The state's policies have not made English (or any other language for that matter) a Singaporean language, and the ramifications are felt at the very heart of the language community in Singapore. The language policies have created a situation in which Singaporeans find themselves without a language they can all their own. In Herderian terms, Singapore is a nation without a language, and therefore without a soul.

What recourse does the community have then? Is it possible for the nation to be articulated without a language? And this is where Singlish enters the fray. Singlish has evolved almost organically, seemingly, with no state effort and planning, though I argue in a paper in 2017 that Singlish is really an illegitimate conception of the state policies, however unintentional it may have been (Y. Y. Tan, 2017). Singlish, which comprises primarily elements of English, Malay, Hokkien, Mandarin-Chinese, and Cantonese, can be said to be a language spoken by almost every Singaporean. The emergence of Singlish did not go unnoticed by the state. The SGEM I described earlier is in fact also a campaign to illegitimatize Singlish (see Rubdy, 2001; Wee, 2014; Y. Y. Tan, 2017 for more on the SGEM). In spite of the authorities' attempts to remove Singlish from the scene, though perhaps as a deliberate act of resistance, in recent years, there has been strong sentiments to push for Singlish as "a cultural marker of Singaporean identity" (R. B. H. Goh, 2016, p. 749). As Goh further observes, there has been "a conscious project of cultural contestation; and these attempts have been driven not so much by everyday users for whom Singlish is the dominant mode of expression, but by an educated class (professionals, journalists, writers) predominantly using standard English" (p. 749). Singlish is a "practical and valuable linguistic [option]" (R. B. H. Goh, 2013, p. 133), and also, as R. B. H. Goh (2016) aptly puts it, is a language "whose authentic performance functions as a shibboleth of 'localness'" (p. 754). This desire for a local language that symbolizes and marks the Singaporean identity harkens back to the Herderian idea I opened this essay with. Can Singlish be the soul of the Singaporean nation? If so, this language is not one that was enforced upon by the authorities, nor was it a product of engineering. It simply is a language that comes from the people, a language that the nation can speak *in*, and a language that can speak *for* the nation. We have here, possibly, the Herderian philosophy in its purest form, where a language emerges unplanned that forms the soul of the nation—a clear, modern example of Herder's mantra in action.

However, we also have here a case where the Herderian idea needs to be carefully negotiated. We have in Singapore an unenviable situation where there is a clash between what the state desires and the linguistic realities of the nation. The carefully crafted multilingual policies are multilingual only in form, but monolingual in practice. Unsurprisingly, Singaporeans are increasingly becoming English monoglots, but English, as a foreign language, cannot be the language of the nation. At the same time, Singlish develops organically from the ground, and is well positioned to be the local language that unites the nation in spirit. And because Singlish is deemed undesirable by the state, it has to be resisted and desisted.

It is precisely the existence of Singlish that makes the myth of multilingualism necessary. The myth of multilingual Singapore must remain for Singaporeans to believe that nation-building and the national spirit is not based on a singular language, but a multitude of languages. In the words of Barthes (1972), "myth does not deny things . . . its function is to talk about them; . . . it gives them a clarity which is not that of an explanation but that of a statement of fact" (p. 143). As has been illustrated in this chapter, multilingualism in Singapore has not been explained empirically by the state, but rather has simply been talked about as if it is a fact. That multilingualism is the national character of Singapore has dominated both the consciousness of the state, its people, and the many others who laud its success. And this myth must persist, for any recourse to a single language in the Herderian fashion would push Singlish to the fore. Singapore therefore is an anti-Herder story, but not because it serves as a counterexample to Herder. In fact, this story unveils how well Herder would work should it be allowed to take flight unhindered.

Notes

1 This research is supported by the Ministry of Education, Singapore, under its Academic Research Fund Tier 1 (RG160/16).
2 The figures make use of the following abbreviations. "MT" = "Mother Tongue"; NTIL = non-Tamil Indian languages; "Dialects" = non-Mandarin Chinese languages; Interest = "interest languages", that is, foreign languages like French, Korean, Japanese, etc.

References

Aye, K. K., & Sercombe, P. (2014). Language, education and nation-building in Myanmar. In P. Sercombe & R. Tupas (Eds.), *Language, education and nation-building: Assimilation and shift in Southeast Asia* (pp. 148–164). London: Palgrave Macmillan.
Barthes, R. (1972). *Mythologies* (A. Laver, Trans.). New York: Farrar, Straus & Giroux.

Bauman, R., & Briggs, C. L. (2003). *Voices of modernity: Language ideologies and the politics of inequality*. Cambridge: Cambridge University Press.

Blommaert, J. (2005). Situating language rights: English and Swahili in Tanzania revisited. *Journal of Sociolinguistics, 9*(3), 390–417.

Blommaert, J. (2009). Language policy and national identity. In T. Ricento (Ed.), *An introduction to language policy: Theory and method* (pp. 238–310). Oxford: John Wiley & Sons.

Bokhorst-Heng, W. (1998). Language planning and management in Singapore. In J. A. Foley, T. Kandiah, Z. Bao, A. Gupta, L. Alsagoff, C. L. Ho, . . . W. Bokhorst-Heng (Eds.), *English in new cultural contexts: Reflections from Singapore* (pp. 287–309). Oxford: Oxford University Press.

Canagarajah, S. (2012). *Translingual practice: Global Englishes and cosmopolitan relations*. London: Routledge.

Cincotta-Segi, A. R. (2014). Language/ing in education: Policy discourse, classroom talk and ethnic identities in the Lao PDR. In P. Sercombe & R. Tupas (Eds.), *Language, education and nation-building: Assimilation and shift in Southeast Asia* (pp. 106–130). Basingstoke: Palgrave Macmillan.

Coulmas, F. (2018). *An introduction to multilingualism: Language in a changing world*. London: Routledge.

Derrida, J. (1998). *Monolingualism of the other, or, the prosthesis of origin* (P. Mensah, Trans.). Stanford: Stanford University Press.

Fishman, J. (1982). Whorfianism of the third kind: Ethnolinguistic diversity as a worldwide societal asset. *Language in Society, 11*(1), 1–14.

Foo, A., & Tan, Y. Y. (2019). Linguistic insecurity and the linguistic ownership of English among Singaporean Chinese. *World Englishes, 38*(1), 1–24.

Gazzola, M. (2006). Managing multilingualism in the European Union: Language policy evaluation for the European parliament. *Language Policy, 5*, 393–417.

Giordano, C. (2014). Epilogue—the dwindling cultural and linguistic diversity of Southeast Asian societies: Comparative reflections from an anthropological perspective. In P. Sercombe & R. Tupas (Eds.), *Language, education and nation-building: Assimilation and shift in Southeast Asia* (pp. 245–261). Basingstoke: Palgrave Macmillan.

Goh, C. T. (1999). *National day rally address by Prime Minister Goh Chok Tong, speech in English on 22 August 1999: First-world economy, world-class home* [Transcript]. National Archives of Singapore Online. Retrieved from www.nas.gov.sg/archivesonline/speeches/record-details/773bbd69-115d-11e3-83d5-0050568939ad

Goh, R. B. H. (2013). Uncertain locale: The dialectics of space and the cultural politics of English in Singapore. In L. Wee, R. B. H. Goh, & L. Lim (Eds.), *The politics of English: South Asia, Southeast Asia and the Asia Pacific* (pp. 125–144). Amsterdam: John Benjamins.

Goh, R. B. H. (2016). The anatomy of Singlish: Globalisation, multiculturalism and the construction of the "local" in Singapore. *Journal of Multilingual and Multicultural Development, 37*(8), 748–758.

Gupta, A. (1998). The situation of English in Singapore. In J. A. Foley, T. Kandiah, Z. Bao, A. Gupta, L. Alsagoff, C. L. Ho, . . . W. Bokhorst-Heng (Eds.), *English in new cultural contexts: Reflections from Singapore* (pp. 106–126). Oxford: Oxford University Press.

Hall, R. A. (1950). *Leave your language alone!* Ithaca: Linguistica.

Herder, J. G. (2002). *Philosophical writings* (M. N. Forster, Ed. & Trans.). Cambridge: Cambridge University Press.

Khoo, C. K. (1981). *Census of population 1980, Singapore: Release no. 2, demographic characteristics*. Singapore: Department of Statistics.

Kosonen, K., & Person, K. R. (2014). Languages, identities and education in Thailand. In P. Sercombe & R. Tupas (Eds.), *Language, education and nation-building: Assimilation and shift in Southeast Asia* (pp. 200–231). Basingstoke: Palgrave Macmillan.

Labov, W. (2006). *The social stratification of English in New York city* (2nd ed.). Cambridge: Cambridge University Press.

Lee, K. Y. (2000). *From third world to first: The Singapore story 1965–2000.* Singapore: Singapore Press Holdings.

Lee, K. Y. (2011, September 6). *Speech for the launch of the English language institute of Singapore (ELIS).* Retrieved from www.moe.gov.sg/media/speeches/2011/09/06/speech-by-mr-lee-kuan-yew-at-elis-launch.php

Mohanty, A. K. (2010). Languages, inequality and marginalization: Implications of the double divide in Indian multilingualism. *International Journal of the Sociology of Language, 205,* 131–154.

Pakir, A. (1991). The range and depth of English-knowing bilinguals in Singapore. *World Englishes, 10*(2), 167–179.

Pakir, A. (2000). Singapore. In W. K. Ho & R. Wong (Eds.), *Language policies and language education: The impact in East Asian countries in the next decade* (pp. 259–284). Singapore: Times Academic Press.

Phillipson, R., & Skutnabb-Kangas, T. (1996). English only worldwide or language ecology? *TESOL Quarterly, 30*(3), 429–452.

Piller, I. (2016, March 4). Herder: An explainer for linguists. In *Language on the move.* Retrieved from www.languageonthemove.com/herder-an-explainer-for-linguists/

Rubdy, R. (2001). Creative destruction: Singapore's speak good English movement. *World Englishes, 20,* 341–355.

Singapore Department of Statistics (2011). *Census of population 2010 statistical release 1: Demographic characteristics, education, language and religion.* Retrieved from www.singstat.gov.sg/-/media/files/publications/cop2010/census_2010_release1/cop2010sr1.pdf

The Straits Times (2011, September 22). Improve teaching of British English. *The Straits Times.* Retrieved August 25, 2015, LexisNexis Academic Database.

Tan, P. K. W. (2014). Singapore's balancing act, from the perspective of the linguistic landscape. *Sojourn: Journal of Social Issues in Southeast Asia, 29*(2), 438–466.

Tan, S. (2011, September 4). Um, er, as I was saying; can eloquence be taught? Many Singaporeans—like me—certainly need help to be more articulate. *The Straits Times,* p. 15.

Tan, Y. Y. (2014). English as a "mother tongue" in Singapore. *World Englishes, 33*(3), 319–339. https://doi.org/10.1111/weng.12093

Tan, Y. Y. (2017). Singlish: An illegitimate conception in Singapore's language policies? *European Journal of Language Policy, 9*(1), 85–103.

Tang, H. K. (2016). *Linguistic landscaping in Singapore: The local linguistic ecology and the roles of English* (Unpublished master's thesis), Lund University, Lund.

Tupas, R. (2018). (Un)framing language policy and reform in Southeast Asia. *RELC Journal, 49*(2), 149–163.

Wee, L. (2002). When English is not a mother tongue: Linguistic ownership and the Eurasian community in Singapore. *Journal of Multilingual and Multicultural Development, 23*(4), 282–295.

Wee, L. (2013). Governing English in Singapore: Some challenges for Singapore's language policy. In L. Wee, R. B. H. Goh, & L. Lim (Eds.), *The politics of English: South Asia, Southeast Asia and the Asia Pacific* (pp. 105–124). Amsterdam: John Benjamins.

Wee, L. (2014). Linguistic Chutzpah and the speak good Singlish movement. *World Englishes, 33*(1), 85–99.

Wong, K., & Tan, Y. Y. (2017). Mandarinization and the construction of Chinese ethnicity in Singapore. *Chinese Language and Discourse*, 8(1), 18–50.

Wright, S. (2004). *Language policy and language planning: From nationalism to globalisation*. Basingstoke: Palgrave Macmillan.

Index

Note: Page numbers in *italics* indicate a figure on the corresponding page.